Captain John Smith

Also by Dorothy and Thomas Hoobler

Nonfiction

Vietnam: Why We Fought
Vanity Rules: A History of American Fashion and Beauty
We Are Americans: Voices of the Immigrant Experience
Real American Girls Tell Their Own Stories
The Chinese American Family Album
The Italian American Family Album
The Irish American Family Album
The Jewish American Family Album
The African American Family Album
The Mexican American Family Album
The Japanese American Family Album
The Scandinavian American Family Album
The German American Family Album
The Cuban American Family Album

Novels

The Ghost in the Tokaido Inn
The Demon in the Teahouse
In Darkness, Death (Edgar Award winner)
The Sword That Cut the Burning Grass

Captain John Smith

Jamestown and the Birth of the American Dream

Dorothy and Thomas Hoobler

WILEY

John Wiley & Sons, Inc.

Published by John Wiley & Sons, Inc., Hoboken, New Jersey
Published simultaneously in Canada

Illustration credits: Pages 123, 130, 195, and 242 courtesy of the Rare Books Division, The New York Public Library, Astor, Lenox, and Tilden Foundations.

For general information about our other products and services, please contact our Customer Care Department within the United States at (800) 762-2974, outside the United States at (317) 572-3993 or fax (317) 572-4002.

Wiley also publishes its books in a variety of electronic formats. Some content that appears in print may not be available in electronic books. For more information about Wiley products, visit our web site at www.wiley.com.

Library of Congress Cataloging-in-Publication Data:

Hoobler, Thomas.
    Captain John Smith : Jamestown and the birth of the American dream / Thomas Hoobler and Dorothy Hoobler.
        p. cm.
    Includes bibliographical references and index.
    ISBN-13 978-0-471-48584-1 (cloth : alk. paper)
    ISBN-10 0-471-48584-5 (cloth : alk. paper)
    1. Smith, John, 1580–1631. 2. Colonists—Virginia—Jamestown—Biography.
3. Explorers—America—Biography. 4. Explorers—Great Britain—Biography.
5. Jamestown (Va.)—History—17th century. 6. Jamestown (Va.)—Biography.
7. Frontier and pioneer life—Virginia—Jamestown. 8. Virginia—History—
Colonial period, ca. 1600–1775. I. Hoobler, Dorothy. II. Title.
    F229.S7H66 2006
    975.5′02′092—dc22
                                                                                    2005017411

Printed in the United States of America

10 9 8 7 6 5 4 3 2 1

In memory of our fathers,
Frederick G. Law and John T. Hoobler,
who believed in the American dream

I am no Compiler by hearsay, but have beene a reall Actor; I take my selfe to have a propertie in [these events]: and therefore have beene bold to challenge them to come under the reach of my owne rough Pen. That, which hath been indured and passed through with hardship and danger, is thereby sweetned to the Actor, when he becometh the Relator. I have deeply hazarded my selfe in doing and suffering, and why should I sticke [hesitate] to hazard my reputation in Recording?

—*John Smith*

Contents

Acknowledgments

We want to acknowledge the invaluable assistance provided to us by Marianne Carter and Cathy Grosfils of the Rockefeller Library of Colonial Willamsburg. We benefited greatly from the efforts of the National Park Service, Colonial National Historical Park at Jamestown. Our sincere thanks also to the knowledgeable and ever-helpful staff of the Irma and Paul Milstein Division of United States History, Local History, and Genealogy at the New York Public Library. We were also ably assisted by the staff of the Deborah, Jonathan F. P., Samuel Priest, and Adam Raphael Rose Main Reading Room of the New York Public Library, and by the staff of the Bobst Library at New York University. Descha Daemgen of New York University made a key contribution to our work at a crucial stage. Our editor, Hana Lane, was understanding, encouraging, and helpful, and as always our agent, Al Zuckerman, was persistent and patient on our behalf. Finally, thanks to our daughter Ellen, a doctoral candidate at Columbia University, for her perceptive reading of an early stage of the manuscript.

Prologue

They said—those who had been here before—that you could smell America before you could see it. "We smelled the fragrance a hundred leagues away," wrote Giovanni da Verrazano in 1524 about his approach to Cape Fear in today's North Carolina, "and even farther when they [the natives] were burning the cedars and winds were blowing from the land." Arthur Barlowe, captain of a reconnaissance voyage sent out from England in 1584, reported, "The second of July, we found shole water, which smelt so sweetely . . . as if we had been in the midst of some delicate garden, abounding with all kinds of odiferous flowers, by which we were assured, that the land could not be farre distant." Two days later, Barlowe reached the North American coast.

Several of the men on board the three small ships that were now, in the early hours of April 21, 1607, groping in the predawn darkness for an American landfall could testify to the truth of this. Gabriel Archer, who had seen America five years earlier, compared the scent of the coast to that of Andalusia in Spain—a blend of fresh flowers, wild fruit, and aromatic woods such as cedar, laurel, and cypress. For nearly a week that drifting fragrance had tantalized the men aboard the *Susan Constant*, the *God Speed*, and the *Discovery* as they made their way north from the West Indies, paralleling the Atlantic coastline of what is today the United States. To them, the name of the land they sought was Virginia, named for—and by—England's virgin Queen Elizabeth, and neither they nor anyone else had any idea of its extent or size. Nor could they possibly have imagined that their mission would prove to be one of the most significant in the history of the world.

Captain Christopher Newport, the gritty, forty-seven-year-old, one-armed "admiral" of the voyage and commander of the flagship *Susan Constant*, knew that land—the sweet-smelling coast of Virginia—certainly lay not far to his west. He was, however, looking for a specific place, a great bay that had been seen twenty-two years earlier by an exploring party from the first English colony in America, whose inhabitants had mysteriously disappeared.

Five days earlier, Newport's ships had encountered a violent storm, "a vehement tempest," one of the colonists described it, "which lasted all the night with winds, rain, and thunders in a terrible manner." The ships were forced to rest on their anchors, because the captains feared they would be blown onto the shore in the darkness. By Newport's calculations, they should now be very close to their intended destination, and the omnipresent scent of land increased his expectations. Every day following the storm, starting with the twenty-second of April, he had ordered his longest lead line tossed overboard to test the depth. Though the line was a hundred fathoms long, time after time it failed to reach the bottom. John Ratcliffe, the captain of the smallest of the three ships, suggested that they give up the search and return to England. Yet Newport must have believed he was very near his goal, so near that he would likely have forsaken sleep, anxious lest he miss it. He sent a boy with young, sharp eyes to sit high atop the mainmast, looking for any sign, even at night. Newport himself paced the deck, staring into the darkness, waiting to hear the lookout's cry.

Another man was certainly lying awake, listening keenly for it too, though he was confined below decks and probably in chains as well. John Smith—*Captain* John Smith as he liked to be called, though he had no rank on this voyage—had a particular interest in the ships' imminent arrival in Virginia, for that was where his enemies would attempt to hang him.

They had tried once before, on the island of Nevis in the West Indies, where the small fleet had anchored for six days to take on fresh water and fruit. Young and brash, red-bearded, notably short of stature, and hot-tempered, Smith had been accused of

plotting mutiny. Very likely his crime had been to offer his opin-
ions and criticism too freely to those who considered themselves
superior to him in rank or birth.

On that earlier occasion, Captain Newport no doubt had
intervened to save Smith from summary execution. However,
Newport's authority was about to lose its force. Everyone on board
was conscious of the sealed iron strongbox in the admiral's cabin,
which contained a list of seven people who would make up the
governing council of the Virginia colony. The names were to be
kept secret until the journey was completed, probably to preserve
Newport's authority over his squabbling passengers. Speculation
as to who might be on that list was no doubt rife, and several
of Smith's enemies on the vessels considered themselves likely
candidates. After the strongbox was opened, someone other than
Newport would have the power either to spare Smith or hang
him, and the latter seemed the more likely outcome.

If Smith felt fear, he never mentioned it in the narrative of
the voyage that he later wrote. He had faced worse situations
during his twenty-seven years of life. If his own account can be
believed, he had already survived mortal hand-to-hand combat,
bloody battles on land and sea, attempts to drown him, and en-
slavement by a Turkish pasha—and those were only a few of the
adventures he claimed to have experienced.

If he can be believed. There's the rub, as Smith's contemporary William Shakespeare wrote in another context. Smith is often
the only witness for some of his most heroic exploits, leading
some even in his lifetime to doubt the truth of his claims, and his
reputation has risen and fallen ever since on the strength of those
doubts. However, the story of Smith's arrival in America—in disgrace, a prisoner, and facing the possibility of execution—is not
one of those doubtful occasions. Others on board vouched for it,
and those who have sought to discredit Smith in the centuries
after his death have sometimes reveled in the fact that he arrived
in the New World "in chains." Ironically, he would become the
person most responsible for the survival of the colony.

As the first sunlight of the day appeared in the eastern sky,
the boy in the crow's nest saw its reflection off to the west, and

gave the signal all had been waiting for: "Land! Land ho!" Others rushed from their cramped bunks below decks, eager to see the New World. Within hours, Newport discovered that he had, through a combination of luck and skill, hit the spot he was aiming for. The great bay that the ships now entered, with an entrance 265 times as wide as the Thames at London, was unmistakably the one called Chesupioc ("great water") by the natives who lived along its shores.

That evening, a number of the gentlemen from the three ships gathered in Newport's cabin. There were at least fifty men aboard who claimed the status of gentle birth, so it is unlikely that all of them could have squeezed inside the small space. Even less likely is that anyone thought to include John Smith in the proceedings. In all probability, he was still shackled below, awaiting his fate.

By flickering candlelight, Newport broke the wax seal on the box and began to read the names on the paper he found inside. His own name, followed by those of Bartholomew Gosnold and John Ratcliffe, the captains of the two other ships, came first. Newport's designation was more or less honorary, since he would return to England after carrying out a few other duties, but Gosnold and Ratcliffe were slated to remain with the colony. Edward Maria Wingfield, the only person on the voyage named as a patentee in the royal charter of the Virginia Company, fully expected to hear his name read and was gratified when it was. Then came the names of John Martin, son of a former lord mayor of London, and George Kendall, supposedly a cousin of Sir Edwin Sandys, a wealthy merchant and member of the Virginia Company that had sponsored the voyage.

So far, no surprises, although there must have been disappointment among those hoping to hear their names read. The seventh, and last, name was likely to be that of George Percy, younger brother of the Earl of Northumberland.

Instead, Captain Newport astounded those assembled by reading the name John Smith. A smile may have crossed Newport's face, for perhaps he knew all along the identity of the council members, and that accounted for his saving Smith from the gallows on Nevis. Possibly someone hoping to curry favor with the new council member slipped off to inform Smith of his designation. Others, in particular Edward Maria Wingfield, who is thought to be the person who accused Smith of mutiny, certainly wondered, who was this nobody who seemed to have such powerful friends, this John Smith? It is a question people have been asking ever since.

I

Dreams of Glory

THE NAME JOHN SMITH IS SAID to be the commonest of English appellations. The man who received it at his baptism in 1580, in the little village of Willoughby-by-Alford, Lincolnshire, spent his life trying to distinguish himself from all the others. He succeeded, and today when people hear his name with the title he earned for himself—*Captain* John Smith—they recognize it. "Oh, *that* John Smith," they say, usually adding, "the one who was in love with Pocahontas." The true John Smith, unfortunately, has been subsumed by the legend that he himself helped to create.

The church in which he was baptized, on January 9, 1580 (1579 in that era's calendar, in which the new year did not begin until March), was dedicated to Saint Helen, the patron saint of travelers. She certainly blessed the infant at the baptismal font that day, for during his lifetime he would travel to four continents. Wanderlust may have been a family trait, because both his parents were newcomers to Lincolnshire, a marshy and isolated county in the east of England. In an era when few people ever ventured more than twenty miles from their birthplace, George Smith, John's father, had moved from Lancashire, more than 140 miles away. Likewise, Alice Rickard, George's wife, had her roots in Great Heck, Yorkshire, in north-central England. What brought them to Lincolnshire is unknown, but in George's case it probably was the opportunity to possess land.

George Smith must have been an ambitious man, for he not only farmed and grazed animals on land of his own, but he also rented out tenements, or houses, to others. In addition, his agricultural enterprises were extensive enough to enable him to lease land from Peregrine Bertie, Lord Willoughby, the largest landholder in the area. Though the village of Willoughby-by-Alford had been the source of the noble lord's title, he had recently built a grand manor house in Eresby, several miles away. So in Willoughby itself, a village of perhaps three hundred to four hundred souls, George Smith was probably the wealthiest person, as the inventory of his possessions in his will indicates.

Yet he was ranked as a "yeoman," slightly below a "gentleman" in the social hierarchy of the time. The important difference, as Sir Thomas Overbury wrote in describing the English yeoman in 1615, was, "Even though he be master, he says not to his servants 'go to the field,' but 'let us go.'" A gentleman was known by his clean, soft hands, for he did no physical labor. George's son John—though he continually showed his disdain for those who would not work—nevertheless yearned for the distinction and respect that gentlemen's sons had from birth.

In this quest, young John had a model: a yeoman's son, like himself, who rose to greatness and wealth through ambition and achievement. This was Sir Francis Drake, who in the year after John Smith's birth completed the first English circumnavigation of the world, a voyage that was primarily undertaken to loot Spanish ships laden with treasure in gold and silver from the Americas. Drake's haul is estimated to have been worth half a million pounds, easily the equivalent of a *billion* dollars in today's money.

The lion's share of this loot went to Queen Elizabeth I, who showed her gratitude by coming aboard Drake's ship, the *Golden Hind*, moored at Deptford on the Thames near London. While Londoners crowded along the docks to watch, Elizabeth dubbed Drake "our golden knight," raising a gilded sword to make him Sir Francis.

An honor like that seldom came to the son of a yeoman, and young John Smith certainly regarded the world-circling Drake as an inspiration. The sea was never far from the thoughts of those who lived in Willoughby-by-Alford, for much of the surrounding land had originally been marsh, which the villagers had reclaimed for agriculture by draining it and then building dikes that kept it from flooding. Regular maintenance of those dikes—probably a communal task—was a constant reminder of the power of the sea only six miles away. John Smith certainly assisted in this work from an early age. As night fell and the villagers started for home, John would have seen the eerie will-o'-the-wisps, swamp gas that briefly ignited, deceiving and frightening the unwary. He became accustomed to them, resisting the teasing of older boys who wanted to scare him. Those who knew John later, both as friend or enemy, attested that he was a man who seldom showed fear.

Elizabeth had been queen of England for twenty-two years when John Smith was born, and she would reign for another twenty-three. The era known as the Elizabethan Age was a time when England took its place as one of the great European powers. Exports of the nation's principal product, wool, increased, bringing wealth to some. Culturally, it was a golden age of drama in which Shakespeare, Christopher Marlowe, and Ben Jonson produced works that have survived the centuries since. When Elizabeth declared in 1559 that England would be officially Protestant, she incurred the enmity of the Catholic countries, primarily Spain. From that point on the two nations would compete commercially and politically, barely avoiding open warfare in a kind of sixteenth-century cold war. Spain had prospered in part because of its New World colonies and had virtually declared America its own territory, to be shared only with its neighbor Portugal. The queen had not dared to challenge Spain openly by declaring war, but she had granted "letters of marque" that gave a cover of legality to the activities of private captains like Drake and Sir John Hawkins who attacked and plundered Spanish ships at sea. To the Spaniards, there was little difference between these "privateers" and pirates, and by 1588 Spain was ready to take action against England.

When John was eight years old, a threat appeared from the sea: an armada of warships sent by Spain to crush once and for all the upstart nation of Protestant heretics whose seafarers had harassed Spanish shipping for most of Elizabeth's reign. King Philip II ordered the governor of the Spanish Netherlands, the Duke of Parma, to invade England the following spring. To move Parma's thirty thousand troops from the Netherlands, Philip would send a fleet of warships and transports up the English Channel to the port of Dunkirk.

It did not take the English long to learn of Philip's intentions, and Elizabeth raised a fleet of her own to defend the Channel against the Spanish Armada. All of the legendary sailors of her age were involved in the preparations—Drake, of course, and Martin Frobisher, who had made several attempts to find a northwest passage through America to Asia, and John Hawkins, whose exploits as a privateer were as renowned as Drake's.

Drake was now an admiral, second-in-command of the English fleet. Some thought his abilities qualified him to be the supreme commander, but Elizabeth's policy was to appoint only men of high birth to such positions. The fleet was thus under the command of Lord Howard, though Howard had the good sense to listen to Drake's freely given advice. (At least Howard was a navy man. Using much the same logic as Elizabeth, King Philip had entrusted his armada to the Duke of Medina Sidonia, a landlubber who protested, "I know by my small experience afloat that I soon become seasick, and always catch cold.")

Preparations for England's defense took place on land and sea. All along the southwest coast, scouts gathered woodpiles that would be set on fire as soon as the Spanish fleet was sighted. Spreading up the coast from bonfire to bonfire, the signals would alert the English ships waiting in the Channel. Even in Lincolnshire, up on England's North Sea coast, people readied for the invasion, for no one knew where the Duke of Parma's troops might come ashore. Like many other places, Lincolnshire raised a volunteer force of "trained and untrained men" who prepared to defend their country with matchlock muskets, pikes, and pitchforks. Eight-year-old John Smith must have regarded it as the most exciting year of his young life.

The Armada appeared off the Lizard, the southernmost point of the British Isles, on the afternoon of July 29, and an epic seven-day battle ensued along the south coast of England. The English were getting the better of it, but eventually the continual bombardments left both sides without enough powder or cannon-balls to continue. Though Medina Sidonia managed to get his fleet to Calais, France, a mere twenty miles from Dunkirk, he was never able to rendezvous with the Duke of Parma and the invasion force the Armada had come to protect. With supplies running low, Medina Sidonia decided to turn north and return home by circling around the top of the British Isles, instead of trying to head back through the Channel the way he had come. He had no way of knowing that storms and shoals would be far more destructive than the English fleet; in rounding Britain, he would lose half his fleet and turn the expedition into a colossal disaster. Only about a third of the twenty-seven thousand men who left Spain with the Armada ever saw home again.

Communications were slow at best in those days. Even after the battle between the two fleets was over, the English were not certain they had won—indeed, rumors spread on the Continent that the Spaniards were the victors. Certainly the ragtag defense force formed by the people of Lincolnshire would have main-tained its guard at the shore. Boys like young John Smith might have served as lookouts—and in any case the temptation to catch a glimpse of the sails of the fearsome Armada would likely have been too great for any boy to resist. In the end, Lincolnshire rejoiced as the news of the fate of the Armada gradually became known.

To most Englishmen and Englishwomen, the arrival of the Armada was a short-lived crisis, not to be compared with the threat to their livelihoods posed by what historians call the en-closure movement. This was the burning economic issue that haunted Englishmen from the sixteenth century to the middle of the seventeenth. Traditionally, the rural population had carried on subsistence farming on strips of land in the common fields, for which they paid their landlords in kind, or produce. Herds of sheep and cattle also grazed on common land. But beginning in about the thirteenth century, some landholders—prosperous yeomen as well as lords—began to consolidate their holdings through purchase or trade, enclosing them with hedges or fences. At first this may have been done to utilize more efficient methods of farming. But as wool became England's largest and most profitable export product (sent to the Netherlands where it was made into fine cloth), landholders started to turn their fields into pasturage for sheep—and sheepherding required far fewer workers than farming. Little by little, the small tenant farmers saw the common land of their villages fenced off. Often they were forced by economic necessity to sell their land rights to yeomen, who were notorious for their acquisitiveness.

John Smith, growing up, witnessed the results. Stripped of their land, the dispossessed farmers looked for work, and when they were unable to find it either relied on the charity of the local parish, became beggars, or turned to thievery. Sir Thomas More, author of *Utopia* and lord chancellor of England before Henry VIII executed him, described those who "must needs depart away, poor, silly, wretched souls, men, women, husbands, wives, fatherless children, widows, woeful mothers, with their young babes. . . . Away they trudge . . . finding no place to rest in." Many headed for London, where the population rose drastically, despite chronically overcrowded conditions and the plagues that regularly wracked its population.

Earlier, the Roman Catholic monasteries had distributed food and given shelter to those who had none. After Henry made his break with Rome and dissolved the monasteries, it became clear that the state itself must take a hand in providing for those unable to help themselves, and Parliament began to pass a series of Poor Laws. Under Henry VIII's first two children to take the throne, Edward VI and Mary, the government appointed collectors of alms to go throughout the realm and raise voluntary contributions for the destitute. It also started to license poor folk to help themselves by begging. Those measures failed. By 1572, the fifteenth year of Elizabeth's reign, Parliament found that the kingdom was overrun "with rogues, vagabonds and sturdy beggars . . . by means whereof daily happeneth horrible murders, thefts, and other great outrages." So the government appointed "overseers of the poor" with the power to assess the local parishes to raise funds to provide work for those who could find none elsewhere. Refusing the offer of work was made a punishable offense. Anyone over the age of fourteen who was convicted of wandering or begging was to be "grievously whipped and burnt through the gristle of the right ear with a hot iron of the compass of an inch about." The penalty for conviction of a third offense was death.

This was the world in which John Smith spent his youth, and years later when he reached America, with its apparently limitless expanses, he would not forget the misery he had seen, the grinding poverty that afflicted those with no land.

Poverty was not a personal concern for Smith. He lived in one of the largest homes in Willoughby-by-Alford, adorned with painted wall hangings. He slept on a featherbed, rather than straw. His father, George, was ambitious for his eldest son—perhaps as ambitious as the "typical" yeoman described by Sir Thomas Smith, secretary to the earl of Essex, in 1583: "[They] commonly live welthilie, keepe good houses, do their businesse, and travaile to get riches . . . by these meanes do come to such wealth, that they are able and daily doe buy the lands of unthriftie gentlemen, and after setting their sonnes to the schools, to the Universities, to the lawe of the Realme or otherwise leaving them sufficient landes whereon they may labour, doe make their said sonnes by these meanes gentlemen."

When John, at the age of six or seven, went to an "ABC school" in the nearby market town of Alford, his father probably had in mind that he was placing his son on the road to becoming a gentleman. At Alford, John learned to write English and some Latin, along with elementary mathematics. Repetition and memorization were the standard teaching methods, and students practiced composition and penmanship by writing letters. The little school, founded with a bequest from a merchant in 1565, went no farther than providing the basics. Most of those who attended probably needed to know only what was necessary for conducting business, calculating profit and loss, buying and selling livestock, seed, and their own harvests.

So it was a significant step forward when John continued his education by entering the boarding school at the larger town of Louth, some twelve miles from his home. Officially known as the King Edward VI Grammar School, the school prepared its students to enter Cambridge, Oxford, or the Inns of Court, which was the entry to a career in law or government. At Louth, Smith encountered the sons of gentlemen and even nobles. Perhaps he was made to feel his social inferiority, and there his lifelong refusal to show "proper" deference to those higher up the scale made its first appearance. Red-haired and notably short, he must have learned early the art of fisticuffs. Certainly none of his teachers or fellow students would have guessed that four hundred years later, a mural at the school would celebrate John Smith as one of Louth's most illustrious pupils.

The King Edward VI Grammar School was a particularly strict institution. Its seal bore the legend (in Latin, from Proverbs 13:24): "He that spareth the rod hateth his son." To emphasize the practical application of the message, a schoolroom scene was depicted on the seal, quaintly described by an early-twentieth-century English historian: "A stalwart pedagogue [is] seated with his legs apart, and on his left knee a boy; the pedagogue's left hand is holding up the boy's garment and baring the parts below the middle, on which a mighty birch erect in the pedagogue's right hand is about to fall. The boy's hands are clasped in a vain appeal for mercy."

Corporal punishment—in the form of "continuall and terrible whipping"—was the usual order of things in Tudor grammar schools. William Bedell, another yeoman's son like Smith but later a respected bishop, attended a school at Grantry in the 1580s. His son recalled that Bedell had "such a love for learning that no harshness of his master could [discourage it]. . . . [One] time he received such a blow from his cholerick master that he . . . had one side of his head so bruis'd that the blood gush'd out of his ear and his hearing on that side was so impair'd that he became . . . wholly deaf as to that ear."

Smith must have had a difficult time accepting such punishments. More than most boys he had dreams of the world outside

The seal of Louth Grammar School, which John
Smith attended in the 1580s. The school was founded
in1552, during the reign of Queen Elizabeth's half
brother, Edward VI. The depiction of a master
whipping a student indicates the school's philosophy
of proper educational method.

the classroom; as he recalled, his mind was "even then set upon
brave adventures." When he was thirteen, he sold (using, like
Julius Caesar, the third person to refer to himself) "his satchell,
bookes, and all he had, intending secretly to get to Sea." His
plans, that time, were thwarted—how, he doesn't tell us. In any
event, he returned to school, and no doubt endured a particularly
severe beating for his vain attempt.

Smith tells us that his parents died that same year, and that
"his father's death stayed him" from his intention to become a
sailor. Contemporary records, however, show that Smith's father
did not die until Smith was sixteen, and his mother lived on for
some years, remarrying less than a year after her husband's death.
What does it say about a man that he forgot when his parents died, and ended his mother's life prematurely—at least in
memory? Considering that Smith was never to form a romantic attachment to any woman, it appears significant. Oddly, the
women he encountered always seemed to have served as saviors,
not lovers—for Pocahontas was not his only rescuer.

It is not clear how long Smith stayed in school after his attempt to run away. Two years later, when he was fifteen, his father apprenticed him to Thomas Sendall, of King's Lynn, in Norfolk, southeast of Lincolnshire across the shallow bay called the Wash. Sendall was, as even Smith admitted, "the greatest merchant of all those parts." This was an excellent opportunity for the young man, and indicates that his father must have had important contacts beyond the local village. It suggests that even as a young man, John Smith may have already attracted the notice of more powerful men—those who could have helped him if he had been the sort of person to want a conventional career.

Apprentice or no, young John still yearned for glory at sea, like the honors won by Drake. He hoped his master would send him on a trading voyage, for Sendall had an import-export trade with the Continent. A year after starting his apprenticeship, however, Smith still found himself doing work he loathed: tallying inventories and cargoes, preparing bills, checking shipments both incoming and outgoing. Each ship that sailed from King's Lynn down the estuary of the Great Ouse River, heading out to sea, carried John Smith's dreams with it—but not the young man himself.

Then, in 1596, his father died. In his will, George Smith downplayed his importance, describing himself as the "poore tenant" of Lord Willoughby. Before mentioning his own family, George left Lord Willoughby "as a token of my dewtifull good will the best of my two yeares old colts." A gift for one's lord was customary—Lord Willoughby himself left "a cup of gold to the value of a hundred pounds" to Queen Elizabeth—but George Smith certainly wanted to ensure Willoughby's continued benevolence toward his children, who included a son and a daughter younger than John. George left his farm to his wife, with the proviso that should she marry again it would pass to his eldest son. (Within a year, when the inventory of George Smith's household goods was taken, Alice Smith had indeed remarried.) John also received seven acres of pasture land, along with his father's admonition: "I chardge and command [him] to honoure and love my foresaide good Lord Wiloughbie duringe his lyfe."

John Smith would follow that advice, to his future benefit, but the possession of a farm and pasture land—a good start in the world for most young men of his time—could not entice him to follow in his father's footsteps. He had no desire to be a farmer. Instead, his father's death and his mother's remarriage freed him to follow a different path.

Because Smith was not yet of age, guardians were named to take charge of his property and money. We know what he thought of them because he wrote, with a touch of sarcasm, "They liberally gave him (but out of his owne estate) ten shillings to be rid of him," and added, with more than a touch of self-pity, "Such oft is the share of fatherlesse children."

But the guardians could not prevent John from leaving his apprenticeship. Apparently soon after his father's death, Smith went to France, where he joined a company of English soldiers, with whom he had his first taste of combat. Queen Elizabeth had sent military forces to the Continent in 1585 to assist the Protestant Dutch in their fight for independence from Spain. Four years later, she also gave military aid to the forces of the Protestant claimant to the throne of France, Henry of Navarre.

Though Smith served in both the Netherlands and France for three or four years, he uncharacteristically left no detailed account of his activities. He failed, evidently, to win the glory he sought. His experiences more likely resembled those of Thomas Raymond, another Englishman who fought in the Netherlands some three decades later. For the average foot soldier, conditions had changed little since Smith's time:

"One night I had nothing to keep me from the cold wet ground but a little bundle of wet dried flax . . . and so with my boots full of water and wrapped up in my wet cloak I lay as round as a hedgehog and at peep of day looked like a drowned rat. . . . And truly, by what I have seen and felt, I cannot but think that the life of a private or common soldier is the most miserable in the world. . . . Soon after our return to garrison to good lodging and diet, many of our soldiers fell into sicknesses and some died. Myself had a huge boil broke out on the inside of one of my thighs from which issued such abundance of filthy matter that I suppose it cleared me from sickness. . . . I had no great fancy to this kind of life but seeing no other way to make out a fortune . . . I buckled myself to the profession."

Smith felt something of a personal connection to the war in the Netherlands, for Lord Willoughby—the man his father had charged him to "honoure and love"—had won renown there. Eleven years before John joined the fighting, Willoughby had led 250 cavalry and 300 foot soldiers against a force of 3,000 Spaniards under the Duke of Parma. Willoughby won a famous victory and a knighthood. He would become celebrated in a song chanted by generations of English schoolchildren, and perhaps even by young John Smith himself:

The fifteenth day of July,
With glistering spear and shield,
A famous fight in Flanders
Was foughten in the field.
The most courageous officers
Were English captains three.
But the bravest man in battle
Was the Brave Lord Willoughby.

By the time Smith arrived in the Netherlands, Lord Willoughby had departed; the queen had rewarded him by making him governor of Berwick-on-Tweed, a military post on the Scottish border. However, Smith received an assignment that indicated that Willoughby not only knew the young man, but trusted him. Willoughby's elder son, Robert Bertie, was now stationed in the city of Orleans, and Smith brought Robert's younger brother, Peregrine, from Lincolnshire to join him.

Robert Bertie, though two years younger than Smith, had already—at the tender age of fourteen!—earned a knighthood for his valor in the capture of the Spanish city of Cadiz by English forces. Smith might well have reflected that the son of a nobleman had greater opportunities for advancement than the son of a yeoman, who was destined to be a foot soldier and not an officer. Thus, when an opportunity for advancement presented itself, Smith seized it. Possibly through the Bertie family's influence, he received a letter of introduction to powerful figures at the court of King James VI of Scotland (who would in a few years become Elizabeth's successor and reign in England as James I). Smith sailed for Scotland, but his boat was wrecked off the English coast. Fortunately, he was saved from drowning, and recuperated for some time on the island of Lindisfarne. Finally reaching Scotland, he found to his disappointment that he had "neither money, nor meanes to make him a Courtier." No doubt he realized that he didn't have the temperament for it either—a wise decision, for the court of King James was, even more than Elizabeth's, a hotbed of intrigue and conspiracy where flattery and backbiting were necessary skills.

Around 1600 John Smith, now twenty, returned home to Willoughby-by-Alford, somewhat deflated and disillusioned by his experiences abroad. Still, he found himself a kind of local hero, in demand at the local alehouse to tell the stories of his adventures for the enjoyment of his friends, farmboys like himself but who had never ventured more than a few miles from home.

The notoriety quickly wore thin. As Smith wrote, "within a short time being glutted with too much company, wherein he took small delight, he retired himself into a little woodie pasture, a good way from any town. Here by a faire brooke he built a Pavilion of boughes, where only in his cloaths he lay." Smith had withdrawn from the world to meditate, study, and—now that he knew the world better than before—decide what his place in it would be. He had already turned down a chance for a higher education, for a merchant's career, or even his father's occupation as a yeoman farmer. He had failed to win a name for himself in battle or to enter the ranks of royal courtiers. Only here, in his retreat near Willoughby, had he found sufficient respect to acquire a local boy, who served as his "page," bringing him food and running errands.

Smith tells us the names of only two of the books he read during his solitary sojourn: "Marcus Aurelius" and Machiavelli's *The Art of War*. These titles are misleading. The work known today as *The Meditations of Marcus Aurelius*, believed to have been written by the Roman emperor of that name, was not translated into English until 1634. It is highly likely that the book Smith read was a work titled *The Diall of Princes*. ("Diall" here refers to a compass, meaning roughly "directions for.") It was written by a Spanish courtier and priest named Don Anthony de Guevara and passed off by him as a translation of Marcus Aurelius's meditations. After the Guevara work was published in Spain in 1529, it won immense popularity and was translated into many languages. Two English translations were extant at the time Smith sought to refocus his life.

The Diall is largely composed of advice given by an older man to a younger one on how to live a noble life, which would certainly appeal to Smith, who was looking for a mentor. Guevara viewed women with a jaundiced eye, and this too may have had a lasting effect on the impressionable English youth. The following passage is typical of the work's antifeminist spirit:

"Always from my youth I had a good mind, and yet, for all that, I have been overthrown with vices. Oh, how many times in my youth I knew women, I accompanied with women, I talked with women, and believed women, the which in the end have deceived me, misused me and defamed me. At the last I withdrew myself and forsook them, but I do confess that if reason kept me from their houses ten days, sensuality kept me with them ten weeks. . . . The frail flesh is somewhat to blame, but much more is the foolish and light woman in fault. For if men were certain that women were chaste . . . they would not dispose their hearts, their bodies, nor . . . consume their time to follow them, lose their goods to serve them. . . . For the hungry worms gnaw in the grave only the frail and slimy flesh of the dead: but you women destroy the goods, honour, and life of the living." There is more—much more—in this vein in *The Diall of Princes*, and it may have reinforced Smith's misogynistic feelings.

The other book Smith recalled reading, Machiavelli's *The Art of War*, contained material that Smith found useful in advancing his career. For the translator of the then current English edition, Peter Whitehorne, had appended another treatise to Machiavelli's work, one that gave detailed instructions on how to make "Saltpeter, Gunpowder, and divers formes of fireworkes or wilde fire." Smith made good use of this information later in life.

One book Smith could *not* have read at that time—because it was not published until 1605 and not in English until 1612—nevertheless comes to mind when one reads his account of his activities during his self-imposed isolation: "his exercise a good horse, with his lance and Ring; his food was thought to be more of venison than any thing else; what he wanted his man brought him. The countrey [people] wondering at such an Hermite." Inevitably this suggests Miguel de Cervantes's fictional hero, Don Quixote, whose devotion to the ideals of chivalry found its outlet in madness.

In England as well as Spain, though the age of chivalry was drawing to a close—if indeed it was not dead already—young men like Smith were still fascinated by it. Many popular books celebrated the deeds of knights-errant, and some were in fact imports from Spain and Portugal, such as the *Amadis of Gaul* and the *Palmerin* romances, the same books that Cervantes was satirizing in his famous epic. An autobiography by an English merchant's son, written in the seventeenth century, describes their effect:

"All the time I had from School . . . I spent in reading these Books; so that I being wholy affected to them, and reading how that *Amadis* and other Knights not knowing their Parents, did in time prove to be Sons of Kings and great Personages; I had such a fond and idle Opinion, that I might in time prove to be some great Person."

In these works of fiction, a knight could gain renown and glory by acts of valor, particularly in battle. Smith had not as yet achieved such feats, even though from boyhood he had before him the real-life exploits of men such as Drake, Hawkins, and, closest to him, "the brave Lord Willoughby." Imagine, then, the effect on him when a visitor of royal blood arrived one day at his hermitage. This was Theodore Paleologue, a man who claimed collateral descent from Constantine XI, the last man to occupy the throne of the Byzantine Empire, who had died defending his realm against the infidel Turks in 1453. Paleologue, a refugee from his homeland, was now riding master to the Earl of Lincoln. He had been sent by Smith's "friends"—no doubt Lord Willoughby or his sons—because they thought Smith needed to be jolted out of his daydreams.

Paleologue took Smith to Tattersall, the Earl of Lincoln's estate, where he gave him riding lessons and talked—telling him better stories, perhaps, than the ones Smith had been reading, and igniting the spirit of the Crusaders within his breast. Smith was to display unusual skill as a horseman; this was the place where he learned it, practicing long hours under the tutelage of Paleologue. At last Smith had a teacher he had to respect and obey. Besides horsemanship, Paleologue gave him a cause to fight for, telling him of the titanic struggle between Christianity and Islam. The Ottoman Turks, who had made Constantinople their capital and renamed it Istanbul, had been defeated on the seas by a confederation of European powers at Lepanto in 1571. Despite this loss, the Turks still controlled many formerly Christian lands in eastern Europe and the Balkans. Rudolf II, the Holy Roman Emperor, was now trying to regain these territories, putting together a coalition of forces that would serve as a counterweight to Turkish power.

Smith tells us that he had disliked fighting in France and the Netherlands because it was a war in which Christians were slaughtering one another. But the Turks—Muslim infidels—were enemies he could oppose without qualm, and before long he was off to Europe, with little more than a vague idea of how to join the battle.

2

"To Conquer Is to Live"

WE HAVE ONLY SMITH'S WORD for what happened to him during the next seven years—a time when he experienced events that were not only spectacular but, to some, unbelievable. Many authors from Smith's own day to ours have called him a braggart who exaggerated, if not invented, his adventures. But it is perhaps a sign of his sincerity that he begins with an episode depicting himself as a naive dupe—more Quixote than Sir Lancelot. "Foure French Gallants," as he described them, one posing as a "great Lord" and the others "his Gentlemen," learned of Smith's quest and invited him to travel with them to France, where they would introduce him to the "Duchess of Mercury," whose husband the duke was a general in the army of Holy Roman Emperor Rudolf II. (Mangling the spelling in his customary way, Smith clearly refers to the Duc de Mercour, a staunch Catholic who had in fact volunteered to help Rudolf.) Smith and his new friends took a ship to the port of Saint-Valéry-sur-Somme in Picardy. There, with the connivance of the ship's master, the "four gallants" had themselves rowed ashore with their luggage—and Smith's. The ship's boat stayed there because of choppy water until the evening of the next day. When Smith finally came ashore he was told his friends had traveled on to Amiens and would meet him there.

Other passengers let Smith know he had been duped. One of them, a soldier, had recognized the ringleader, who was not a lord but merely "the sonne of a Lawyer." Smith was left with only the clothes on his back and a little pocket change, but poverty never seemed to bother him, for he had the knack of making friends and the luck of encountering kind people. He lists the names of many who helped him as he traveled south, "wandring from Port to Port." Sometimes his account has the ring of the tales of chivalry he loved, as when he lay "in a Forest, neere dead with griefe and cold, a rich Farmer found him by a faire Fountaine under a tree. This kinde Pesant releeved him againe to his content." Smith even encountered a real French nobleman, the count of Plouër, who provided him with a new outfit and supplies for his journey. Years later, the count would receive his reward when Smith named a point of land in America after him.

After reaching Marseilles, Smith caught another ship, bound for Rome. Given the destination, it is not surprising that most of the other passengers were, as Smith wrote, "a rabble of Pilgrimes of divers Nations"—in other words, Roman Catholics. When a storm blew up, causing the captain to anchor offshore in hopes of riding it out, the passengers took it as a sign of God's displeasure that an English Protestant was among them. According to Smith, "his Nation they swore were all Pyrats, and so vildly railed on his dread Soveraigne Queene Elizabeth." Finally some declared "that they never should have faire weather so long as hee was aboard," and flung Smith over the rail.

Fortunately, a small uninhabited island lay nearby and Smith was able to swim to it. The next morning, he hailed a passing ship. As luck would have it—and Smith's luck was always phenomenal—the captain, a Breton named LaRoche, was a friend of the Count of Plouër. Any friend of the count's . . . and so Smith was invited to join the ship's company in delivering a cargo to Alexandria, at the eastern end of the Mediterranean. He accepted, listing in his autobiography the names of ports the ship stopped at along the North African coast, but unfortunately describing none of them.

The cargo delivered, Captain LaRoche turned back, now following the northern coast of the Mediterranean. When the ship reached the Adriatic Sea, it encountered a Venetian argosy, one

An illustration from Smith's 1630 autobiography shows him thrown into the Mediterranean by fearful pilgrims, and then, after swimming to an island, giving thanks to God. The "map" framing the scene shows the coast of Europe to the right, and Africa to the left.

of the large merchant ships that the wealthy island-state of Venice sent out to all parts of the Mediterranean world. Captain LaRoche sent a boat to communicate with the argosy, which responded in hostile fashion; Smith says the Venetians slew one of LaRoche's men, but perhaps he was only trying to excuse what happened next.

Captain LaRoche let loose three volleys of cannon fire, "the broad-side, then his Sterne, and his other broad-side also," displaying remarkable maneuverability. The Venetians first tried to run, but their sails and tackle were so shredded by LaRoche's volleys that they were compelled to turn and fight. The French closed with the Venetian ship and boarded it, upon which the Venetians set fire to their own vessel, hoping the French captain would have to draw clear. Instead, the French extinguished the fire and, seeing that their ship was near sinking, the Venetians surrendered. Smith—modestly or discreetly—did not describe his role in the battle, but he details the plunder with a keen eye: "Silks, Velvets, Cloth of gold, and Tissue [cloth woven with gold or silver thread]," along with a hoard of Spanish, Venetian, and Turkish coins. It took the French sailors a full day and a night to unload their booty, until, "tired with toile," they cast the ship off, leaving behind, Smith wrote, "as much good merchandize" as would have filled another ship the size of the French one.

That Smith did take a hand in the fighting we know, for when the French captain put him ashore at Antibes in Piedmont (today part of France, but then in the domain of the Duke of Savoy) Smith took with him "five hundred chicqueenes [gold coins] and a little box God sent him worth neere as much more."

Flush now with what God and a bit of piracy had given him, Smith took the opportunity "to better his experience by the view of Italy," or, in other words, to go touring, which was what he often did when he had an abundance of money. Once again, unfortunately, he only lists places he visited, except when he arrived in Siena, where he encountered the Bertie brothers. The elder, Robert, had become Lord Willoughby on the death of his father in 1601. According to Smith, his two friends had been "cruelly wounded, in a desperate fray," but apparently did not require his assistance, and after a few days he continued his journey.

Finally he reached Rome, where the splendor seems to have inspired him to detailed description and a bit of touristy lore: "it was his chance [good fortune] to see Pope Clement the eight, with many Cardinalls, creepe up the holy Stayres, which they say are those our Saviour Christ went up to Pontius Pilate, where bloud falling from his head, being pricked with his crowne of thornes, the drops are marked [on the stairs] with nailes of steele, upon them none dare goe but in that manner, saying to many *Ave-Maries* and *Pater-nosters*, as is their devotion, and to kisse the nailes of steele: But on each side is a paire of such like staires, up which you may goe, stand, or kneele, but divided from the holy Staires by two walls: right against them is a Chappell, where hangs a great silver Lampe, which burneth continually, yet they say the oyle neither increaseth or diminisheth."

While in Rome, Smith recalled, he "saluted" Father Robert Parsons, whom he identifies as "that famous English Jesuite." This considerably minimizes Parsons's reputation, for Parsons would have faced the death penalty had he been caught in England. A 1568 graduate of Oxford, he had accepted the Anglican faith, but six years later, accused of "popery," was forced to leave his teaching post. He went to Italy that summer, where he became a member of the Society of Jesus and helped establish a college in Rome to train English students for the priesthood. In 1580 he and another English Jesuit, Edmund Campion, slipped into England in disguise. They set up an illegal printing press to produce Catholic tracts, and they did missionary work. Campion was apprehended and executed, while Parsons fled his homeland forever. In Rome he continued to work for the eventual establishment of a Catholic monarch on the throne of England after "the death of that wretched woman," as he referred to Queen Elizabeth. Parsons endorsed the mission of the Armada as well as Philip II's claims that his daughter was England's rightful ruler, and English popular opinion regarded him as a traitor. When an early version of Smith's autobiography appeared in 1625, the editor omitted all reference to Parsons, even though the Jesuit had been dead for fifteen years, for his name was still anathema in England.

For that matter, it was also unusual for an English Protestant like Smith to stroll unannounced into the English College in Rome and ask to see Father Parsons, for the Inquisition actively persecuted heretics who fell into its hands. An Englishman named John Mole died in Rome in 1638 at the age of eighty, after thirty years in jail. A Scottish Presbyterian named William Lithgow visited Rome in 1609, some nine years after Smith was there, and wrote, "I hardly escaped from the hunting of these blood-sucking Inquisitors, of which the most part were mine owne Country men, the chiefest of which was Robert Mophet a Jesuit born in St. Andrewes, and of our Colledge there. . . . And to speake trueth, if it had not beene for Robert Meggat . . . who hid me secretly for three dayes at the top of his Lords Pallace, when all the streets and ports of Rome were layd for me . . . I had doubtlesse dyed."

Smith may have escaped such treatment because of his sincerity; he asked Father Parsons to help him join the forces opposing the Turks. Any forces would do, Catholic or Protestant. Parsons was impressed, and he seems to have sent Smith on his way with a letter of referral to an Irish Jesuit in the city of Graz, in Styria (part of today's Austria), who in turn "acquainted [Smith] with many brave Gentlemen of good qualitie." Smith managed to join a regiment commanded by the Count of Modrusch, a Protestant.

The Eastern Roman Empire had fallen to Mehmet the Conquerer in 1453, when Constantine XI Paleologue was killed defending Constantinople. Mehmet's great-grandson, Suleiman the Magnificent, continued the conquest of eastern Europe, nearly reaching Vienna before his death in 1566. Most of this conquered territory had been part of the domain of the Holy Roman Emperor. The latest man to hold that title, Rudolf II, was now fighting to reclaim his lands, assisted by a number of European commanders and rulers—among them his cousin Ferdinand, in whose army the Count of Modrusch served.

Modrusch's forces went to help break a Turkish siege of the city of Lower Limbach. After Smith learned that the Christian governor inside the city was Lord Ebersbaught, one of the "brave Gentlemen" he had met in Graz, he went to his commander with a plan. Using a code he and Ebersbaught had discussed earlier, the relief force could use torches to coordinate its movements with the defenders inside the town. This was straight from the textbook on warfare that Smith had read during his self-imposed sojourn in a glade near Willoughby-by-Alford.

That same book also inspired a diversionary trick that Smith now proposed. The firearms then in common use were matchlocks, in which a mechanism lowered a slow-burning fuse to ignite the powder that propelled the bullet. Smith argued that if several thousand burning fuses were set out in a line at night, the Turks would turn their defenses toward them, enabling the main offensive force to attack from another direction. Meanwhile, the torch signals would notify Ebersbaught of the planned attack, which he could then support with his own troops. Smith's plan worked: the

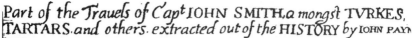

Part of the Trauels of Capt IOHN SMITH, a mongst TVRKES, TARTARS. and others. extracted out of the HISTORY by IOHN PAY

How hee releeued OLVMPAGH by a stratagem of Lights Chap 4

Again from Smith's autobiography, this scene shows his stratagem of using torches to send messages to the besieged Christian forces inside the town of Lower Limbach. The relief force, of which Smith was a part, could thus coordinate its actions to launch a two-pronged attack on the Turks who had surrounded the town.

Turks were forced to withdraw and the siege was lifted. Impressed, Modrusch gave Smith a reward: an officer's rank that he claimed ever after. From then on he was Captain John Smith.

Modrusch attached his regiment to a larger force led by the Duc de Mercour, whose current objective was to retake the city of Stuhlweissenburg, ancient capital of the kings of Hungary, from the Turks. In early September 1601, the duc's forces assembled outside Stuhlweissenburg's walls. Modrusch introduced his "fire-workes" expert to the chief of artillery, and Smith proposed using what he called "fiery Dragons": earthenware pots filled with an explosive mixture and lined on the outside with metal fragments. As he recalled, when these were set on fire and launched over the walls of the city with catapults, it was "a fearfull sight to see the short flaming course of their flight in the aire, but presently after their fall, the lamentable noise of the miserable slaughtered Turkes was most wonderfull to heare."

Smith's most spectacular military exploit was still to come. The sudden death of the Duc de Mercour led to Modrusch's decision to attach his forces to Zsigmond Bathory, Prince of Transylvania. Zsigmond was an erratic figure who had wedded the Holy Roman Emperor's cousin, but left her without consummating the marriage because he wanted to become a priest. (He failed at that too.) Because Transylvania bordered Ottoman territory, it had come under the sway of the Turks even though its population was Christian, but Zsigmond—for now—acknowledged the overlordship of the Holy Roman Emperor and needed military support.

In the spring of 1602, wrote Smith, "The earth no sooner put on her greene habit than the Earle [Modrusch] overspread her with his armed troopes." Heading for the city of Alba Iulia, which was Zsigmond's capital, they marched through a place Smith called the "Plains of Regall," possibly the Transylvanian Basin in today's Romania. A walled city stood in their path, and Modrusch settled in to besiege it. Mózes Székely, a Transylvanian general, arrived with reinforcements that doubled the size of the Christian forces. According to Smith, they "spent neere a month in entrenching themselves," so that the Turks jeered from the city walls, claiming that they were growing fat from lack of exercise. Finally, the Turks sent a challenge to the Christian camp:

"That to delight the Ladies, who did long to see some court-like pastime, the Lord Turbashaw did defie any Captaine . . . [to] combate with him for his head." Several of the Christian officers wished to accept the challenge, so they drew lots for the honor. The winner was Captain Smith.

The scene that followed could be taken from any youth's fantasy of a medieval tournament. Along the ramparts of the city's walls appeared "faire Dames" in finery, while the Christian forces, in battle array, awaited the appearance of the challenger, Lord Turbashaw. A blast of hautboys, oboe-like instruments, announced his appearance as he rode through the city gate. He was splendidly accoutered, making an impression on Smith that remained vivid twenty-five years later: "[O]n his shoulders were fixed a paire of great wings, compacted of Eagles feathers within a ridge of silver, richly garnished with gold and precious stones." As chivalric custom demanded, Turbashaw was accompanied by an aide bearing his heavy wooden lance. Two more assistants, on either side, led his horse. Smith, in his memoir of the event, still sounded chagrined that he himself had "only a Page" to bear his lance.

The Christians responded. Trumpets sounded from their ranks and Smith urged his horse forward. Both he and his opponent were in armor, and saluted as they rode past each other. In a formal tournament a barrier, or tilt, would have stood in the middle of the field to keep the horses from crossing each other's path. Likewise, the wooden lances would have had safety tips to ensure that they could not pierce the armor of the combatants, but merely unhorse them.

However, this was not a joust *à plaisance*, one held for ceremony or sport. Those kinds of tournaments were still popular throughout Europe; in Elizabethan England, they were occasions for the queen's knights to show their devotion to her. Sometimes elaborate allegories were part of the festivities, as in 1581 when the Duke of Alençon sent ambassadors to seek Elizabeth's hand in marriage. Four English knights, portraying the "foster children of desire," laid siege to the "fortress of perfect beauty," which had twenty-two defenders. The attackers and defenders jousted and fought with swords. No one was seriously injured, and at the end the four "attackers" knelt in submission to the queen.

Smith may have daydreamed of such tournaments, but now he faced a conflict *à outrance*, in which there were no rebated weapons. This would be a fight to the death. As Smith turned his horse to face his opponent, waiting for the signal to charge, he must have reflected that he would never have a better chance to win glory. His page handed up the lance, which was about eleven feet long and quite heavy. Lord Turbashaw certainly had experience in jousting, or he would not have issued the challenge. No doubt he thought Smith inexperienced; in that, Smith had an advantage, for he had been well drilled in the skills of lance warfare by Theodore Paleologue.

Smith lowered his face mask, raised his shield with one hand and the lance with the other, struggling to keep it level with the ground. A trumpet sounded: he spurred his horse onward and squinted through his visor at his onrushing foe. The sounds of heavy hoofbeats competed with shouts from both sides of the field.

Paleologue, Smith's trainer, may well have familiarized him with the work of Duarte, king of Portugal, who wrote a classic book on jousting technique, published in 1434. Smith would have recalled Duarte's advice:

"[T]hose who joust can fail in four different ways:

"Firstly, because they want to avoid the encounter.

"Secondly, because they veer away, fearing the moment of encounter.

"Thirdly, by failing to keep their body and lance steady because of the effort required.

"Fourthly, they are so anxious to gain an advantage over their adversary that they end up by failing."

Smith kept his eyes open and did not shy from the contact. He knew that quite likely his lance would shatter harmlessly against the largest target in sight: Lord Turbashaw's heavily armored torso. The lord was vulnerable at only one spot. In 1589, at a French royal tournament, the Duc de Montgomerie had inadvertently delivered a fatal blow to King Henri II when his lance—even though it had a rebated, or protective, tip—pierced the king's visor. The shocking mishap was widely known, and Theodore Paleologue may have told Smith of it.

So that was where Smith now aimed his lance, holding it high as the two riders approached each other at a gallop. It hit its mark, passing through Turbashaw's "face, head and all, [so] that he fell dead to the ground." Trying to control his elation, Smith dismounted and handed his lance to his page. Approaching his lifeless enemy, he exercised the right of the victor: he drew his sword to cut off Turbashaw's head and, followed by a cheering crowd of companions, presented it to General Székely.

That was not the end of Smith's heroics. Lord Turbashaw had a friend, Grualgo, who became, says Smith, "enraged with madnesse," and "directed a particular challenge to the Conquerer"— as Smith now termed himself—"to regaine his friends head, or

His three single Combats Chap. 7.
His Encounter with TVRBASHAW Chap. 7.

The first of the jousts that Smith engaged in while encamped outside a Turkish-held city on the "Plains of Regall." His opponent, Turbashaw, had issued a challenge to the Christian forces, and Smith won the right to respond. He managed to pierce the Turk's armor at its weakest point: the visor that allowed the rider to see.

lose his owne." To sweeten the challenge, Grualgo offered his horse and armor should Smith emerge the victor.

A second time, then, the field of battle was marked off. The cheers from either side were shriller, more desperate, now that death had made its dramatic appearance, and making the tournament far more than a game. After the trumpets' call, the two riders galloped toward each other, lances straight ahead—and both struck their targets, but this time it was the lances that gave way. Shattered into splinters, they fell to the ground. The riders turned for another pass through the list, as each man drew his pistol. The Turk aimed for Smith's body, and the pistol ball struck his chest. Fortunately for Smith, his armor was heavy enough so that even though the ball dented his steel breastplate, it did not pierce it. Smith's own shot nearly went astray, but passed through Grualgo's arm, making it impossible for the Turk to control his horse.

His Combat *with* GRVALGO. Capt *of* threehundred horſmen. Chap · 7 ·

As depicted by engraver Martin Doeshout in Smith's 1630 *True Travels*, Smith battles Grualgo, "captain of three hundred horsemen," in the second epic challenge. In this joust both men's lances shattered, and they drew their pistols. After taking his opponent's shot on his armor, Smith responded, piercing Grualgo's arm and unhorsing him. On the ground, the Turk was easy prey for Smith to finish off.

He was thrown to the ground, where he was struggling to get up when Smith dismounted and approached with his sword. In his account of the event, he stated simply that Grualgo "lost his head, as his friend before him; with his horse and Armour; but his body and his rich apparell was sent backe to the Towne."

Sullen now, the Turks within the town sought to avenge their fallen champions by staging surprise sorties against the Christians. These having little effect, the two sides settled in to the static state of siege once again. Now Smith grew bolder, perhaps pushing his luck. As a twenty-two-year-old who had already survived several brushes with death, he may have felt invulnerable. He obtained permission from his superiors to send a challenge of his own—in Smith's words, so "that the Ladies might know he was not so much enamoured of their servants heads, but if any Turke of their ranke would come to the place of combate to redeeme them, should have [Smith's] also . . . if he could winne it."

A man Smith calls Bonny Mulgro accepted. This time no lances were employed, because Mulgro as the challenged party decided Smith had demonstrated too much prowess with them. Instead, the combatants began with pistols, but neither man scored an effective shot, and on the next pass through the list, both brandished the most fearsome weapon yet employed: battle-axes with hooked blades that could tear a man asunder if struck from a galloping horse. The disadvantage of using the heavy weapons was that the momentum of their swing might cause a rider to lose his seat. Several times Smith and Mulgro passed each other, delivering and dodging blows, until Smith was struck so hard that he dropped his ax, and struggled to keep himself from falling to the ground as well.

Turning, Smith heard the shouts of triumph from the "ladies" on the ramparts of the town. Chivalric honor demanded that he ride past Mulgro once again, and the Turk was still armed with his deadly ax. Smith's only remaining weapon was a falchion, a short, broad sword effective when fighting on foot (and in taking heads), but virtually useless against an opponent in full armor. All the spectators on both sides knew, as the two combatants rode toward each other again, that Smith was rushing toward his death.

"The Turk," wrote Smith, "prosecuted his advantage to the uttermost of his power." Yet Smith's training under Paleologue served him well once again: "by the readiness of [Smith's] horse, and his [own] judgment and dexterity . . . beyond all mens expectation, by Gods assistance," he managed to dodge the blow from Mulgro's ax, and as the horses swept past each other he turned and deftly slipped the point of his falchion between two plates of armor on the Turk's back. Mulgro fell, but managed somehow to get to his feet. Yet as Smith declares, "he stood not long ere hee lost his head, as the rest had done."

The cries of triumph that greeted Smith were overwhelming. Riding at the head of a crowd of thousands, followed by three riderless horses, each carrying a Turk's head mounted on a lance,

How he flew BONNY·MVLGRO·Chap · 7 ·

In the final joust, the outcome looked bleak for Smith as he emptied his pistol and then lost his battle-ax. Dodging his opponent's blows, he managed to slip the point of a falchion, or small sword, under the rear of his opponent's breastplate. Note the crescent and cross, representing Islam and Christianity, above the head of each contestant.

he went to General Székely's tent. The general embraced the "conquerer," and presented him with a horse, swords, and a "belt worth 300 ducats." (Smith, the yeoman's son, was ever conscious of the price of his awards.)

As Smith tells the story, the Christian forces soon went on the offensive. Székely's father had been killed by Turks in a previous encounter, and now the general showed no mercy. He "did his best to wipe the town off the face of the earth." Before long the streets ran with blood, and hundreds of Turks' heads were impaled on stakes around the town walls.

Székely's men moved on, sweeping aside Turkish resistance, capturing and sacking three more towns. Triumphant, they made camp and Prince Zsigmond arrived to review his forces. Informed of Smith's exploits—not only the taking of the Turks' heads but his ingenuity with "fire-workes"—Zsigmond awarded him a coat of arms, Zsigmond's own portrait in gold, and a yearly pension of three hundred ducats. By one estimate, this was the equivalent of fifteen pounds, or about one-fifth the value of the property inventoried in Smith's father's estate. The yeoman's son was now a gentleman, and had found not only glory but a degree of wealth.

Smith was later able to obtain written confirmation of the prince's awarding him a coat of arms, and subsequently in 1625, he submitted it to the College of Arms in England, where the document was accepted as genuine by Sir William Segar, the Garter King of Arms, along with a drawing of the arms, bearing three stylized Turks' heads, and a motto Smith chose: *Vincere est Vivere*—"to conquer is to live." This document provides the only independent confirmation of Smith's military record, although another has been reported. Samuel Purchas, the editor of the first published version of Smith's memoirs, noted that he also consulted a history of the war written by Prince Zsigmond's secretary, Francisco Ferneza, an Italian. Purchas claimed to have a copy of the book, which he translated into English, but no trace of it has been found by any researcher since Edward Arber stated in his 1884 edition of Smith's works that he knew of a printed Spanish translation of Ferneza's book. That too is now lost. If found, it would greatly add to the credibility of Smith's account of his military career in eastern Europe.

After Zsigmond presented Smith with his reward for valor, the campaign took a new turn. Because Zsigmond was so erratic in his behavior, having resigned his office twice before and now showing signs of negotiating a separate agreement with the Turks, Emperor Rudolf II sent General Giorgio Basta with an army to establish imperial control over Transylvania, and Zsigmond promptly departed.

Modrusch and his men, including Smith, joined Basta's forces. They became involved in a struggle for Walachia, just south of Transylvania, where in September 1602 Basta's army won a major victory. Modrusch's forces, about eleven thousand strong, were assigned to pursue Turkish stragglers. They rode into a deadly trap. The Turkish ruler of Walachia had escaped after the battle and regrouped an army of fifteen thousand men. Worse, an even larger force of about forty thousand Crimean Tatars led by a Turkish ally nicknamed Bora ("the Drunken Camel") was moving toward Modrusch's line of march.

Modrusch's scouts warned him of the approaching menace, and he headed for Red Tower Pass—or Rottenton, as Smith called it—where the Aluta River crosses through the Transylvanian Alps on the border between Transylvania and Walachia. An enemy force was waiting in the pass to ambush Modrusch, but Smith came up with another "fire-workes" stratagem. Attaching metal casings filled with explosives to the tips of several hundred lances, Modrusch's men charged out of the night and routed their enemies.

But the victory came too late, for the Drunken Camel's forces had by now caught up to Modrusch. The Christians did the best they could. As Smith recalled, "It was a most brave sight to see the banners and ensignes streaming in the aire, the glittering of Armour, the variety of colours, the motion of plumes, the forrests of lances." But the odds were too great, and "the most of the dearest friends of the noble Prince Sigismundus perished."

They had made the Tatars pay dearly for the victory, and on the "bloudy field, neere thirty thousand lay, some headlesse, armlesse, and leglesse, all cut and mangled." Among them was Captain John Smith, wounded but not dead. Pillagers roamed the field after the battle looking for booty. Seeing Smith's armor (won from a Turk), they assumed he would be worth more alive than dead. Often the friends or relatives of Christian hostages ransomed them from their captors. So Smith's wounds were bound up, and when he was restored to health, he and others were brought to a slave market, "like beasts in a market-place, where everie Merchant, viewing their limbs and wounds, [set] other slaves to struggle with them, to trie their strength."

The Ottoman Empire was not the only part of Europe where human beings were bought and sold publicly. There was a busy slave market in Naples, and another in Lisbon where a traveler reported seeing men and monkeys sold side by side. But fear of the Muslim invaders fueled tales of their particular brutality.

Smith, a prisoner, his head shaved and an iron ring around his neck, is led into slavery by his Turkish captors.

Fynes Moryson, an Englishman who published an account of his wanderings through Europe during the 1590s, reported:

"The Marchants . . . buying these Captiues, lead them bound one to another in Chaynes, forcing the sick and weake with whips to march as fast as the rest, or els cutt their throates if they be not able to goe, and at night when they are brought into a stable, and might hope for rest, then they suffer hunger, the men are scourged with whips, the women and boyes are so prostituted to lust, as their miserable outcryes yeild a wofull sound to all that are neere them."

Smith was purchased by a man he calls Bashaw (or Pasha) Bogall, who sent his newly acquired possession as a gift to a young woman living in Constantinople. Smith recalled marching to the city with other slaves, "by twentie and twentie chained by the neckes." Delivered to his mistress, he understood her name to be Charatza Tragabigzanda, apparently a Greek phrase that may mean nothing more than "the girl from Trebizond."

Evidence that Smith's story is true comes from the fact that in 1614, when he was sailing the coast of New England, he gave the name Trabigzanda (leaving out a syllable) to the point of land north of Boston that is now known as Cape Ann. That was eleven years before the first time he mentioned her in print, indicating that she must have been part of his memories.

With Charatza, a pattern in Smith's life made its first appearance. In the chivalric tales, knights traditionally save damsels in distress. In Smith's experiences, a damsel often appears at a critical time to save *him*. We do not know how old Charatza was, but it is apparent that she was a young woman whose mother still supervised her closely.

Having been informed by Bashaw Bogall that he had personally taken Smith prisoner in battle, Charatza wished to know the circumstances. Through some of her friends who spoke English and Italian, she learned the true story of Smith's military adventures. "She tooke," Smith wrote, "much compassion on him," and found excuses to meet him in private. Finally, fearing that her suspicious mother would sell him, Charatza sent him to her brother, a *timor*, or government official, supervising a farm in another part of the Ottoman Empire. Her motives are made clear when Smith relates that she intended "he should there . . . sojourne to learn the language, and what it was to be a Turke, till time made her Master of her selfe." Presumably she would then reclaim and free him. This was not an impossible idea; some Christian captives, after converting to Islam, did in fact make careers for themselves in the Ottoman Empire.

Once outside Charatza's protection, however, Smith was shocked back to the reality of his slave status. He recalled that "within an houre after his arrivall," he was stripped naked, his beard and head shaved, and "a great ring of iron . . . riveted about his necke." He was given a raw, untanned sheepskin to wear. Several hundred other slaves, some Christian, some "Turkes and Moores," worked on the timor's estate. Smith, "being the last, was slave of slaves to them all . . . no more regarded than a beast."

Smith was in a territory he called Cambria. Not found on any map today, it was evidently north of Constantinople near the western shore of the Black Sea. Other Christian slaves advised him it was impossible to escape, for there was no safe place to flee. Smith saw the truth of this and remembered thinking that his only hope "to be delivered from this thralldom" was "the love

Sent to work in the fields of his owner's plantation, Smith seizes the opportunity to use his threshing bat on his master. In the background, Smith rides off, headed north to find refuge in the nearest Christian country—Russia.

of Tragabigzanda," but that she must be unaware of his harsh treatment.

One day Smith's temper overcame reason and caution. He was sent to thresh wheat in a field far from the main house. His master the timor, evidently fearing that Smith might be slacking, rode out to check his progress "and tooke occasion so to beat, spurne, and revile him." Smith, seeing that the two of them were alone, took advantage of the situation and "beat out the Tymors brains with his threshing bat."

Knowing that he would certainly be put to death for this offense, Smith took the only alternative. He dressed himself in the timor's clothes, mounted his horse, and rode off. It was a desperate attempt, for he was easily identifiable from his shaved head and the iron ring around his neck. He could ask no one for directions, and so headed north, where hundreds of miles away lay a Christian nation, Russia.

Smith stumbled upon a traders' road that was marked with signposts bearing symbols. The direction of Turkey was indicated by a crescent, of Persia by a black man with white spots, of China, the sun, and Muscovy (or Russia), a cross. For sixteen days he pursued the cross until at last he reached a Russian military garrison on the Don River. There the governor listened to his tale and had the iron ring removed from his neck. Smith also found another sympathetic woman, "the good Lady Callamata [who] largely supplied all his wants." What those wants might have been he refrains from telling, but by the time he left the fort he was again supplied with clothing and money.

With a safe-conduct pass signed by the governor, Smith rode west across the vast Russian heartland, where "in two days travell you shall scarce see six habitations." He noted and described log cabins that required no nails in their construction. (But it would not be Smith who introduced this form of dwelling to America; the Swedes built the first ones in Delaware in 1638.) He was headed back to Transylvania, for he wanted that precious piece of paper signifying he was now a gentleman with a coat of arms. Prince Zsigmond, however, had abdicated for the third time, so Smith pressed on in search of him through Hungary, Moravia, and the imperial capital of Prague. Finally he found Zsigmond in Leipzig. The prince recognized Smith and graciously gave him another copy of the paper attesting to his achievements and right to arms. For good measure he also presented Smith with "fifteen hundred ducats of gold to repair his losses." Presumably this was also the prince's way of discharging his earlier promise of three hundred ducats a year, considering his now reduced circumstances. By all available evidence, Smith never received any further payments from Zsigmond.

Smith left Leipzig as free as a man could be and embarked on another tour of Europe. In his memoir, he does little more than name the places he passed through, and it makes an impressive list—from the German states to Paris and other French cities, then on through Spain (again risking the wrath of the Inquisition, as an English Protestant with no excuse for being there). It is a pity that he tells us nothing about his activities or his impressions, for they would throw more light on a man who remained essentially private. It seems doubtful that he squandered his wealth on drink or women or gambling; friends who knew him not long afterward attested that those were not pleasures he enjoyed. He traveled out of curiosity: to see and to understand places and cultures that were different from those he knew. That curiosity, and the openness that accompanied it, would serve him well when he encountered the native peoples of America.

Ultimately, the lure of action proved stronger than the pleasures of tourism. Hearing that a war of succession had broken out among the three sons of the recently deceased king of Morocco, Smith went there with a dozen other men, presumably soldiers of fortune like himself. He found, however, that the warfare was not to his liking: "perfidious, treacherous, bloudy murthers rather than warre." Hoping to go elsewhere, he boarded a ship at the port of Safi. Its captain's name was Merham; Smith calls him an "old fox," and apparently his business was privateering, of a kind somewhat closer to outright piracy than usual. Smith professes to have been unaware of this, going aboard merely on Merham's invitation and then finding himself detained when a storm blew the ship out to sea.

Merham revealed his true colors when he captured and looted a ship loaded with casks of wine. The casual plunder of unwary vessels continued until Merham's vessel encountered two Spanish military men-of-war disguised as merchant ships. A violent battle ensued. When the ships closed with one another, Merham's crew fought back so ferociously—disregarding at one point a flag of truce offered by the Spaniards—that one Spanish ship was on the verge of sinking and both were forced to withdraw.

Smith ends his account of his early career with that episode. He doesn't mention making any money from the voyage, so it presumably wasn't very profitable. The clash with the Spaniards may in fact have frightened him—an unfamiliar emotion—for he describes it in more detail than any of his other military exploits. In any event, he decided that having seen much of the known world, he was tired of travel for the moment. Around the beginning of 1604 he went home to England.

3

Voyagers West

O N HIS HOMEWARD JOURNEY Smith would have come
up the Thames to London. Like any newcomer, he
must have been awed by what he saw. At the beginning
of the seventeenth century, London was a city of some 200,000
inhabitants—more than ten times the size of any other English
town. It was England's capital, principal port, and center of com-
merce, and it was dangerously overcrowded. Gutters stinking
with sewage and garbage ran down the center of every street.
Householders were forced to erect posts in front of their dwellings to protect them against the press of passing carts and animals.
Plague was rampant in the city. More than 30,000 Londoners
had died of it in 1603 alone, yet each year more people poured in
from the countryside, searching for work.

Houses, both humble and great, were built right to the edge
of the Thames, which rose and fell with the tide, even though
it was fifty miles from the sea. At flood tide, the water rushing
through the arches of London Bridge made a roar that could be
heard throughout the city. On either side of the roadbed of the
bridge stood shops and houses that rose as high as seven stories,
the buildings on opposite sides joining overhead, forming a tun-
nel through which people traveled back and forth from London
on the north bank to the less reputable towns of Southwark and
Bankside, where the city's prisons, brothels, hospitals, poorhouses,
bear-baiting arenas, and theaters were located. Those crossing

the bridge from the south were treated to the sight of the severed heads of criminals and traitors, which stood, rotting, on stakes above the entranceway.

Smith may well have stepped ashore at Billingsgate, a busy landing place not far from the bridge, and the site of a raucous fish market. The noise was legendary, referred to in several contemporary plays, and the continual cursing of the fish vendors made "billingsgate" a synonym for coarse language. Smith might have sought refuge from the din at the Blue Anchor Tavern, a well-known spot for travelers to refresh themselves and learn what had happened in their absence. Here he would have heard for the first time that Elizabeth was dead.

The old queen had passed away in the early morning of March 24, 1603. An astrologer—perhaps her favorite, John Dee—had predicted that she would die in bed, and for this reason during her last illness she had taken to sleeping in a chair or on cushions on the floor. Finally a courtier had persuaded her to lie down, and two days later she breathed her last.

She was seventy and had ruled England for nearly forty-five years. Most of her subjects could not recall a time when Elizabeth was not their sovereign. Their initial reaction on hearing the news was disquiet—fear that the bloody disputes over religion that had marked the reign of her Catholic sister Mary would now resume. But Robert Cecil, Elizabeth's wily secretary of state, had plotted to avoid any uncertainty over the succession. Cecil was not one of the handsome young men whom Elizabeth picked as her favorites. He was, in fact, five feet three inches tall and had a spinal deformity that made him appear to be a hunchback. But he had made himself exceptionally valuable through his keen intelligence and shrewd judgment. He had corresponded with the likeliest Protestant heir to the throne, King James VI of Scotland, who, like Elizabeth, could trace his ancestry back to Henry VII, the first Tudor king. Cecil obtained from Elizabeth a deathbed declaration naming James as her successor—or so Cecil claimed. Ironically, Elizabeth had ordered the execution of James's mother, Mary, Queen of Scots, a Catholic who had allegedly plotted to seize the English throne.

James had been a king—as he often reminded people—since his infancy. Within a year of his birth, his father had been killed, strangled by assassins after an explosion drove him from his house. Before another year had passed, his mother, Mary, Queen of Scots, had fled Scotland, suspected of having arranged her husband's death. She left her infant son behind, and James was raised by a series of guardians, several of whom also met violent deaths.

His precarious childhood, and perhaps congenital illnesses as well, took a toll on the boy. James became a strange mixture of brilliance, eccentricity, and fearfulness. Among other habitual precautions, he always wore a thick quilted doublet to ward off dagger thrusts. His appearance inspired neither confidence nor love. Observers noted that his tongue seemed too large for his mouth, causing a speech impediment, and also made him slobber when he drank from a cup. His legs were weak, causing him to lean on other men's shoulders and walk in a circular fashion. When upset, he fiddled nervously with his codpiece, and his large, curious eyes followed strangers who entered his presence, making them uncomfortable.

Yet James had real achievements. He wrote learned treatises on a number of subjects, from witchcraft (which he believed in) to tobacco (which he condemned, calling smoking "loathsome to the eye, hateful to the nose, harmful to the brain, dangerous to the lungs.)" As king of England, he sponsored a new translation of the Bible that remains one of the great literary works in the English language.

James also had definite ideas on what England's foreign policy should be. In the first year of his reign, he secured a peace treaty with Spain, ending fifteen years of warfare. Not all his courtiers were pleased; some attributed the negotiations to cowardice on James's part. Nevertheless, by the time Smith reached London, ambitious and adventurous men like him were coming to grips with a new reality. Fortunes were no longer to be made by privateers preying on Spanish shipping, for the peace treaty expressly forbade the practice.

The agreement was, however, silent on the possibility of England's establishing its own colonies in the New World, neither forbidding nor permitting them. James would, of course, try not to irritate the Spanish needlessly, but it seemed that England could turn its gaze westward, across the Atlantic, and consider how to compete with Spain in the Americas.

At some point soon after his return to England, Smith encountered a man who had already been to America and back: Bartholomew Gosnold, onetime law student, privateer, and explorer, who was now seeking the backing for a major attempt to settle a colony in America. Gosnold would change Smith's life, giving him a focus that he never lost, and in the process changed the world as well. Perhaps Gosnold enticed Smith by telling him the story of England's previous contacts with the New World.

Some thought England should have been first to America. In 1488, Bartholomew Columbus, brother of Christopher, had approached King Henry VII, who had seized the throne of England only three years earlier. Henry was preoccupied with securing his hold on the country, and thus turned down Columbus's proposal that the English outfit a fleet that would reach the Indies by sailing west. Later, of course, Columbus and his brother found their sponsors: Ferdinand and Isabella of Spain.

Others believed that even in 1492, Columbus was far behind sailors from the British Isles. For centuries, fishermen from the west coasts of England and Ireland had ventured out on the chilly waters of the Atlantic to learn if there was anything beyond the limitless horizon. England's most serious claim to America resulted from the 1497 voyage of Giovanni Caboto, a Venetian citizen known as John Cabot to the English. Henry VII, hearing of Columbus's discoveries, had decided it was time to invest a little of his prestige in these new lands across the Atlantic. No royal money went toward the project; that would have been uncharacteristic of the tightfisted Henry. It was, in fact, the merchants of Bristol, England's largest west coast town, who raised the money for Cabot's voyages. They would share in the profits, after a one-fifth share went to King Henry. This was to set the pattern for English voyages of exploration: royal consent, but private funding, with an eye toward profits. It contrasted with Spain's policy of supporting exploration and colonization entirely with royal funds.

Cabot left Bristol with one ship, the *Matthew*, on May 2, 1497, and in less than two months reached land, which he gave the name Land First Seen. A nearby island he dubbed Saint John, because he had found it on that saint's feast day. His maps, copies of which survive, make it clear that he had reached Newfoundland. To Cabot, it was "the country of the great Khan," even though he saw no evidence of the civilization described by Marco Polo. He returned to Bristol on August 6 and immediately began to promote another voyage, with more ships and supplies so that he could fully exploit his discovery. Cabot had little trouble doing this, for his reports were persuasive—as was the crew's testimony that the waters off the Land First Seen teemed with fish, leading the Bristol merchants to see at least one sure way to make money off the voyage.

Cabot left with five ships in May 1498, and there disappears from history. A contemporary wrote that he found "new lands nowhere but on the very bottom of the ocean." The loss of John Cabot's fleet seems to have cured the Bristol merchants of exploration fever, at least for the time being. However, ships from the city evidently continued to sail west to exploit the teeming fishing grounds, the Grand Banks, that Cabot had discovered off Newfoundland. Since it was to the advantage of the English seamen not to reveal the location of these grounds, little about these later voyages was ever set down on paper.

The next serious attempt at American colonization did not come until the reign of Elizabeth I, who took the throne in 1558. Elizabeth had grown up in the shadow of her two half siblings, Edward VI and Mary, both of whom ruled before her. Officially declared a bastard at the age of two after her mother, Anne Boleyn, was executed for adultery, Elizabeth nonetheless grew up in comparative comfort, taking care never to attract the suspicion of her Catholic sister, known for good reason as "Bloody" Mary. One of Elizabeth's closest companions was Humphrey Gilbert, the nephew of her governess. After Elizabeth became queen, she put Gilbert in command of a military force in Ireland, where

Shane O'Neill was leading a rebellion against English rule. Gilbert distinguished himself for brutality; according to a contemporary account (by an Englishman), he lined the path to his tent with the freshly severed heads of enemies—men, women, and children. Elizabeth, hearing of this, was pleased.

One of the tactics England was using in its attempt to subdue the Irish was colonization. The English government had seized the lands of the O'Neills and other Irish lords. Favorites of Elizabeth received the property with the understanding they were to establish "plantations" on it. By the time Gilbert, newly knighted for his services, returned from Ireland in 1570, he had developed the idea of planting such colonies in the New World as well. He wrote, "We might . . . settle there such needy people of our countrey which now trouble the Commonwealth." England was suffering from overpopulation, and gangs of beggars and brigands roamed the countryside.

After much persuasion, Elizabeth granted Gilbert a patent to settle a colony in the New World. Like her grandfather, she was loath to contribute funds for such a venture, but Gilbert had a rich wife, and he pledged her property as collateral for loans. In addition, he found backers among friends and relatives, including his half brother, Walter Raleigh. Raleigh, then only twenty-four, was rewarded with his first command: the ship *Falcon*. Seven vessels set sail from Dartmouth, on England's south coast, in September 1578. Gilbert commanded the largest ship, the *Ager*—named for his wife's family, an honor that was possibly the only thing his colonial efforts ever brought her. The ship's prow also bore Gilbert's personal motto: *Quid non*—"Why not?"

That question was soon answered, for the voyage was an unmitigated disaster. The ships were leaky and the captains disloyal. Raleigh alone kept his ship at sea for six months, although in all that time he never ventured any farther west than the Cape Verde Islands, about 280 miles from the west coast of Africa.

Undaunted, Gilbert immediately began making plans for a second voyage. Creditors harassed him; he complained to a friend that he had to sell the clothes off his wife's back (not off his own, apparently). The only way he could get out of debt was to exploit the patent on colonization, so he began to sell "rights" to the land he assumed he would colonize—land that neither he nor anyone associated with him had yet seen. In August 1580, John Dee wrote in his diary that Gilbert had granted him "all to the North above the parallel of the 50 degree of latitude." Dee does not say what he paid for this huge parcel, which included most of Labrador.

The queen did not, however, wish to allow Gilbert himself to accompany his latest expedition, for as she pointed out, he was "a man noted of not good happ by sea." Gilbert replied in the tone of a man whose pride had been hurt, and Elizabeth relented. Raleigh, who by now had caught the queen's eye, did not sail on this voyage, though he contributed a ship of his own design, dubbed the *Bark Raleigh*.

In June 1583 Gilbert set out with five ships and some 260 men, including what Edward Hayes, one of the passengers, called "Minerall men and Refiners," because the colonists hoped to find gold or silver—the two New World commodities that had enriched Spain for nearly a century. While the Spaniards had subdued the Native American Aztecs and Incas by force, Gilbert hoped to win the natives' favor with gifts and music, bringing a small band of musicians and a supply of toys on the voyage.

The *Bark Raleigh* soon had to turn back, because many of its crew had fallen ill. This was a serious blow, for it was the largest vessel of Gilbert's fleet and had been carrying important supplies. The other four ships sailed on, heading due west and passing "mountaines of yce" in the North Atlantic. In early August, after seven weeks at sea, they reached the harbor of St. John's, Newfoundland. Here Gilbert discovered how frequently fishing boats of many nations were already making the transatlantic crossing. Hayes records seeing "36 sailes" in the harbor. The would-be colonists were welcomed with gifts sent from the other ships.

Gilbert went ashore to erect a pillar of wood with the English royal coat of arms engraved on it, claiming the land in the name of Queen Elizabeth. After exploring the island, the "minerall men" reported they had found silver ore, and Gilbert rejoiced at the possibility of profit. That was to be the high point of his American ventures.

The colonists, however, showed a lack of enthusiasm. (Some were criminals released from jail to provide manpower for the voyage.) Hayes wrote that some passengers conspired to steal a ship and return to England, and a "great many more of our people stole into the woods to hide themselves," hoping to hail a fishing vessel to take them away. A "flux," or dysentery, struck the company, and people began to die of it. Finally Gilbert was forced to assign one of his ships to transport the sick and discontented back to England. Then he lost his flagship in an incident that seems sadly typical of him. As the band was giving a concert on deck, the helmsman's attention was distracted and the ship drifted into shallow water, struck a shoal, and broke apart. According to Hayes, about a hundred men lost their lives in the disaster, including the mineral men and along with them the ore that was meant to substantiate their claims.

After that, "Our people lost courage," wrote Hayes, for even though it was late August, they felt winter drawing on. The remnants of the colonizers begged Gilbert to return to England. He agreed, though he promised optimistically to bring them back to America the following spring. Defying the pleas of his officers, Gilbert chose to sail home in the smaller, frailer of his two remaining vessels, the *Squirrel*. Sailing past the Azores, the travelers encountered "very foule weather, and terrible seas," wrote Hayes. "Men which all their life time had occupied the Sea, never saw more outrageous Seas." In the afternoon of September 9, Hayes and the others aboard the larger vessel caught sight of Gilbert sitting nonchalantly on the deck of the *Squirrel* with a book in his hand. The two ships were close enough so that they could hear as he called out to them, "We are as neere to heaven by sea as by land." That night, the lookout of Hayes's ship saw the lights of the *Squirrel* suddenly disappear. "In that moment," Hayes recalled, "the Frigat was devoured and swallowed up of the Sea." All aboard were lost.

With the death of Gilbert, leadership in the effort to plant English colonies in America passed into the hands of twenty-nine-year-old Walter Raleigh, who had become the favorite of

Queen Elizabeth, a position both profitable and precarious. The fifty-year-old queen had shown her admiration for—infatuation with, some said—Raleigh by bestowing on him certain licenses and monopolies that enabled him to become a wealthy man. He needed the money to keep up the display required of Elizabeth's courtiers, but he also used his fortune to establish at his London home, Durham House, what one writer has called the first "think tank." Raleigh surrounded himself with—and paid generously— men who had knowledge or skill in many fields and were willing to put their talents to work for his numerous projects. The spirit of inquiry that reigned in his household sometimes endangered him; in an age that regarded heresy as a crime punishable by death, it was whispered that in "the school of night" at Durham House, Raleigh and his friends even discussed atheism.

Within a year of Gilbert's death, Raleigh had obtained from the queen an extension of his half brother's patent on American colonization. Raleigh wanted to look farther south, where English sailors had not yet ventured, fearing repercussions from the Spaniards, who had established a fort at St. Augustine, Florida. Spanish soldiers had wiped out a French Huguenot colony on today's Parris Island, ruthlessly executing all its inhabitants, who had surrendered. The Spanish commander, Pedro Menéndez de Avilés, claimed "divine inspiration" as his motive, because the Huguenot colonists were Protestant. (Of course, Raleigh himself had, under orders from *his* commander, carried out the slaughter of the entire Italian and Spanish garrison at the Irish fort of Smerwick in 1580, as well as Irishmen and -women who had sought shelter there—*after* the Catholics had surrendered. It was not a gentle age.)

In July 1584, Raleigh's reconaissance ships, piloted by Simon Fernandes, a Portuguese navigator and reputed former pirate, arrived at the Outer Banks of today's North Carolina. A Spanish expedition had visited here in 1566, formally annexing the area, but Spain had done little to follow up the claim. It should not have been difficult to guess why, for from a navigator's viewpoint there could hardly have been a worse place for a colony. The Outer Banks are long, narrow, sandy islands that extend for about two hundred miles along the Carolina shore; between them and the mainland is Pamlico Sound, a shallow, mostly swampy body of water that deep-draft ships enter at their peril even today. On the ocean side of the Banks, storms blow up unexpectedly, often driving ships to their doom against the reefs. Thanks to Fernandes, all of Raleigh's attempts to plant a colony would die here.

On this first occasion, Fernandes found a passage through the reef, and the ships anchored at the north end of the island of Hatteras. Arthur Barlowe, captain of one of the ships, wrote a report in which he described the country in the most glowing terms: "We found such plenty . . . that I think in all the world the like abundance is not to be found." Friendly natives appeared, bartering animal skins for English metal objects, such as knives, dishes, and kettles. The natives brought the English deer, "conies [rabbits], hares, fish, the best of the world." Even the soil, according to Barlowe, was "the most plentiful, sweet, fruitful, and wholesome of all the world."

This enthusiastic report was not penned until Barlowe returned to England, and it is clear that he had help from both Raleigh and a man who would become the chief promoter of England's destiny as a colonial power. This was Richard Hakluyt, graduate of Oxford, Anglican priest, and assiduous collector of accounts of sea voyages to all parts of the world. As a boy Hakluyt had visited the law offices of his cousin and guardian (also named Richard Hakluyt), where he examined the older man's extensive collection of maps. Turning from the maps, his cousin, recalled Hakluyt, "brought me to the Bible . . . where I read, that they which go down to the sea in ships, and occupy by the great waters, they see the works of the Lord, and his wonders in the deep." Inspired, young Richard resolved that "I would by God's assistance prosecute that knowledge." He made exploration (on paper) his life's work. Few people have had so great an influence on the history of the world. Without him there would have been no British Empire, and the United States of America would never have been born.

Hakluyt became the first professor of geography at Oxford, and sought to accumulate narratives about the voyages that had enlarged Europeans' understanding of the world. Considering that the details of exploration were often carefully guarded state secrets, he was remarkably successful. In 1582, he published his first collection of these narratives, *Divers Voyages Touching the Discoverie of America*. This became the beginning of the massive work known today as *Hakluyt's Voyages*.

In July 1584, Hakluyt met Raleigh, who needed someone to help him convince Elizabeth that America was of vital importance. Hakluyt swiftly wrote a report outlining the political and economic benefits of "Western Planting," that is, of establishing colonies in America. The arguments he presented were not new, but had never been assembled in so orderly and forceful a manner. In summary, they were:

First, to bring Christianity to North America—more specifically, to enlist the Native Americans as Protestant allies in the war against Spain and Roman Catholicism.

Second, to establish settlements as bases of operations for privateers. The Spanish treasure ships annually brought back from America a fortune in gold and silver from the mines of Mexico and South America. English privateers waited to pick off any ships that became separated from the fleet and its accompanying warships. If the English had a colonial port close to the Caribbean, that would give the privateers a base from which to operate. By striking at the Spanish king's sources of wealth, the English could weaken his empire.

In addition, Hakluyt argued, overseas colonies would enable the English to acquire products that England itself could not produce, and thus reduce the need to import goods from the other European countries. In turn, the natives of America would make up a new market for English goods. Since the primary English export was woolen cloth, England should aim to build colonies in northern, colder climes where the Spaniards had not bothered to settle.

Finally, the colonies could serve as a social safety valve. Vagrants, debtors in prison, unemployed soldiers, Catholics, and Puritans—all sources of domestic unrest—could be sent there.

Because of the inflammatory nature of Hakluyt's report— Spain formally claimed all of America, north and south—it was kept a state secret for nearly three centuries. Raleigh, of course, made sure that it reached Elizabeth, and after Captain Barlowe returned in October 1584, Raleigh was able to emphasize Hakluyt's arguments with a flourish. Hakluyt had predicted that the Native Americans would be peaceable and present no obstacles to colonization. Barlowe confirmed this by bringing home two quite friendly natives named Manteo and Wanchese.

According to Barlowe, the king of the area he visited—"as mannerly and civill, as any [monarch] of Europe"—was named Wingina and his country known as Wingandacoa. (Raleigh later discovered this latter word only meant, "You have nice clothes.") Queen Elizabeth and Raleigh, who were fond of wordplay, must have noticed the similarity of the king's name to an English word. Historians have often credited Raleigh with the proposal to name the North American coast Virginia, in honor of Elizabeth, the Virgin Queen. Barlowe's account leaves open the possibility that the queen herself suggested it. In any event, to the English, the entire Atlantic coast between Spanish Florida and Newfoundland was henceforth to be known as Virginia.

Despite Raleigh's flattery and Hakluyt's reasoned arguments, the queen was still unwilling to back the venture with her own money, though she bestowed a knighthood on Raleigh and permitted him to inscribe on his coat of arms, "Lord and Governor of Virginia." Forced to raise funds from others, Raleigh held out the lure of immediate profits. Quietly he let prospective investors know that his ships would be doing double duty as privateers, making it easier to imagine that the voyage would reward its backers. Thus, when he assembled seven ships at Plymouth harbor in April 1585, not everyone on board was thinking of colonization. In all, the ships carried about six hundred men and boys—no women. The governor-designate of the colony was Ralph Lane, recently recalled from service in Ireland by Elizabeth specifically to serve on this voyage. He was to use the same brutal methods in America that the English had employed in Ireland.

Though Raleigh himself wanted to accompany the expedition, the queen refused permission. She remembered what had happened to Gilbert. So Raleigh recruited a distant cousin, Sir Richard Grenville, to command the ships. At age forty-one, he was ten years older than Raleigh, had served as a soldier in Hungary and Ireland, and had a reputation as a man with a violent temper. A Dutchman who had seen Grenville at a dinner with some Spanish officers recalled that the Englishman tried to impress them by consuming the glasses in which wine was served. Grenville would "take the glasses between his teeth and crash them in pieces and swallow them down so that sometimes the blood ran out of his mouth." Though Grenville had never crossed any body of water larger than the English Channel, he did not have to navigate; that role was again assigned to Simon Fernandes, the Portuguese who had piloted the reconnaissance voyage the previous year.

Two of those on board were part of Raleigh's scientific team, and they would provide the only enduring value from the voyage. One was John White, an artist who had been on an earlier expedition that had searched for the Northwest Passage. The other was Thomas Harriot, a brilliant young man of twenty-five who was part of the circle of people who gathered at Durham House. Harriot had worked with Manteo and Wanchese to compile a dictionary of Algonquian, the language spoken by the natives encountered by Barlowe's ships the year before. The two Native Americans were being returned to their homeland on this year's expedition.

After leaving Plymouth, the seven ships soon became separated, evidently because their captains went freelancing after the Spanish treasure fleet. When Grenville's flagship, the *Tiger*, reached the Outer Banks in June, Fernandes was unable to find the former passage through the offshore islands. The ship plowed onto a sandbar, which ground a hole in its hull. Though the crew managed to salvage the ship, its cargo of wheat, rice, salt, and other vital supplies was ruined by seawater.

Undaunted, Grenville took a party of men ashore for a march through nearby villages. After leaving one of the native settlements, he discovered that a silver cup was missing. His demand for its return was met with obstinate denials, so he ordered his

The arriual of the Englifhemen   II.
in Virginia.

John White, artist for Walter Raleigh's first attempt to found a colony in America, made this fanciful drawing of the English ships' arrival off the coast of present-day North Carolina. Then as now, vessels had to thread their way through the treacherous Outer Banks to reach the mainland. Note the sea monster and the sinking ships, warnings to those who would approach the Banks. The colonists established a settlement at the north end of an island the natives called Roanoke (at left in the drawing).

men to destroy the village and uproot the cornfields growing nearby. To Grenville, such a display of force was the only way to deal with the natives; it was the same way the English treated the Irish. With Manteo as interpreter, however, he had a successful meeting with Chief Wingina, who agreed to let the English build shelters on Roanoke, an island inside Pamlico Sound. Feeling that he had accomplished his mission, Grenville departed on August 25, leaving Ralph Lane in charge of 108 colonists.

Under Lane's firm hand, the colony at first gave every sign of thriving. Houses with thatched roofs were built and a stockade surrounding the settlement erected to ward off attacks. The colonists had cannons; a forge to make nails, tools, and weapons; and a large pitsaw to transform logs into timber. The English traded with the natives for corn, venison, fish, and oysters. No one went hungry and the colony survived the winter. In the spring, Wingina's people gave the English seed corn and taught them how to plant it.

Meanwhile, White was making a detailed record of the Native Americans and their customs. In his drawings, it does appear to be an idyllic society, where the barely clad inhabitants are depicted as perfect physical specimens living in a state of nature. A selection of engravings based on White's work was published in 1590, along with an account by Harriot titled *A Briefe and True Report of the New Found Land of Virginia*. Harriot was the first Englishman to note a possible cash crop for the Virginia colonists: tobacco. He wrote, "There is an herbe which . . . is called by the inhabitants Uppowoc . . . the Spaniards generally call it Tobecco. The leaves thereof being dried and brought into powder, they use to take the fume or smoke thereof by sucking it through pipes made of clay, into their stomach and head, from which it purges superfluous phlegm and other gross humours, and openeth all the pores and passages of the body." Ironically, Harriot may also have been the first European to die from the effects of smoking, for it was a tumor in his nasal passages that killed him in 1621.

During the winter of 1585–1586, Harriot and White accompanied an exploring party that went north from Roanoke and discovered Chesapeake Bay. Lane's report to Raleigh would praise the region around the bay ("not to be excelled by any other whatsoever") and urge him to settle the next colony there. It was this spacious bay that Captain Newport was trying to relocate twenty-one years later, with the *Susan Constant, God Speed,* and *Discovery.*

Grenville failed to return to Roanoke with additional supplies in the spring of 1586, because renewed tensions with Spain had put England on a war footing. As the months dragged on at Roanoke, relations between the colonists and the natives deteriorated. Wingina's people no longer had a surplus to trade and they resented the continual English demands for food. Lane took a group of men north to map the region and look for new trading partners. When he returned, he heard that Wingina was preparing to attack the colony. Deciding to act first, Lane led his soldiers into the chief's village. When he shouted the signal, "Christ Our Victory," the English soldiers fired their muskets, slaughtering many. The chief himself ran off but a soldier chased him and returned with Wingina's severed head. The "golden age" predicted by Captain Barlowe was over.

This brutal demonstration of military superiority only made it more difficult to obtain food from other natives. Thus it seemed a godsend when a fleet of twenty-four ships appeared on the horizon in early June. They were commanded by Sir Francis Drake, who had been attacking Spanish settlements in the West Indies. Lane proposed moving the entire colony north to the Chesapeake Bay, and Drake was willing to provide transport. But a powerful storm, no doubt a hurricane, blew up and many of Drake's ships went out to sea to avoid being dashed onto the reefs of the Outer Banks. Fearful, the colonists panicked and demanded to be taken aboard a ship returning to England.

Once back home, the former colonists spread the word that Virginia was in no way the earthly paradise that Barlowe and Hakluyt had described. Harriot, still in Raleigh's employ, chided these complainers in print: "Because there were not to be found any English cities, nor such fair houses, nor . . . any of their old accustomed dainty food nor any soft beds of down or feathers, the country was to them miserable." Even so, the bad word of mouth made it difficult for Raleigh to recruit new colonists—and to find financial backers for a second trip. All the profits of the voyage had come from Grenville's capture of Spanish ships, so it seemed sensible to invest in privateering ventures alone, and not bother with colony schemes.

Meanwhile, the queen granted Raleigh and two partners about forty-two thousand acres of land that had been confiscated from Irish lords in Munster. Here it was that Raleigh first planted potatoes from America—probably gathered by Harriot—which were to have an enormous effect on the Irish economy. Probably because of his experiences in this venture, Raleigh conceived a new approach to American colonization. It should follow the pattern of the English colonies in Ireland and become an agricultural enterprise.

On the next attempt, Raleigh would offer ownership of land as an incentive: five hundred acres to each man who signed on, and additional acres to those who invested money in the enterprise. To encourage the colonists to stay, Raleigh would allow them to bring their families. He drew up a charter establishing the "Citie of Raleigh in Virginia," giving the residents a certain amount of self-government. Though Raleigh was to fail, all of his innovations would later be imitated by successful colonies.

Raleigh appointed the artist John White as the first governor. To set an example of domestic tranquillity, White brought along his married, pregnant daughter and her husband, Ananias Dare. Manteo, one of the Roanoke natives who had gone to England on one of Drake's ships, would be returned to Roanoke Island, where the colonists would establish him as lord of the Roanoke region. Then they would proceed north to Chesapeake Bay, a great natural harbor with no hazardous sandbars.

There would be only three ships—two of them quite small—and 150 colonists, including seventeen women and nine boys. They set sail from Plymouth on May 8, 1587. From the outset conflicts arose between Governor White and Simon Fernandes, who was once again Raleigh's choice for the expedition's pilot. Since White had no training as a navigator, Fernandes effectively took charge of the voyage.

When the ships reached Roanoke, Fernandes announced that the summer was too far gone to proceed farther. (It was only July 22.) Therefore he would land the colonists here at Roanoke and not at the Chesapeake Bay area. White was livid, but the crews supported Fernandes's decision, and White was powerless.

By White's own account, the artist-governor made mistakes. He sent messengers to several of the local *werowances*, or tribal leaders, inviting them to a conference. Receiving no replies to this friendly gesture, White decided to adopt Lane's harsh tactics. He planned a surprise night attack on the same village that Lane

A Native American town as depicted by John White. The elements
have been compressed so that all of them can be shown. The letters
correspond to a key that explains what is happening. For example,
at upper right, labeled "F," a boy is stationed at a cornfield as a
human scarecrow to chase off birds or animals.

had targeted the previous year. Unfortunately, the earlier residents had abandoned the place, and it was now occupied by
members of Manteo's tribe. Before the mistake was discovered,
one of the locals was killed. White tried to make amends, but the
relationship between the English and the natives had gotten off
to a bad start.

There were two bright moments in the colony's brief history.
On the thirteenth of August, Manteo was baptized a Christian and

given the title Lord of Roanoke. He had convincingly showed his loyalty by blaming his own people for provoking the English attack on their village a few days earlier. Later English colonists demonstrated their gratitude by naming a town on Roanoke Island for him. It is not known what happened to him after his protectors disappeared.

Five days later, on the eighteenth, Governor White's daughter, Eleanor Dare, gave birth to a daughter—"the first Christian born in Virginia," her grandfather noted. It was a happy occasion, signifying, the colonists believed, the survival and future growth of the colony.

A more pressing concern called for White's attention. Fernandes was finally preparing to depart, and the colonists began to worry that they might not have sufficient supplies to last them through the winter. The relief ship Raleigh had promised might well head for Chesapeake Bay, where the colonists were supposed to be, and never stop at Roanoke. According to White, "the whole companie . . . came to the Governour, and with one voice, requested him to returne himself into England, for the better and sooner obtaining of supplies." White at first turned down the request, but finally let himself be persuaded, on condition that the colonists all sign a document affirming that it was only at their entreaty that he had returned to England.

So it was that White, after officiating at his granddaughter's christening—she was baptized with the name Virginia—set sail for England on August 27 on a small "fly-boat," a ship he does not name. Fernandes took the two larger vessels and headed south toward the Spanish Main, where he expected to find treasure ships to plunder. As for those 114 colonists who stood on the shore at Roanoke, watching the sails disappear over the horizon—none of them was ever again seen by White or any other Englishman.

When White arrived in England in November, the nation was preparing for war. Spain was assembling its mighty armada, and every available English ship was being called upon for defense. Despite White's pleas, Raleigh was unable to outfit a relief expedition until late in the following April—and even then,

White was given only two small ships. As before, the captains proved to be more interested in privateering than rescuing colonists. But this time the tables were turned when White's ships encountered French privateers, who captured the English vessels and massacred most of their crews. White was spared and made his way back to England, where he fretted helplessly for two years, trying in vain to find some way to bring supplies to those he had left at Roanoke.

By 1590, Raleigh himself, distracted by his larger ventures in Ireland, had virtually written off the Roanoke colony. He placated White by turning the problem over to his London business manager, William Sanderson. Sanderson found a ship, the *Moonlight*, to carry the colonists' needed supplies, and engaged a London privateering syndicate to provide three additional ships with battle-hardened crews as escorts.

White's frame of mind must have been blindly optimistic, for somehow he recruited additional settlers to go on this voyage. But the leader of the privateer fleet, Abraham Cocke, flatly refused to take the passengers on board—an act of kindness, for as anyone but White could have foreseen, the purpose of the voyage would be primarily privateering, not resupplying the colony.

So it proved to be. Though White sailed with his protectors from Plymouth on March 20, 1590, he did not see Roanoke until August 16. Cocke and his captains spent the months in between searching for and attacking Spanish treasure ships. The richest prize they captured was the *Buen Jesus*, which was three times the size of any of the privateer vessels. Shortly afterward, the English attacked an even larger ship, the *Nuestra Señora del Rosario*, whose crew put up such fierce resistance that the ship and its cargo went to the bottom. Nonetheless, Cocke assigned two of his ships to accompany the *Buen Jesus* back to England.

That left Cocke with only one ship, the *Hopewell*, to fulfill his contract to escort White and the *Moonlight* to Roanoke. The weather in August was stormy along the Outer Banks, but as they approached Roanoke Island a lookout reported seeing smoke rising from the shore—a good sign, for it must mean that someone was tending a cooking fire. At dusk the ships anchored offshore, and White spent the night looking forward to the following day when he would rejoin his friends and family.

The next morning, the ships fired their guns to attract attention, while White, the officers, and some crew members set out in two small boats to make their way up the shallow channel to Roanoke Island. Again they saw smoke, but in a different direction from the day before. This took them on a wild-goose chase inland, where they discovered only a small brush fire. They had to return to the ships for the night.

After the search party set out again on the following day, a storm blew up, sending their small boats perilously close to the shoals. One overturned, and the crew of the other struggled frantically to rescue their companions. But the gale blew so fiercely that most of them were swept away. Seven men drowned, including the captain of the *Moonlight*. The remaining sailors now threatened mutiny, and Captain Cocke had to exert all his authority to bring them into line. Reluctantly they proceeded toward their destination, even though night was falling. In the darkening twilight, the English could see the lights of fires in the woodland to the north. The crew anchored and, as White recalled, "sounded with a trumpet . . . and afterwards [sang] many familiar English tunes of songs and called to them friendly, but we had no answer."

In the morning, White at last stepped ashore on Roanoke. On the ground he could see the tracks of bare feet, but none of people who wore shoes. A little to the north of the former fort, he found the letters "CRO" carved on a tree. Inside the fort itself was a tree with its bark stripped off, and the full word carved into the wood: "CROATOAN," which was the name of the place where Manteo's people lived. In his account, White says this was "a secret token agreed between them [the colonists] and me at my last departure from them, which was that . . . they should not fail to write or carve on the trees or posts of the doors the name of the place where they should be seated. . . . [I]f they should happen to be distressed . . . that they should carve over the letters a cross . . . but we found no such sign of distress."

That appeared to be good news. Other signs indicated the colonists had not left in haste. The houses had been taken down and the furnishings removed. Also gone were the blacksmith's forge and most of the small cannons from the fort. It looked as if the settlers had intended to make a permanent move, and the markings on the tree seemed to indicate that they could be found at Croatoan Island, not far away.

The next day White and the others planned to sail along the coast to Croatoan, but again the skies turned gray and stormy. Captain Cocke's ship, the *Hopewell*, lost two of its three anchors, and to avoid being blown onto the reefs it had to head out to sea. The *Moonlight*, with a reduced crew and a less experienced captain, was also forced to retreat from the hazardous Outer Banks. Cocke argued that the best course was for the *Moonlight* to return to England while White, Cocke, and the *Hopewell* headed south to the Caribbean to make repairs and take on needed supplies. They could then return to resume the search for the colonists. Even though White was reluctant to abandon the search when he had waited so long to reach Virginia, he had no choice but to agree.

His doubts were well founded, for the *Hopewell* soon met a large English fleet commanded by Sir John Hawkins, England's premier privateer. Cocke, forgetting his promises to White, found the lure of making profits too strong and added his own ship to Hawkins's band. Unfortunately, the Spanish treasure fleet eluded them. By then, the *Hopewell* was closer to England than America, and Cocke headed for home. The ship landed at Plymouth on October 24, 1590.

White never managed to mount another expedition to America. The hostilities between England and Spain were making privateering too profitable, and colonial voyages too dangerous. The onetime governor spent his remaining years in Ireland, writing the account of his search for the lost colonists. He died in 1593 without ever learning the fate of his family and friends. It was a mystery that John Smith, among his other achievements, would solve in America.

4

The "First Mover" of Jamestown

WHILE ELIZABETH WAS ALIVE, conflict with Spain precluded any further serious English attempts at American colonization. Richard Hakluyt nevertheless continued to work toward the time when English sailors would again devote their energies to exploration. The queen had granted him a "living," or clerical post, at the Bristol cathedral, which paid him a good income and left him free of time-consuming duties. He devoted his energies to collecting manuscripts, translating some, editing others for the great work he was composing. By 1600 he had published three volumes—comprising 1.6 million words— of *The Principal Navigations, Voiages, Traffiques and Discoveries of the English Nation, made by Sea or over-land, to the remote and farthest distant quarters of the Earth, at any time within the compass of these 1500 yeeres.* The title gives an idea of the scope of his ambition.

Hakluyt's books sparked a new wave of interest in trade and exploration, not only in America but worldwide. In 1600 Queen Elizabeth had granted a group of investors the right to form a company to open the lucrative spice trade with the East Indies. Hakluyt was made secretary of this East India Company; its members chose Thomas Smythe, one of the wealthiest common- ers in England, as the governor, turning down the queen's sug- gestion that they name a gentleman knight to the post. That the shareholders found it necessary to risk offending the queen shows how highly Smythe was regarded.

The queen's charter gave the East India Company the sole right to trade with the East Indies. Anyone trying to compete with it was subject to having their ships and cargoes seized. The formation of the company was a milestone in the history of capitalism, for shares in its voyages were available to the public; tradesmen and gentlemen alike were attracted by the prospect of profits, and initially some 125 investors put up capital of £72,000. During the company's first years of existence, shares were sold for specific voyages, but in 1612 it became a joint-stock company, more like a modern corporation, in which the shareholders had a stake in all the company's activities.

The immediate success of the East India Company—its early voyages usually returned 100 percent profits for investors—led Smythe, Hakluyt, and others to once again contemplate an American venture. They selected thirty-year-old Bartholomew Gosnold, a former law student turned privateer, to lead a new colonizing effort. Gosnold had important connections to both Smythe and Hakluyt. He had grown up in Suffolk, where Hakluyt was the rector of a church in the town of Wetheringsett, and from him may have acquired the curiosity about distant places that made Gosnold leave a law career for the sea. If so, those ambitions were only encouraged by his marriage to Mary Golding in 1595, when he was twenty-four. Three of his wife's first cousins were sea captains; she also had an uncle who had been a captain on one of Sir Humphrey Gilbert's expeditions to the New World. Most importantly, another of her cousins was Thomas Smythe himself.

Unlike the East India Company's voyages, this venture was to be privately financed. The lion's share of the money came from Henry Wriothesley, Earl of Southampton. He is best known today for having been Shakespeare's patron and possibly the person for whom the Bard wrote his sequence of sonnets. At the time of Gosnold's departure, Southampton was, unfortunately, in the Tower of London under a death sentence, convicted of having taken part in the Earl of Essex's plot to overthrow the queen. (Smythe too had been imprisoned on suspicion of being involved in the conspiracy, but was able to demonstrate his innocence, and was soon freed.)

Southampton's incarceration, and thus his inability to contribute more funds, may have been one reason why Gosnold's expedition was small, seemingly too small for its intended purpose. He set out in March 1602 in the ship *Concord* with a crew of eight and twenty-three passengers, the would-be colonists. Certainly following Hakluyt's advice, he crossed the Atlantic by going directly west to the northern part of Raleigh's "Virginia." This area, Hakluyt knew, had in 1524 been visited by Giovanni da Verrazano, an Italian sailing for the French king. Verrazano had dubbed the area Norumbega; today we know it by the name John Smith gave it later: New England. The Italian explorer had sailed partway up a large river (thought to be the Hudson), which Hakluyt suggested to Gosnold might prove to be the gateway to the Northwest Passage, the chimerical water route around or through the American continent that would lead directly to Asia.

Approaching the mainland near today's Casco Bay in Maine, the English sailors were surprised to see a "Biscay shallop"—a small European boat with a sail—coming toward them, with six to eight men in it. Gabriel Archer, one of the *Concord*'s passengers and later to be a Jamestown colonist, wrote, "we supposed [them] at first to bee Christians distressed. But approching us neere, wee perceived them to bee Savages. . . . One that seemed to be their Commander wore a Waste-coate of blacke worke, a paire of Breeches, cloth Stockings, Shooes, Hat, and Band." The natives also understood "divers Christian words," apparently from previous contacts with Europeans, probably fishermen and fur trappers. Clearly, Europeans—fishermen no doubt—were still coming to the area, but not publicizing their voyages.

Gosnold followed the coastline from Maine south to the end of the great hook of land that he named Cape Cod. After rounding the cape, he landed on a large island, where he found a profusion of grapevines clinging to trees in the dense forest inland. The dark, verdant scene revived a memory of Gosnold's eldest daughter, who had died in childhood, and he named the place after her: Martha's Vineyard.

Gosnold next landed on one of the Elizabeth Islands (again, named by him) at the mouth of Buzzard's Bay. The English established friendly relations with the local natives, obtaining furs from them, along with a promise that later in the year furs would be more plentiful. Gosnold's men treated some of the natives to a dinner. According to Archer, "they sate with us and did eate of our Bacaleure [codfish] and Mustard, dranke of our Beere, but the Mustard nipping them in their noses they could not indure: it was a sport to behold their faces made being bitten therewith." Gosnold organized the construction of a palisaded fort and planned to stay there with eleven of his men to found a colony, while the others returned to England for more supplies. The work was in vain, however, for when it came time for the ship to depart, Gosnold's companions got cold feet and insisted on being taken aboard.

Though Gosnold had spent only a month and three days in America, his expedition accomplished much. It demonstrated that trade could be carried on with the natives—an important point to English merchants who wanted to find new markets for their goods—and it showed that a New World voyage could bring immediate profits for its backers. Besides furs, Gosnold's men had collected cedarwood, prized for its fragrance, and sassafras roots, thought to be medically useful against the "French pox" (syphilis) and the plague, which was still a scourge in England.

The voyage also shifted the monopoly on American colonization out of Raleigh's hands. When Raleigh heard of the arrival in England of a cargo of sassafras, he knew that it could only have come from America. He wrote to Sir Robert Cecil, the queen's secretary of state, declaring that his exclusive patent on American exploration and settlement had been violated and demanding that the Concord's cargo be confiscated.

Cecil faced a dilemma. He was a close friend of the Earl of Southampton—he had in fact engineered the commutation of his sentence to life imprisonment—and knew that the earl stood to profit from the sale of Gosnold's cargo. Raleigh too felt he could rely on Cecil's friendship, but Cecil was looking to the future. Cecil had read Hakluyt's report on the advantages of establishing

American colonies and had been impressed. Raleigh, now nearly fifty, had done nothing with his American patent in fifteen years, and his associates Grenville, Lane, and White were all dead. Cecil felt it would be a wise course to shift the enterprise to younger men. With Hakluyt's help, he placated Raleigh by arranging for him to receive a share of the profits from Gosnold's voyage. In addition, Archer's account of the expedition was published with a respectful dedication: "By the permission of the honourable Knight, Sir Walter Raleigh." (The account, interestingly, omitted key navigational details so that others could not easily follow in Gosnold's wake.)

Within a year, Raleigh's star was on the wane. After Elizabeth's death, his enemies had taken every opportunity to whisper calumnies against him into the ear of the new king from Scotland. James needed little encouragement to dislike the elegant, fastidious Raleigh; by contrast, as one courtier recalled, James "never washt his hands, onley rubbed his fingers ends slightly with the wet end of a napkin." Raleigh's advocacy of the use of tobacco also set him at odds with James, who was the first person ever to condemn tobacco for reasons of health.

Gosnold, probably encouraged by Hakluyt, was seeking to follow up his first voyage with another venture that would succeed in establishing a colony. However, the backers who had financed him before were not available. Gosnold's wife's wealthy cousin Thomas Smythe had gone to Russia as England's ambassador. The Earl of Southampton, freed from the Tower after James's accession to the throne, was currying favor with the new monarch. Southampton dared not risk offending the king by promoting another voyage to America before James made his feelings about colonization known—and James had not yet made up his mind.

Frustrated, Gosnold sought out new backers. It was during this time that he encountered John Smith, newly returned from three years of soldiering in Europe and casting about for a quest that would satisfy his yearning for adventure and glory. It is not known how the two met. Smith relates that he had a considerable amount of money when he returned to England. Perhaps he chose to treat himself to the pleasures of London; that might have meant a visit to the Globe Theatre, where the Chamberlain's Men were presenting a revival of *The Merry Wives of Windsor*, supposedly written by William Shakespeare in fourteen days at the request of Queen Elizabeth, who wanted to see the blustering Sir John Falstaff, a character from the earlier play *Henry IV*, fall in love. Smith might have run into Gosnold there or at the bear-baiting arena next door; both were on the south bank of the Thames, a livelier and less reputable place than London proper on the north bank. That may have been why the rotting heads of executed criminals were displayed on stakes above the southern entrance to London Bridge, not on the northern side.

Over cups of ale—or ginger beer, for Smith was not a drinker—the two adventurous young men might have traded stories as Gosnold described his trip down the coast of America and Smith his escapades in eastern Europe and Turkey. Others might have called Smith a braggart, but Gosnold saw the gold in his character and invited him to sign on for the next voyage to America. Smith had already visited three continents, and no doubt he decided, why not another? He had no way of knowing that America would become his preoccupation for the rest of his life.

Still in his early twenties, Smith was confident in his ability to meet almost any challenge. A man who had survived hand-to-hand combat, slavery, and a variety of efforts to kill him was not likely to be deterred by the hazards of a trip across the Atlantic. Once committed to Gosnold's proposal, Smith was impatient to get started. Indications are that he spent some of his own money and helped Gosnold recruit colonists.

But time was needed to gain the financial backing for such a voyage. Gosnold, who was better connected than Smith with the kinds of people likely to have sufficient wealth, knew that these things proceeded slowly. Wealthy merchants, nobles, and courtiers had to be approached and persuaded. Finally, King James himself must give his permission, if not his financial help, and the king had proved to be a notoriously cautious individual; such an endeavor, which carried the possibility of offending Spain, might be too risky for his taste.

One obstacle to Gosnold's effort to find investors was the well-known failure of Raleigh's colonizing ventures. Some of the

resulting disillusionment had seeped into the public conscious-
ness. In 1605, while Gosnold and Smith were trying to drum up
interest in their project, London theatergoers were enjoying a
new play coauthored by Ben Jonson. Titled *Eastward Ho*, it
poked fun at the promoters of American colonization by depicting three gullible would-be "adventurers" carried away by fanta-
sies of making fortunes in Virginia. "Captain Seagull" lures them
into the venture with a description of the natives of America:
"Why, man, all their dripping pans and their chamber pots are
pure gold; and all the chains, with which they chain up their
streets, are massy gold; all the prisoners they take are fettered in
gold; and for rubies and diamonds, they go forth on holidays and
gather 'em by the seashore, to hang on their children's coats."

Well-informed people knew that Raleigh's people had found
no such wealth in Virginia, but there was always the possibility
that rich sources of silver and gold, like those the Spanish ex-
ploited farther south in Mexico and Peru, could be found. And
there were other ways that an American colony could be profitable. Hakluyt continued to maintain that colonies were necessary if
England was to become a leading nation in trade. The long-sought
Northwest Passage remained a lure for those who saw America as
the gateway to the East Indies, and some thought a base in America could become a supply port for ships taking that route.

Finally, English Catholics, facing prejudice in their homeland and disappointed in their hopes that Elizabeth's successor
would be a Catholic, considered establishing refuges for their co-
religionists in America. Sir Thomas Arundell, a Catholic and the
brother-in-law of Gosnold's patron the Earl of Southampton,
commissioned an expedition to seek out someplace in America
where English Catholics might form such a colony. Commanded
by Captain John Waymouth, the ship *Archangell* set out in early
1605. Waymouth spent two months along the coast of Maine,
sailing up (and naming) the St. George River; he took careful
note of the tall trees in the area, which would make excellent
masts and planks for shipbuilding. He encountered some peaceful Penobscots, and violated their trust by luring five of them
aboard and taking them back to England. Their arrival was to
have world-shaking consequences.

Waymouth returned home via the port of Plymouth, on the southwest coast of England, from which ships had for many years regularly sailed to the fishing grounds off Newfoundland. The governor of Plymouth Fort, Sir Ferdinando Gorges, had quietly observed the transatlantic comings and goings, and had taken an interest in America. He later wrote of the arrival of the five native Americans on Waymouth's ship, "this accident must be acknowledged the meanes under God of putting on foote, and giving life to all our Plantations." In other words, it sparked the English colonization of America.

Gorges had been looking for some way to draw attention to the possibilities of New World plantations. He took control of the natives from Waymouth and sent two of them to Sir John Popham, the lord chief justice of England. Popham, "a huge, heavie, ugly man," was deeply concerned about the rising tide of crime in England. Rumor had it that in his youth Popham had himself been a highwayman, but as a judge he handed down harsh sentences. Earlier, as a member of Parliament, he had drafted a bill to prevent "idleness" by forcing the poor to work, and had proposed to punish "rogues and vagabonds" by sending them "into such parts beyond the seas as shall be at any time hereafter for that purpose assigned."

Assisted by one of Waymouth's crewmen, who had picked up some of the natives' language, Popham questioned the Penobscots about conditions in America. He learned that the land was sparsely populated, and that it held a great many resources that England could use. To him, establishing colonies was a practical solution to many of the nation's problems.

Popham was the right person to bring the dream into reality. Before long, a letter went to Robert Cecil, who had smoothly made the transition from Elizabeth's reign to the new one, becoming King James's closest English adviser. (Because of his diminutive size, Cecil received the fond nickname "my little beagle" from the king.) Popham knew that with Cecil's support the king would give his blessing to the plan. He proposed bringing together all those who would be willing to provide backing for a colonial venture. Making a profit was not *his* primary motivation, but he knew it would be for others, and he recognized that the more money raised, the greater the chance of the colony's success. As the experiences of Gilbert and Raleigh had shown, it ought not to be a mission that relied primarily on the finances of one person.

Before Cecil could act on Popham's proposal, however, an assassination attempt rocked the nation and put all other government activities on hold. On October 26, 1605, a servant of Lord Monteagle, a Catholic member of Parliament, was handed a letter by a stranger in the street. It warned Monteagle not to attend the opening session of Parliament ten days later. No one has ever discovered who wrote the letter, but it foiled an elaborate plan by radical Catholics to gain control of England.

Monteagle, whose loyalty to his country overcame his loyalty to his fellow Catholics, took the letter to the king's palace at Whitehall and showed it to Cecil. That set in motion an investigation that resulted in the discovery of a man named Guy Fawkes hiding in a cellar under Parliament House. To invoke a modern term, he was a suicide bomber—with thirty-six barrels of gunpowder ready to ignite when King James arrived to open the session.

James was deeply shaken by the news of the so-called Gunpowder Plot. Nothing could have aroused his fears more, for it brought back a horrific memory of the explosion that had destroyed his father's house when James was an infant. Soon, however, the faithful "little beagle" Cecil succeeded in hunting down the rest of the conspirators. Those involved were either killed while resisting arrest or were tortured, hanged, drawn, and quartered. To this day, English schoolchildren celebrate Guy Fawkes Day on November 5 by burning effigies of Fawkes in the streets.

A grateful King James rewarded Cecil by giving him a noble title: Lord Salisbury. Thus when Salisbury raised the issue of approving a colonial enterprise, the king was amenable. On April 6, 1606, James authorized two "companies" to form American colonies. Though privately financed through a joint-stock arrangement similar to that of the East India Company, the two companies would be governed by a thirteen-member council appointed by the crown. This gave James control without the necessity of financing the operations.

Each company was assigned a certain length of the "Virginia" coast. One had the right to plant a colony in "northern Virginia," between 38 and 45 degrees north latitude (approximately from present-day Baltimore north to Newfoundland). The other company had the rights to "southern Virginia," between 34 and 41 degrees north latitude (from the southern border of today's North Carolina to New York City). Because the areas overlapped, the two companies were directed to build their colonies no closer than one hundred miles to each other.

The king's charter named four people from each company to whom the patents for colonization were officially granted. Four were from the cities of Plymouth and Bristol, and they were assigned the territory in northern Virginia; their group was henceforth known as the Virginia Company of Plymouth. The other four, who were Londoners, were given southern Virginia, and their organization was dubbed the Virginia Company of London. Only two of these eight patent-holders were well-known. The Reverend Richard Hakluyt was the most prominent of the four members of the London Company, and George Popham, a nephew of the lord chief justice, was the leading representative of the Plymouth Company.

In reality, all eight members named in the charter were front men. Lord Salisbury himself and Sir Thomas Smythe, now returned from Russia, were the prime movers of the London Company, just as Chief Justice Popham and his friend Sir Ferdinando Gorges were the guiding spirits behind the Plymouth Company. But Salisbury and other members of His Majesty's government— and certainly His Majesty—were still somewhat nervous as to how Spain would react on learning that England was making a try at establishing colonies in America. It was thus deemed politically unwise to declare openly that men of such high stature were the true leaders of the colonizing ventures. The fewer significant names listed on the patents, the easier to claim royal deniability. If Spain objected too strenuously, or other unforeseen difficulties arose, His Majesty's government could wash its hands of the whole affair.

As it happened, Spain was not only interested but also well informed about England's plans. Don Pedro de Zuñiga, the Spanish ambassador to England, was also an efficient spy—the eyes and ears in London of King Philip III. A full month *before* King James issued patents to the two Virginia companies, Zuñiga had written his monarch:

"Sire, . . .

"They also propose to do another thing, which is to send 500 or 600 men, private individuals of this kingdom to people Virginia in the Indies, close to Florida. . . . They brought 14 or 15 months ago about ten natives, that they might learn English, and they have kept some of them here [in London] . . . teaching and training them to say how good that country is for people to go there and inhabit it. The chief leader in this business is the Justiciario [Chief Justice Sir John Popham], who [says] that he does it in order to drive out from here thieves and traitors to be drowned in the sea."

To John Smith, the issuance of the king's charter for Virginia came as a great relief. For more than a year he had been cooling his heels and waiting for action. Leisure was never something he felt comfortable with. In his autobiography, he writes little about this period, except to give Gosnold credit as "one of the first movers of this plantation [Jamestown], having many yeares solicited many of his friends, but found small assistants [assistance], [until] at last prevailed with some Gentlemen, [such] as Captain John Smith . . . and divers others, who depended a yeare upon his projects, but nothing could be effected, till by their great charge and industrie, it came to be apprehended by certaine of the Nobilitie, Gentry, and Marchants, so that his Majestie [gave] his letters patents [for the colony]."

No one has learned specifically what "charge and industrie" Smith carried out on Gosnold's behalf. Very likely he recruited some colonists and crew. The only people of influence he knew were the Willoughby family, but they seem not to have had a role in the Jamestown venture. In addition, Smith almost certainly met Henry Hudson at this time. Hudson was preparing his first voyage in search for the Northwest Passage, a venture sponsored by the Muscovy Company, another of Sir Thomas Smythe's many enterprises. John Smith was later to send Hudson a letter from Virginia, suggesting that Chesapeake Bay might be the entry to the waterway that could take ships through America and on to Asia.

Pretty clearly, Smith also learned the principles of surveying and mapmaking during the three years before he left for Virginia. He displayed these skills once he reached America, and there seems to be no other period in his life when he might have acquired them. That has led to speculation that his teacher might have been Hudson, Hakluyt, or even Thomas Harriot, who had left Sir Walter Raleigh's employ and was now serving the Earl of Northumberland. The earl's younger brother, George Percy, would be one of the most prominent of the Jamestown colonists. When Smith reached America, he apparently had a rudimentary command of the language spoken by the native people; it is quite possible that he learned it from Harriot. Who might have taught him is less important than the fact that during these years he had continued to prepare himself for this new venture.

Gosnold, and Smith too, may have been surprised to learn that they were not to be going to northern Virginia—what we call New England—which Gosnold had visited earlier. Hakluyt and Sir Thomas Smythe, Gosnold's mentors, were involved with the London Company of Virginia, which had been allotted rights to southern Virginia, encompassing the area that Raleigh's men had tried to settle earlier. Hakluyt for one was no doubt pleased, but Gosnold was probably disappointed.

In due course, the King's Council for Virginia came forth with firm directives. In Smith's eyes Gosnold deserved to be recognized as the "first mover" of the Virginia colony, but at age thirty-five Gosnold was judged too inexperienced to command such an expedition. That post was assigned instead to a man whose very presence commanded respect—even from a brash young adventurer like Smith. This was forty-six-year-old Christopher Newport, with twenty years' experience as a ship's master, fifteen of which he'd spent as a privateer, preying on Spanish shipping. Newport had been to Virginia before, as captain of the *Little John*, one of the ships Abraham Cocke had assembled on the privateering venture/rescue mission that set out to find White's lost colonists in 1590. Newport had a permanent souvenir from that trip: a pinned-up right sleeve in place of an arm he had lost in an attempt to capture the Spanish treasure ship *Nuestra Señora del Rosario*.

Known for his courage, Newport had earlier fought alongside Drake in the famous raid on the Spanish port of Cadiz in 1587, when a small English fleet had destroyed part of the Armada. It had been Newport too who led the flotilla that captured the treasure-laden Spanish carrack *Madre de Dios* in 1592 (earning the modern equivalent of $100 million for his backers). Having made many trips to the West Indies, Newport knew those waters as well as any English seaman, but since the signing of the peace treaty he had turned from raiding Spanish Main towns to carrying English trade goods to and from them.

Newport had returned from the latest of these trading voyages in September 1605, bringing two live alligators and a wild boar as presents for King James. The king loved exotic creatures; his prize was a tame cheetah—a gift from the ambassador of the Duke of Savoy—that he took on deer hunts. The alligators no doubt pleased him greatly, and may even have had something to do with Newport's appointment as commander, or admiral, of the voyage to Virginia.

Newport would be master of the flagship, a vessel of 120 tons named the *Susan Constant*. (In the seventeenth century, tonnage referred to the cargo-carrying capacity of the ship; originally it was based on the number of tuns, or casks, of wine a ship could carry in its hold.) Bartholomew Gosnold was to command the second ship, the forty-ton *God Speed*. Finally, the expedition would be accompanied by a twenty-ton pinnace, the *Discovery*, under John Ratcliffe, a man who has defied the attempts of scholars in subsequent centuries to learn anything about him, except that his real name was Sicklemore.

A better idea of the size of these ships can be gained by visiting the site of Jamestown, the colony they crossed the Atlantic to found. As one looks at the actual-size replicas of these three ships, moored in the James River of Virginia today, one's first reaction is surprise at how small they seem—and then awe at the courage it must have taken to set out on the ocean in craft like these. The *Discovery* measures only thirty-eight feet long at the waterline, the *God Speed* forty-eight, and the *Susan Constant* seventy-six. At top speed, a champion sprinter of today could run from the flagship's stem to stern in less than three seconds.

And yet seventy-one people crossed the Atlantic in the *Susan Constant*, sleeping in the hold along with food supplies, casks of water, tools, livestock such as chickens, sheep, and goats, as well as whatever possessions each man thought necessary to take along when moving to a new world. The *God Speed* carried fifty-two men and boys, and twenty more made the journey in the tiny, two-masted *Discovery*. There were no females on the voyage. Privacy was impossible, and during the five long months at sea it would have taken a very mild-mannered person not to irritate or offend someone else. John Smith was far from mild; some regarded his self-confident air as braggadocio, and he was particularly likely to antagonize those who prided themselves on their refinement and social status.

In November, the royal council had issued specific instructions for the colonists. Each of the vessels carried a copy, for it was not unusual for ships to become separated at sea, or lost entirely. Briefly, the council instructed the colonists to "find out a safe point in the entrance of some navigable river," preferably a river that appeared to run far inland. If more than one such river was available, the colonists were to choose the one that flowed most toward the northwest, the direction of the supposed passage to Asia. Captain Newport was directed to spend two months exploring such rivers, looking for trade goods and commodities as well as the Northwest Passage. He was to return with a full hold of such "Merchandizes."

The royal council also named seven men on the voyage as a council of governors for the colony. These names, however, were to be kept secret until after the colonists reached Virginia, presumably to preserve Newport's authority during the voyage. The local council members, when their names were revealed, were to take an oath of loyalty to King James. Among the declarations

sworn to by those who took the oath was to "keep secret all matters committed and revealed unto me." Even the embarkation of
the three ships was a hush-hush affair. There were no fanfares
nor public farewells for the men who sailed off to plant on a far
shore the new British flag.

On a chilly December day, John Smith stepped into one of
the hundreds of small rowboat-taxis, called wherries, that swarmed
along London's riverfront. A wintry fog rose from the water, and
most of the royal swans—protected from harm by law—that usually crowded the Thames had flown south. Though the river
itself was not yet frozen, it might well be in another month, post-
poning departures and arrivals of ships till the spring. Smith and
his companions hoped to be in Virginia by then. Sitting back into
the upholstered passenger seat, Smith asked to be taken downriver to Deptford, mooring place of the *Golden Hind*, the ship in
which Sir Francis Drake had circumnavigated the globe a quarter
century before, when Smith was an infant. Now permanently
docked, and destined to remain there until it finally rotted away
in the next century, Drake's ship had become a place where seafarers setting out on a long journey met for a last meal at home,
but of course it had particular significance for Smith: a reminder
of the heights to which a yeoman's son could rise.

After Smith and the others had enjoyed their feast aboard the
Golden Hind, they went farther downriver to Blackwell, where the
ships were anchored. Climbing aboard, they waited for the tide
to turn in the morning and sweep them toward the sea. The
British Empire (a term first used by John Dee in a letter to King
James the following year) was about to begin.

5

A Charge of Mutiny

O N DECEMBER 19, the captains of the *Susan Constant*, the *God Speed*, and the *Discovery* gave the orders to raise the anchors and set the sails. River pilots had been taken aboard to guide the ships down the twisting Thames to the sea. The three little ships flew a flag that had only come into existence that year; it combined the red English Cross of Saint George with the white-on-blue Scottish Cross of Saint Andrew, to signify the uniting of the two kingdoms under James's rule. Officially, he had taken the title King of Great Britain, the first monarch to do so.

As the ships wound their way through the lower reaches of the Thames, Smith and his companions encountered reminders of the greatness Britain aspired to. Along Gravesend Wharf the air was filled with the scent of cinnamon, cloves, and nutmeg. Here were the docks of the East India Company, whose backers hoped to build a spice trade that would compete with that of Portugal and the Netherlands. One day, perhaps, longshoremen would also be unloading products here from America.

Past Gravesend, the sailors could see sheep grazing beyond the marshes on the south bank of the Thames—reminders that virtually the only item England produced for export was wool. A foothold in America would give England access to the potentially vast resources of that land and might enable the nation to create new industries. The nearly treeless hills and dales south of the Thames were typical of the countryside. Over centuries, many of

England's forests had fallen to the woodsman's ax. One of the thoughts in the minds of those who sent the three little ships on their way was that America's virgin forests would provide the timber to build the English navies of the future.

The Thames was crowded with vessels, and the fifty-mile journey from London to the sea was a slow one. At last, however, the voyagers came in sight of the buoy that marked the Nore, the sandbar in midstream at the mouth of the Thames. After navigating past it, the ships put ashore their river pilots. The America-bound colonists were now at sea.

To reach the Atlantic, the ships first had to round the southeastern point of England through a channel called the Downs. Unfortunately, the cold December winds here blew strongly against their course, bringing storms with them. The captains of the three ships were forced to trim their sails and lower their anchors to avoid being blown onto the shore. Bobbing like corks in the water, they had to wait for better weather. It was not a short wait—they were stuck there for six weeks.

Smith was an experienced sailor and the choppy seas would have given him little discomfort. But many of the would-be colonists had never gained sea legs and suffered dreadfully from seasickness. Among them was the Reverend Robert Hunt, the lone clergyman in the company. His malady was severe enough so that Smith recalled it years later when writing an account of the colony's early days: "by unprosperous winds [we] were kept six weeks in the sight of England, all which time Master Hunt, our preacher, was so weak and sick that few expected his recovery." Smith noted the irony that the ships were only twenty miles from Hunt's home in Kent.

Six full weeks lost fighting a contrary wind must have seemed a most inauspicious way to begin. More ominously, it might have been regarded as a sign of divine displeasure with the voyage. Many of those on board had no doubt consulted fortune-tellers or astrologers before setting out; merchants and marine insurance brokers commonly used them to determine the most favorable times for voyages to leave. John Dee, Queen Elizabeth's personal stargazer and now an adviser to James, had prescribed his advice for earlier expeditions to America, although it is not known what he said about this one. For the same reason, some of the colonists must surely have made offerings at churches or shrines. Elizabethans felt strongly that the spirit world closely interacted with the material. In his writings, Smith often interprets favorable or unfavorable turns of events as signs of God's approval or disapproval.

Now, seeing Hunt, the man of God, suffering so greatly, some on board began to question his effectiveness as a spiritual conduit. Smith refers cryptically to "the scandalous imputation of some few (little better than atheists) of the greatest rank amongst us, suggested against him [Hunt]." Smith was shortly to have his own problems dealing with the high-ranking colonists, but it may be that someone, or two or three, made sarcastic comments about the feebleness of Hunt's ability to petition God with his prayers. Smith became his defender.

Smith praised the clergyman's staunch faith: "all this could never force from him [Hunt] so much as a seeming desire to leave the business [i.e., go home] but [he] preferred the service of God in so good a voyage before any affection [desire] to contest with his godless foes; whose disastrous designs, could they have prevailed, had even then overthrown the business . . . had he not with the water of patience and his godly exhortations . . . quenched those flames of envy and dissension." This makes the issue sound like a great deal more than a squabble over the power of prayer. It can best be understood in that the godless foes' "disastrous designs" were soon to find another target: Smith himself.

Despite Sir John Popham's oft-expressed hope of using America as a dumping ground for English criminals and indigents, a sizable number of the colonists were considered "gentlemen." No complete list of the passengers and crew exists, but of the sixty-seven men and boys whose names Smith set down later from memory, he lists thirty-six as gentlemen, fourteen as having a skilled trade, and only seventeen as laborers. Before many months had passed, this preponderance of gentlemen would prove disastrous for the colony. The chief characteristic of a gentleman, according to William Harrison, a sixteenth-century writer, was that he "can live without manual labour." That might be possible in England, where there was a surplus of laboring men and women, but in America the group's very survival would require everyone to work.

Early in the voyage, divisions began to appear between Smith and some of the others on board. Smith, though he ranked as a gentleman, had not been one by birth or inheritance. He had known the life of a farmer before he took up arms, and for that reason the "true" gentlemen would always look down on him. Smith's superior qualities—as a soldier, a leader, and a man—did not guarantee him the respect he craved.

At last the storms abated and a kindly wind sent the ships through the Downs and the English Channel into the Atlantic. Captain Newport set a course heading south. So much food and fresh water had been consumed during the six-week delay that Newport decided to take on more supplies at the Canary Islands. While a look at a map would seem to indicate that his small flotilla was going out of its way, in reality Newport had always intended to take the southern route, watering at the West Indies before turning north to Virginia. It was the route that was most familiar to him, for he had often followed it on his ventures to the Spanish Main.

During the layover in the Canaries, Smith made an important enemy. With him on board the flagship *Susan Constant* was Edward Maria Wingfield, one of those "of the greatest rank" who slighted Smith and aroused his dislike. Graying and with the erect bearing of a military veteran, Wingfield had a strong sense of his own worthy heritage. His father and grandfather had been knighted; his middle name reflected not only his family's Catholic background, but also the fact that Queen Mary, England's last Roman Catholic monarch, had been godmother at his father's baptism. Despite his religion, Wingfield had demonstrated his loyalty to Queen Elizabeth by serving as a soldier in both Ireland and the Netherlands. He was the only one of the four named members of the London Company who was actually making the voyage. As such he was the highest-ranking person on board the three vessels—except for Newport, and the captain's status was only temporary. Apparently Wingfield was not reticent about asserting his importance.

It is unclear what precisely set Wingfield against Smith at the Canaries. Though their social backgrounds were quite different, the men might have found a common ground in their military experience. Wingfield was around twenty years older, but age alone would not have earned Smith's respect. That Smith was friendly with so many of the men aboard may have made Wingfield jealous and then suspicious. Possibly he overheard a flippant remark that Smith made to one of the men he had recruited, perhaps commenting on some fault Smith found with the leaders of the voyage. More likely Smith remembered Wingfield as one of those who had earlier ridiculed Hunt, and now gave him back a little of his own during the stopover.

In any case, Wingfield lodged a charge of mutiny against Smith, specifically (according to Smith's account) that "he intended to usurpe the [colonial] governement, murder the Councell, and make himself king." That was a shocking accusation, and if Captain Newport had believed it, he certainly would have treated it more seriously than he did. The sentence for such an offense was death.

Newport would have had no hesitation about severely punishing a mutineer, particularly one who had many potential allies among the passengers. As an alternative, if Newport felt Smith were a genuine threat, he could simply have left him in the Canaries. Instead, Smith writes that he was "restrained as a prisoner" from the time the flotilla left the Canaries, but there was no brig in any of the ships, so it is difficult to guess how his freedom might have been limited.

The ships now headed due west across the Atlantic. Their next landfall was 3,200 miles away, and the voyagers spent two rough and tedious months on the open sea before reaching it. The tight confines aboard ship must have exacerbated what was now an ugly feud. Neither Smith nor Wingfield would make any effort to patch it up, and there was not enough room on the small *Susan Constant* for them to avoid each other. Day after day Wingfield grew more indignant that this commoner upstart was being permitted to escape punishment for his mutinous schemes. Smith, resentful at the false accusation (he would later charge Wingfield with slander), would not offer an apology. Tensions ran high, and both men most likely sought allies in their feud. Unfortunately for Smith, his most powerful friend on the expedition, Bartholomew Gosnold, was captain of another ship and for the time being was unable to provide assistance or mediate the dispute.

The men of the little fleet sighted the island of Mattanemio (today's Martinique) on March 23 and began to make their way north along the Antillean archipelago. Though Spain claimed these islands, most of them were either uninhabited or occupied only by a few indigenous people. Newport was familiar with them from his days as a privateer, when he often found it necessary to seek a safe haven or a place where the ship's freshwater casks could be refilled without hindrance from a Spanish garrison.

Much of what we know about this part of the journey comes from the account of George Percy, the youngest brother of the Earl of Northumberland and the only colonist from a noble family; in terms of social rank, no one on any of the ships was his equal. (His ancestor was the Harry Hotspur who appears as a character in Shakespeare's *Henry IV*.) At the time, however, the earl was still imprisoned in the Tower of London, accused of having played a role in the Gunpowder Plot. The Percy family had clung to the Roman Catholic faith for several generations, and Percy's father and grandfather had both been executed for their plots against the Tudors. That political and religious background was, no doubt, why George Percy found it advisable to leave England for a distant shore at this time.

Nonetheless, Percy had other reasons for wanting to visit America. Since his boyhood, he had known Sir Walter Raleigh, a frequent visitor to the Northumberland castle. Percy's brother, like Raleigh, was a patron of Thomas Harriot, the official surveyor of the first Roanoke colony, who had published his *Briefe and True Report of the New Found Land of Virginia* in 1588. Young George (eight years old at the time, the same age as John Smith, who was worlds away in terms of status) had not only gone through its profusely illustrated pages, but as he grew up had often listened to Harriot's firsthand tales of America's native people and natural wonders.

Throughout his youth Percy had been dreaming of America, and the sight of it did not disappoint him. He described Dominico (Dominica), the first island they landed on, as "very Faire . . . the Trees full of sweet and good smels inhabited by many Savage Indians." In fact the "savage" natives were too timid to board the English ships, despite the sailors' coaxing. Percy learned later that they had been cruelly treated by the Spanish. When the natives came to believe that the English did not intend to harm or enslave them, they brought gifts: "many kinds of sundry fruites, [such] as Pines [pineapples], Potatoes, Plantons [plantains], Tobacco . . . and Roane Cloth [Rouen linen, which the natives had recovered from Spanish ships that had been wrecked on the island]."

Despite the natives' friendly gestures, Percy saw them through prejudiced eyes. He wrote, "These people and [those in] the rest of the Ilands in the West Indies, and Brasill, are called by the names of Canibals, that will eate mans flesh, these people doe poyson their Arrow heads, which are made of a fishes bone: they worship the Devill for their God, and have no other beliefe." Percy could have learned almost none of this from personal observation, because the English ships stayed at Dominica only a day or two. He was no doubt repeating what he had heard back in England.

On March 28 the colonists reached the island of Mevis (today's Nevis). Newport decided to anchor in its harbor and allow his crews and passengers to go ashore. He planned a week's stay to give them time to recover their strength and to resupply the ships with water and firewood. Here Smith and Wingfield once more squared off against each other.

The colonists dispersed to different parts of the island. Some caught an alligator and feasted on the strange creature's meat. Percy recalled going with another group of men to "a Bath standing in a Valley . . . where wee bathed our selves and found it to be of the nature of the Bathes in England, some places hot and some colder." As Percy wrote, the island was "convenient for our men to avoid diseases, which will breed in so long a Voyage." Some men "went a hunting, some a fouling, and some a fishing." And others—unnoticed and unmentioned by Percy—went after John Smith.

Newport was evidently distracted, probably occupied with supervising the resupply efforts, and Wingfield saw an opportunity finally to exert his authority as chief representative of the Virginia Company of London. He enlisted the support of several like-minded "gentlemen," pronounced Smith guilty of mutiny, and set out to execute him at once. They hurriedly raised a gallows, which may not have been much more than a rope around a tree branch.

Smith, perhaps brought from the ship in shackles, proved a match for his enemies. He had allies of his own standing by. This time, Gosnold was ashore, as were the men Smith had personally recruited for the voyage. They came forward to protect him, and he actually seems to have mocked Wingfield and those who stood ready to hang him. Many years later, in Smith's autobiography, he tossed off the whole incident in less than a sentence: "A paire of gallowes was made, but Captaine Smith, for whom they were intended, could not be perswaded to use them." That act of defi-ance, of course, would only have enraged Wingfield all the more.

Newport, on learning of all this, must have been annoyed and exasperated. He may even have intervened in the attempted exe-cution, but he certainly had more important tasks to attend to than keeping the colonists from killing one another. Again, New-port's favorable bias toward Smith seems puzzling. Though com-mander of the expedition, the one-armed captain was also an employee of the Virginia Company, and it seems odd that he refused to give in to Wingfield's desire to see Smith swinging from the end of a rope. The reason may have been that he knew, as Wingfield did not, the contents of the sealed box in his cabin.

No matter how much satisfaction it gave Smith to defy Wing-field, it shows a lack of prudence on his part, for he had made a vindictive and powerful enemy. Once the ships reached Virginia, Wingfield would be certain to revive the case against him. Smith had a friend in Gosnold, possibly another in Reverend Hunt, but neither could continue to protect him from Wingfield's wrath, for the other members of the ruling council were certain to be gentlemen, Wingfield's natural allies. Even Newport, the only person to command universal respect, would be leaving Virginia once he had carried out his orders to explore the local river system.

But Smith had already cheated death so many times in his brief lifetime that he must have felt, even more than most twenty-six-year-olds, that he was invulnerable. He had survived being thrown off a ship in a storm, faced the ends of Turks' lances and prevailed in three deadly jousts, been wounded and left for dead on a battlefield, escaped from slavery, and made his way through 2,500 miles of unfamiliar territory in eastern Europe while wearing leg chains and not knowing a word of the local languages. To him any threats Wingfield could offer must have felt less fearsome than those he'd already faced and survived.

There was a reminder, shortly after the ships left Nevis, that death was always hovering in the background. At one of the last islands the colonists visited—Mora, just west of Puerto Rico—the first fatality struck the colonists. Percy recorded it, and its cause: "Edward Brooke, gentleman, whose fat melted within him by the great heat and drought of the country." It probably had not helped poor Brooke that, like all the colonists, he wore a full outfit of woolen cloth, with padded doublet and hose—not exactly suitable for the tropics. Before the year was out, more than half of those who reached Virginia would follow in his wake.

Once again the ships headed onto the open ocean, following a northerly course toward a destination none of those on board had ever seen. Smith was probably shackled below decks now, either at Wingfield's insistence or because Newport wanted him to stay out of the older man's way. It is one of history's ironies that the person who, more than any other, guaranteed the success of English settlement in America arrived as a prisoner under sentence of death.

6

Disease, Dissension, and Death

A S THE THREE SMALL VESSELS SAILED into Chesapeake Bay on the morning of April 26, 1607, passengers and crewmen breathed a sigh of relief. It had been a grueling trip. The ships had left London more than four months earlier; it had been sixteen days since the men aboard had seen any land at all. Now here at last was their destination—that green paradise of which an earlier English visitor had written, "for temperature of climate, for fertility of soil, and for the commodity of the sea . . . not to be excelled by any other whatsoever." The colonists could hardly wait to set their feet on land, and Newport led some of them ashore at a place they named Cape Henry, after the eldest son of King James I. After Virginia itself, it was the first place in the world outside England to be given an English name—but hardly the last.

There, George Percy described his first sight of Virginia's "fair meadows and goodly tall trees, with such fresh waters running through the woods as I was almost ravished at the first sight thereof." The other Englishmen had similar reactions as they wandered happily about for most of the day. Perhaps their only disappointment was in not finding nuggets of gold lying on the ground, as many of them had hoped.

Meanwhile, other eyes were observing the scene from the cover of the trees and high grass. At dusk, when the Englishmen prepared to board the small boats that would take them back to their ships, Percy wrote, several "savages" came "creeping upon all four from the hills like bears, with their bows in their mouths," and suddenly let fly with a volley of arrows. Two of the Englishmen received "dangerous" wounds, though not fatal. The others, after recovering from their surprise, responded with fire from their matchlock rifles. The natives, having "felt the sharpness of our shot," Percy wrote, "retired into the woods with great noise, and so left us."

That was a disconcerting end to what had started as a joyous day, and as later events in the colony would show, there was never any reluctance to criticize the leadership when things went badly. Now that Newport had accomplished his task of bringing the colonists to America, someone may have reminded him, he was supposed to reveal the names of the governing council. Newport, though acceptable as a ship's captain, was not a "gentleman," and plenty of those aboard ship felt it was time he turned his power over to them. For his part, Newport may have been glad to rid himself of the responsibility.

The revelation made by candlelight in Captain Newport's cabin on the colonists' first night in Chesapeake Bay—that John Smith had been named to the seven-member governing council of Virginia—did not result in a reconciliation between him and Wingfield. By all accounts, Smith remained under suspicion, if not in chains, and at first he was not permitted to take the oath of office prescribed in the Virginia Company's instructions.

The other six council members were sworn in a week after arriving in Virginia, and those six then elected Wingfield as their president. (The title of governor was not then used.) He thus became the first elected official in what is now the United States, a claim that his admirers (and Smith's detractors) seldom tire of repeating, ignoring the fact that the electorate was somewhat limited. None of the accounts that survive, not even Smith's, explain why Smith was not allowed to be sworn, perhaps because by the time those accounts came to be written and edited, the deliberate snub had become embarrassing to all. It is clear, however, that despite the high esteem that someone at the Virginia Company had for him, Smith was still under a cloud in Virginia itself.

The colonists had used the first week to construct a shallop, a shallow-draft boat that had been disassembled in England and stored on board one of the ships. An exploring party used it to sail or row up the nearest river, the one they named for King James, searching for an appropriate location to establish their colony. Gabriel Archer, who had been with Gosnold in New England in 1602, sighted a "point of land," which according to Percy "was sufficient with a little labour to defend our selves against any enemy." Percy dubbed it "Archer's Hope," not to describe the enthusiasm of its discoverer, but because *hope* was an old word for a haven.

Archer's hopes for his hope were soon dashed as Wingfield forcefully objected to his suggestion that the colonists build there. Gosnold seems to have taken the side of his old friend—besides the 1602 trip, he and Archer had attended both Cambridge University and law school together—and that in turn bred hard feelings between Gosnold and Wingfield. It became a power struggle, not the last that would occur in the colony, and strengthens the impression that Wingfield was a man who felt that the expedition should follow military discipline, with him as the chief officer.

On this occasion Wingfield, as president, got his way. He chose a location two miles upriver from Archer's Hope. It was a wooded peninsula about two miles long by one mile wide. This was the site that became Jamestown (ambitiously titled "James Citee" by some), named in honor of England's current king. Wingfield felt that it fulfilled the specifications set forth in the Virginia Company's instructions. Though it resembled an island, it was in fact connected to the mainland by a narrow sandbar (today the sandbar has been eroded away and visitors come to Jamestown via a bridge). Thus it seemed to be an easily defensible location. In addition, the channel of the James River was quite deep here, making it possible for the ships to anchor close to the shoreline, where they could be easily unloaded.

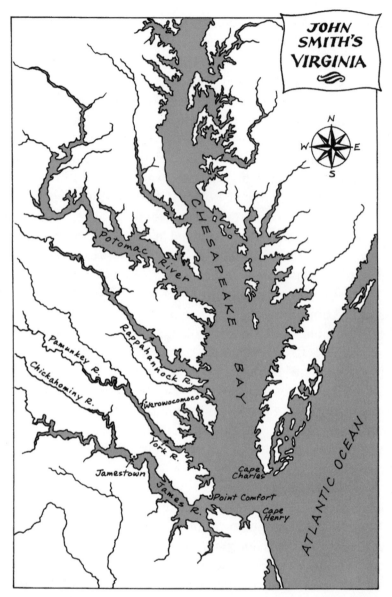

Before John Smith left Virginia, he would explore much of the area shown on this map.

John Smith, for once, agreed with Wingfield, calling the site "a very fit place for the erecting of a great city." Both were wrong. Unfortunately, Jamestown had crucial disadvantages as well, some of which were not evident on first inspection. First of all, even this far from the ocean—it was fifty-seven miles to Cape

Henry, the entrance to the bay—the James is still a tidal estuary, and its water, used for drinking by the colonists, is brackish. It was even more so in the spring of 1607, for the region had been suffering from a prolonged drought, as modern scientists have found from tree ring measurements. That dry spell also concealed the fact that in times of normal rainfall, Jamestown resembled a swamp. Also, though the little plot of land appeared deserted and unclaimed, it very likely had been used as a hunting ground by the Paspahegh people who lived nearby. It would not be long before the Paspaheghs showed up to discuss the English appropriation.

Once the site had been chosen, "Now falleth every man to worke," a colonist recalled later, perhaps overstating the case in retrospect. According to Smith, the gentlemen were reluctant to work, and not much got built. After clearing the ground, the colonists erected only tents to shelter themselves from the elements, and, at first, not even a palisade to protect themselves against the natives. Wingfield felt that the instructions of the Virginia Company to take "Great Care not to Offend the naturals [natives]" would be violated if the colonists built a fort. George Kendall, one of the other council members, forcefully objected and won permission to use tree boughs to build a barrier in the shape of a half-moon partially encircling the encampment. Considering that the very first encounter between English and the "naturals" had resulted in conflict, Wingfield's position appears foolhardy. This was not the last time that instructions written in London conflicted with what the colonists on site found necessary for their survival.

Less than a week after the English had begun to unload their supplies at Jamestown, they had two visitors—"Commanders," wrote Percy, "with Crownes of colored haire upon their heads." They were in fact messengers from the Paspaheghs' werowance, a word familiar to Percy and anyone else—probably including Smith—who had read Harriot's account of the Native Americans. Literally, the werowance was a man of wealth, although the term was generally used to mean the leader of a group, a "king," according to Harriot. The messengers announced that their werowance would soon arrive to welcome the English, and, wrote

Percy, he was bringing the makings of a feast: he "would be merry with us with a fat Deare."

It was a good thing the werowance brought his own food, for when he arrived two days later he was accompanied by one hundred men armed with bows and arrows; the English would have been hard pressed to feed them all. Percy gave an ominous interpretation toward their bearing arms, writing that the Paspaheghs thought "at that time to execute their villainy." The English certainly had their arms at the ready too, and the werowance requested that they lay them aside. Neither side trusted the other to that extent, and the weapons remained in hand.

It soon became evident that the werowance had come to negotiate land usage. He "made signes," wrote Percy, "that he would give us as much land as we would desire to take." Seemingly that was a generous offer, but before it could be discussed, one of the natives picked up a hatchet—probably out of curiosity, for the Paspaheghs had no metal tools. In Percy's view, the man "stole" the hatchet. (To emphasize the point, the first publisher of Percy's report added a marginal note to the reader: "These Savages are naturally great theeves.") Another colonist saw the native take the hatchet, snatched it back, and struck the man on the arm for good measure. One of the other natives started to retaliate; he "came fiercely at our man with a wooden sword, thinking to beat out his braines." By that time, everyone assembled on both sides was ready to fight, but the werowance led his men away with a few angry gestures.

Two days later, he sent forty men back to the English with a deer—probably a peace offering, but Percy did not interpret it that way. He wrote, "They came more in villanie than [because of] any love they bare us." The natives had aroused Percy's suspicions by asking to remain in the English camp all night. "Wee would not suffer them [to do so]" he wrote, "for feare of their treachery."

The English, thinking to impress their guests with a demonstration of strength, set up a target, one thick enough so that not even a pistol ball could penetrate it, and invited the natives to try their skill with their bows. To the surprise of the English, the first arrow, "about an ell long [forty-five inches]," went clear through the target and stuck out the other side by a foot. Not wanting to be bested, the English then set up a steel target; this time the arrow broke into pieces when it struck the metal surface. The man who had shot it "presently pulled out another Arrow and bit it in his teeth, and seemed to bee in a great rage," and finally stalked off.

Captain Newport prepared to carry out the last of his instructions from the Virginia Company: to explore any river that tended to flow from the west, looking for a possible link to the South Sea, or Pacific Ocean. The English had no idea of the extent of the North American mainland, and it seemed possible to Hakluyt and others that one or more of the rivers that flowed into the Atlantic could prove to be a gateway to the opposite side of America. On May 21, a month after the colonists first arrived, Newport chose twenty-three men to accompany him upriver in the shallop. Most of them were sailors, men Newport knew he could count on; five others were gentlemen, including Percy, Archer, and Smith, who was probably selected because Newport feared for his safety if left under Wingfield's authority. For similar reasons, Newport left Gosnold behind, though the company's instructions said that Gosnold should accompany the party looking for the South Sea. Newport no doubt felt that Gosnold's calming influence would keep Wingfield from becoming embroiled in more disputes.

By nightfall, according to Archer's account, the explorers had traveled upriver eighteen miles, to a place Archer called Wynauk, the native word for sassafras. The people who lived here entertained the English "with Daunces and much rejoycing." Word had already spread upstream that Newport generously distributed trinkets such as little bells, pins, and Venetian-made beads to those who showed friendliness. Smith commented that Newport's liberality made the natives "follow us from place to place and ever kindely to respect us."

The next day, the travelers encountered several men in a canoe. As they approached, the English hailed them with the Algonquian word they knew meant "friend": *wingapo*. The natives and Englishmen went ashore for a parley, and Newport conveyed that he wanted to discover the extent of the river. One of the men offered to draw a map in the sand; instead Archer provided pen and paper. Undaunted by these new tools, the man "layd out the whole River" from Chesapeake Bay to the fall line where it would become necessary to portage or leave the boat behind (about the location of today's city of Richmond). Above the falls, he told the English, there were two kingdoms, and, "a great Distance off," mountains named Quirank. He added something that led the English to believe that beyond those mountains lay the great salty water that must be the Pacific.

That was enough to persuade Newport to hurry on at once, although the mapmaker tried to get him to stay and trade. Nonetheless, the shallop was so slow that the man was able to load his canoe with baskets of dried oysters and catch up with the English a little later in the day. Archer even reports that after trading his oysters, the man overtook the English a second time, now carrying a cargo of mulberries, "little sweete nuttes like Acorns," and some beans. The ease with which he moved up and down the river should have caused the English to question the efficiency of their lumbering shallop, but apparently Newport felt that the larger boat offered both cargo space and safety. (The English nearly always slept in it at night, anchored in midstream.)

Even though their boat was slow compared to a canoe, the English made fair progress. On the third day of the journey, Archer estimates they traveled thirty-eight miles, coming to a place he named in descriptive fashion "poore Cottage." Here they once more met the mapmaker, who had spread word of Newport's generous trade practices. The werowance of the local area, named Arrohattoc, treated Newport as an equal, ordering a mat of reeds similar to his own to be spread on the ground for the English captain, and even presenting Newport with a crown made of deer hair dyed red. The assembled company feasted on roasted venison, and the women made cakes for their guests.

It was here, evidently, that Percy reported seeing a boy about the age of ten, who "had a haire of a perfect yellow and a reasonable white skinne, which is a Miracle among all Savages." The obvious conclusion does not seem to have occurred to Percy: that this boy must be a descendant of the lost Roanoke colonists. This lapse is all the more remarkable because the Jamestown settlers had been instructed to keep an eye out for their earlier counterparts, who might well have made their way up the coastline to the Chesapeake area, which was, after all, their original intended destination in 1587. As we shall see, there are good reasons for thinking that some of the Roanoke refugees or their offspring were in fact in the region at the very moment Smith and his companions arrived, but if the Jamestown colonists seriously looked for them on first arrival, no one who wrote of their experiences mentions it.

While the English were finishing the banquet, watching dances, and smoking tobacco provided by their hosts, word came that the "great king" of the region, Powhatan, was approaching. This was the first time Smith and the others had heard of the man who held sway over much of the region. As it happened, the visitor was not Powhatan, but Powhatan's son Tanx-Powhatan ("Little Powhatan"). The paramount chief himself was intensely cautious—no doubt a survival skill—and was gauging the intentions of the newcomers before meeting them. It would be seven months before Powhatan allowed any of the Englishmen into his presence.

Noting that all the natives except Arrohattoc rose to their feet at the arrival of Tanx-Powhatan, the English pointedly remained seated. Even so, they presented him with "gyftes of dyvers sortes ... more amply then [than] before." Tanx-Powhatan in return appointed five of his men as guides to lead the English up the river; one was the mapmaker, who had apparently taken the colonists under his wing, thinking to enhance his own prestige as a result.

They went some ten miles farther, accompanied by curious natives paddling alongside, before arriving at another island, probably the one called Mayo's Island today, where, according to Archer, Tanx-Powhatan had his residence. (Again, the English were misled—probably deliberately—on this occasion. The paramount chief's actual home village lay to the north, across the strip of land between the James and York rivers.) More feasting followed, during which Tanx-Powhatan confided that the "Chessipians," or Chesapeakes, people who lived downriver near the entrance to the bay, were enemies of his kingdom. Archer took the hint, saying that the English "had warres with them also," and even showed the wound, only partly healed, that he had received when the English had been attacked during their first exploration of the shore. On that shared note, the king proposed a "league of friendship," and Newport sealed it by accepting the king's gown, presented with the words *wingapo chemuze*—"the best of friends."

The English were eager to go on, and left Tanx-Powhatan's island to make their way upstream. They soon came to the falls that their native mapmaker had described and saw that they were indeed impassable. Undaunted, the English found a place to anchor for the night, thinking to portage around the falls in the morning. One of the guides, a man named Nauirans who was Arrohattoc's brother-in-law, asked if he could sleep aboard the English boat. Permission was granted, and the man "proved a very trustye friend," as Archer declared. Later, his actions would signal to them that something was wrong.

Tanx-Powhatan began to discourage the English from going above the falls, arguing that they did not have enough supplies to reach the mountains and that the Monacans who lived there were enemies who regularly invaded Powhatan's domain when the leaves fell. Newport decided it was important to maintain the chief's goodwill, and agreed not to go farther on this occasion. However, he promised to return with a large enough force (five hundred men, according to Archer—something of a rash pledge, or perhaps one intended to convince Tanx-Powhatan that the English had overwhelming power) to overcome the Monacans and make Tanx-Powhatan king of their country.

Newport showed his true intentions, however, when he set up a wooden cross at the base of the falls, inscribed with the year, the name of King James, and Newport's own name. As Percy wrote in his journal, by doing so "we proclaimed James King of England to have the most right unto [the river]." Pointedly,

Tanx-Powhatan absented himself from this ceremony; the cheers of the English had given him an idea of their purpose.

The English, having gone as far as they could, now turned downriver on what took on aspects of a triumphal tour, stopping and feasting at villages along the banks. While in Arrohattoc's camp, one of the English seamen became involved in a dispute with a native. Newport, says Archer, bound his own man to a tree and beat him with a cudgel—demonstrating English discipline. Not to be outdone, Arrohattoc went after the offending native, who fled. Arrohattoc chased him down personally, impressing Archer with his speed. Archer commented that the werowance could have given any of the Englishmen a sizable head start and still overtaken them.

In one of the places the English visited, a woman was werowance. "A comely young savage," according to Smith (but described by Archer as "a fatt lustie manly woman"), this "Queen of Apamatuck" wore a crown and necklaces made of copper and had a group of female attendants waiting on her. She requested that Newport discharge one of his firearms and he complied. At the sound of the shot, Archer noted, "she shewed not the like feare as Arohattock, though he be a goodly man."

Nauirans, the brother-in-law of Arrohattoc, had continued to accompany the English everywhere, but one day abruptly announced he had to return home. His sudden departure aroused Newport's suspicions, making him fearful that something had occurred back at Jamestown. The English made their way back as swiftly as they could, and found that two hundred natives had attacked the day before. "They came up allmost into the Fort," reported Archer, "shott through the tentes . . . hurt 11 men (whereof one dyed after) and killed a Boy." An arrow had passed through Wingfield's beard but left him unharmed. The natives were driven off only after the colonists fired small cannons at them.

After that scare, Wingfield could no longer maintain that the fort should not be reinforced as strongly as possible. Now the men set to work building a three-sided structure, palisaded with small tree trunks driven into the ground. Atop each corner of the structure was an observation post. While construction was going on, sporadic attacks continued, seemingly with the intent to harass rather than overrun the English. However, a man named Eustace Clovell wandered too far beyond the fort, and came running back with six arrows sticking out of his body. He lingered for eight days before dying. Because the fort was surrounded by tall grass, it was easy for the natives to approach closely without detection. Another unfortunate colonist, venturing out "to doe naturall necessity," as Archer described his purpose, received an arrow in the head "and through the Clothes in two places, but missed the skynne."

The almost daily attacks started to wear on the Englishmen's nerves. The day Clovell died, two unarmed natives approached the fort while shouting, "Wingapo!" A sentry, apparently not acquainted with the Algonquian for "friend," took a shot at them. The two men ran off, still calling back, "Wingapo!"

The tension had one beneficial effect. "A murmur . . . against certayne preposterous proceedings" spread through the company, and a petition was presented to the council, demanding that Captain Smith be sworn in as a member. Apparently Smith's record as an effective soldier convinced the others that his services were desperately needed now. Archer says that Captain Newport argued in favor of the petition, and on June 10 Smith at last was allowed to take his rightful place on the council.

Neither he nor anyone else was able to stop the ongoing attacks on Englishmen who ventured outside the palisade. Two more men were shot at on the thirteenth of the month. Then on Sunday, June 14, a visitor arrived—the unnamed mapmaker who had helped the English up the river. On learning of the difficulties, he surveyed the situation and gravely announced that the colonists should simply cut down the tall grass that surrounded the fort, making it impossible for attackers to hide there. It is difficult to say who might have been more embarrassed—the English at having overlooked the obvious for so long, or the native guide at having to counsel such tenderfeet. The grass was duly cut down, and the daily attacks on settlers ceased.

Newport now prepared to depart. We know that he worried about what might happen once he left, for Wingfield wrote a self-justifying account later in which he said Newport met privately with him and asked how secure he thought himself as head of the colony. Wingfield replied that the only two people who might cause him difficulties were Gosnold and Archer, "for the one [Gosnold] was strong with friends and followers, and could if he would; and the other [Archer] was troubled with an ambitious spirit, and would if he could." It is telling, first, that Wingfield didn't mention Smith, and, second, that he feared Gosnold—who by all accounts wished only the best for the colony—merely because the younger man had friends and followers.

Newport made matters worse by going to both Gosnold and Archer and repeating what Wingfield had said. His intentions were good, for he entreated them "to be mindful of their duties to His Majesty and the Colony." But learning of Wingfield's insecurity could hardly have increased their respect for him, and it is possible that others regarded the grizzled old soldier as more bluff than substance.

Taking the two larger ships and leaving the pinnace at Jamestown, Newport set sail for England on June 22. He had a cargo of clapboard, thin slats of wood that the colonists had managed to carve up from oak trees; in England they would be useful for making barrels. The ships also brought back some two tons of wild sassafras that the sailors had gathered for their own profits. The clapboard was all that the Virginia Company could show in return for the money its investors had put up for the voyage. There was no chance that would be enough to turn a profit. Of course, the colony would survive for a time on promises: that gold and silver might yet be found, that other economic benefits could accrue, that Jamestown might one day be a landing place for ships on their way to Asia. Newport also carried Archer's optimistic account, as well as a letter from the council in Virginia throwing the best possible light on the colonists' limited achievements. (Smith stepped forward to sign his name to the document directly below President Wingfield's.) "Wee moste humblie praie the heavenly Kings hand to blesse our labours with such counsailes and helpes, as wee may further and stronger proceede in this our Kinges and Contries service," wrote the new Virginians.

As the sails of Newport's ships disappeared over the horizon, however, the 104 men left behind must have felt misgivings. They had enough food to last them perhaps thirteen to fourteen weeks, and Newport promised to return before that time had passed. But it had taken him four months just to make the one-way journey from England to Virginia. The example of the lost colonists could hardly have been far from the settlers' minds. Their own circle of safety barely encompassed the confines of the tiny fort; beyond lay a continent filled with unknown dangers.

Misfortune struck the colony almost as soon as Newport had left, and was wholly unexpected. A mysterious illness swept through the fort. "Within ten dayes," wrote Smith, "scarce[ly] ten amongst us could either goe [walk], or well stand, such extreame weaknes and sicknes oppressed us." Smith thought he knew the reason for the epidemic: lack of proper food. As long as the ships had been moored off Jamestown, the sailors supplied the colonists with extra rations of ship's biscuit (in return for "money, Saxefras, furres, or love"). When this source of food disappeared, the colonists were left with the contents of "the common Kettell." The daily ration, distributed by President Wingfield, was "halfe a pint of wheat, and as much barley boyled with water." Moreover, the dry wheat and barley, "having fryed some 26 weekes in the ships hold, contained as many wormes as graines."

Smith doesn't hesitate to place the blame on Wingfield, accusing the president of hoarding beef, eggs, oil, and strong drink for himself and his close friends. As for the rest of the colonists, "our drinke was water, our lodgings Castles in the ayre," for there had still been no progress in building houses for them to live in. Very likely, the heat of the summer made a contribution to the colonists' weakened condition, and they had brought nothing but heavy woolens to wear.

The effects were harrowing. A full fifty men—half the company—died from June to September. Percy listed the names of many in his journal, as dispassionately as the tolling of a bell. "The fifteenth day, their died Edward Browne and Stephen Galthrope. The sixteenth day, their died Thomas Gower Gentleman. The seventeenth day, their died Thomas Mounslic . . . ." Once,

Percy allowed himself a cry of frustration: "There were never Englishmen left in a foreign Countrey in such miserie as wee were in this new discovered Virginia." Scholars have puzzled over the cause of the epidemic. Percy describes a few symptoms: "swellings, flixes [diarrhea], burning fevers . . . but for the most part they died of meere famine." He notes that the water was salty and full of slime and filth. Hunger and unsanitary conditions were doubtless factors, but most modern authorities think there must have been a disease to account for the sudden deaths of so many apparently healthy men. Food was available to them; Smith mentions that some colonists supplemented their diet with sturgeon and sea crabs. Adding to the mystery is that twenty-five years earlier, the Roanoke colonists, who also settled on an island with much the same climate, suffered only four deaths from disease, and three of those who died had been sick when they arrived in America.

Gordon W. Jones, a twentieth-century Virginia physician, applied the skills of an epidemiologist and historian to analyzing the illness that struck the 1607 Jamestown settlers. He discounted malaria, despite the swampy location, because neither the disease nor its carrier (the anopheles mosquito) had yet been introduced to America. The symptoms described by Percy, particularly the fever and diarrhea, suggested to Dr. Jones a diagnosis of typhoid fever, accompanied by beriberi. Yet the fever did not make its appearance until Newport left. The reason, Dr. Jones speculates, was that typhoid thrives under unsanitary conditions. Competent sea captains like Newport had learned to keep their crews alive by enforcing cleanliness, including swabbing the living quarters with vinegar and airing the bedding. Bodily wastes were deposited directly into the ocean. It is probable that Newport was able to insist on such standards of sanitation, to some degree, while he remained at Jamestown. After he left, Wingfield may have let those standards slide, and of course as the weather grew warmer, so did the likelihood of the spread of bacteria in the drinking water and food. Moreover, the dead were buried inside the fort, secretly, at night, "trailed out of their cabins like dogs," according to Percy. This was in line with the Virginia Company's instructions to conceal any deaths from the native people, but having the decaying bodies within the confines of the living quarters was a potential hazard. It was a combination of all these factors, rather than any hoarding of food and drink, that brought on the epidemic.

Yet typhoid is a contagious disease that requires a carrier, and since the disease was unknown among the Native Americans, that carrier had to have been one of the Englishmen. Dr. Jones points out that only one person had been known to be ill on the journey: the Reverend Robert Hunt, while the ships were becalmed off the coast of England. (Jones ignores Edward Brooke, the man who died on the island of Mora. Presumably he felt the evidence indicates he expired from heatstroke.) Smith, in his account of the voyage, noted that during Hunt's shipboard illness, some had urged him to "give up the business," and allow himself to be put ashore, but Hunt steadfastly refused. Smith saw this as the admirable tenacity of a man of God determined to carry out his duties, but there was another reason—a secret kept from the colonists.

Hunt never returned to England from Jamestown. The circumstances of his death are unknown, but he had made a will less than a month before leaving England, and it was probated July 14, 1608, so news of his death must have reached home before then. Its contents are revealing. After bequests to servants, his daughter, and his son, Hunt left the bulk of his estate to his wife Elizabeth, with a striking proviso: that if she should commit "the act of incontinency" or should be suspected of such an act during his lifetime, *or, even after his death*, if Elizabeth should live in the same house with "John Taylor the eldest Sonne of John Taylor of the parish of Heathfeild" [*sic*], then she should be deprived of any of Hunt's property or estate.

Hunt could hardly have been more specific regarding his suspicions about his wife's unfaithfulness. The gentle preacher depicted by Smith had felt himself a cuckold, and he resented it. So do the minor details of life influence the big events: Had Hunt's wife been faithful, he might not have resisted going ashore during his illness. Had he not accompanied the colonists to Virginia, the typhoid bacillus would not have arrived along with him. The fifty men—half the colony—would not have died, nor would many from subsequent voyages who also suffered from the mysterious illness.

And John Smith might have remained an obscure figure in history. For he was ultimately to benefit from the colonists' distress. The disease that was spreading relentlessly through the camp created an atmosphere of fear. Wingfield reported that one of the English boys fled the camp, choosing to take his chances among the natives rather than remain among the disease-ridden colonists. (The Paspahegh werowance had the boy returned to Jamestown.) Almost no one was able to escape the illness; Smith himself contracted it, though he recovered. At one point, it was reported that there were only six able-bodied men to defend the camp in case of attack.

On August 1, Bartholomew Gosnold fell ill. This was a serious blow, for he commanded the respect of nearly everyone and served as a voice of moderation. Smith and Wingfield met, and clashed, in Gosnold's tent while the dying man listened helplessly. Wingfield believed that Smith was spreading calumnies against him (probably true). We have only Wingfield's description of the event, and it is worth reporting in full to give the tone of the older man's hurt and anger:

"Master Smyth in the tyme of our hungar had spred a Rumor in the Collony that I did feast my self and my servantes, out of the Comon stoare, with entent (as I gathered) to have stirred the discontented Company against me. I tould him privately in Master Gosnolds Tent, that indeede I had caused half a pinte of pease to be sodden [soaked] with a peese of porke of my owne provision for a poore old man, which in a sicknes (whereof he died) he much desired, and [I] said that if out of his [Smith's] malice he had given it out otherwise, that hee did tell a lye. It was proved to his face, that he begged in Ireland like a rogue, without lycence, to such I would not my name be a Companyon."

The last sentence, with its insult, completely irrelevant to the accusation but rather intended to put Smith in his (lower-class) place, seems typical of Wingfield. Scholars have searched in vain for any proof that Smith was ever in Ireland, though there are gaps in his life history during which he could have been there. It is difficult to see how Wingfield could have proved it, "to his face" or otherwise. The key point, for Wingfield, was that Smith wasn't worthy to be his companion. One imagines Smith's response to this: a grim smile and a silent promise that the slight would not go unavenged. Wingfield would in time need "companyons," particularly those with steel in their spines. Smith would in time obtain satisfaction and see Wingfield brought low.

Gosnold died on August 22 and was buried with military honors. Even Wingfield knew he had lost a valuable man "upon whose lief stood a great part of the good succes, and fortune of our government and Collony." Wingfield now expected his authority to be challenged, but the first attack came from someone other than Smith.

There were now five council members: Wingfield; Smith; John Ratcliffe, the captain of the small pinnace; John Martin, the son of the lord mayor of London; and George Kendall, who had taken the initiative in reinforcing the palisade surrounding the fort. Given the service that Kendall had clearly done for the struggling community, it is surprising that he should have been accused of disloyalty, but so it was. The reasons, along with the precise charges, are obscure ("hainous matters which was proved against him," wrote Percy), but they were sufficient to cause the others to depose him from the council. A document later found in the archives of the Spanish government, supposedly an interview with an Irishman who was at Jamestown at this time, indicates that Kendall may have been an agent of Spain. Again, it is difficult to see what evidence could have convinced the others of this, but finger-pointing and paranoia had increased during the months when disease carried off so many of the colonists. Wingfield wrote that Kendall tried "to sowe discord betwene the President and Councell," but hard feelings along those lines needed no encouragement from anyone. For the time being, Kendall was imprisoned aboard the pinnace, still anchored in the James River.

Striking down one council member made it easy to attack another. On September 10, according to Wingfield's account, Ratcliffe, Smith, and Martin came to his tent "with a warrant subscribed under their handes to depose the President, sayeing they thought him very unworthy to be eyther President or [a member] of the Councell, and therefore discharged him of both." Smith claimed later that Wingfield, one of the few men who had never contracted the mysterious illness, had planned to take the pinnace and a few of his friends and abandon the colony. It had been the discovery of this plot that caused the others to depose and imprison him.

Wingfield, who wrote a defense of his conduct (or more accurately, a condemnation of others' conduct) for the Virginia Company in London, took a sarcastic tone toward the proceedings. He claimed to have told the others "that they had eased him of a great deale of Care and trouble," adding his advice, as from someone who wished them well: take care in what they were doing. "But they told him," he reported, "if they did him wrong, they must answere [for] it."

The following day, Wingfield was called to face his accusers publicly. He notes that "Master Archer" had been made recording secretary of Virginia, and Archer wrote down virtually any charge that anyone in the colony cared to bring. Acidly, Wingfield says it was "naturall to this honest gent Master Archer to be allwayes hatching of some mutany; in my tyme, hee might have appeered an author of 3 severall mutynies." Indeed, the former law student Archer was to prove a treacherous individual to virtually anyone who headed the colony, including Smith.

Wingfield lists some of the objections that others raised against his conduct, making many appear so trivial and petty as to be ridiculous. Ratcliffe, who had been elected as the new president, "said that I had denyed him a penny whistle, a Chickyn, a spoonfull of beere, and served him with foul Corne." Ratcliffe, says Wingfield, even took some of the corn out of a bag and displayed it to the assembled colonists. Martin had a more serious charge: he blamed Wingfield for the death of his son, one of the colonists, alleging the former president had "denyed him a spoonefull of beere." Martin even made a threat that friends of his in England would take revenge on Wingfield if he ever ventured to London—where, everyone knew, his father had been the lord mayor.

Smith's charges of misconduct were somewhat different: he claimed to have been slandered by Wingfield on two occasions.

First, in Gosnold's tent, Wingfield had accused Smith of lying and added (as Smith recalled the story) that he was not fit to be the companion of Wingfield's servant, much less of Wingfield. Second, and more seriously, on the voyage from England, Wingfield had accused Smith, not of mutiny, but of concealing mutiny. Smith demanded that Wingfield prove his allegations, or pay for them. A few days later there was a trial on these charges, and a jury found Wingfield guilty, awarding Smith two hundred pounds in damages, a considerable sum. Even in his own account of the proceedings, Wingfield could find no one to support the accusation of mutiny (or concealing mutiny) that had nearly cost Smith his life on Nevis.

Archer had recorded many other charges and complaints against Wingfield, but Wingfield's request for a copy so he could answer them in detail was denied. He was summarily imprisoned in the pinnace, and Kendall—for the time being regarded as not so dangerous—was released, though he was forbidden to carry weapons.

It was September by then, and unexpectedly the natives came bearing gifts of food—primarily corn that Smith regarded as unripe. He was not accustomed to eating fresh corn on the cob (or corn in any form, since it was not yet grown in Europe), imagining that it was more useful dried and ground into flour. Still, he regarded the natives' generosity as a good sign, brought about because "God the patron of all good indevors . . . changed the hearts of the Savages." The corn, along with wildfowl and some fish that the English had managed to catch, provided a better diet for all, and the sickness that had raged through the colony now began to abate. Very likely, everyone in the fort had now been exposed to it and the survivors had acquired immunity.

The council was reduced to three, and Martin, who was in his forties and not robust, was still weak from illness. Smith airily recalled that his two fellow councilors were "little beloved, of weake judgement in dangers, and lesse industry in peace." They were content to let Smith take over active management of the colony. Winter was coming, and Smith knew that the flimsy tents in which the men had been living were inadequate to protect them against the cold weather. He took firm charge, giving orders to all, setting "some to mow, others to binde thatch, some to build houses." Smith led by example, doing as much work as he asked anyone else to do, even though he was a gentleman. Not all of the upper-class colonists were so willing, but at last Jamestown began to resemble a settlement more than a temporary campsite.

That task accomplished, Smith set out with six or seven men, hoping to obtain more food from the natives. His official title in the colony was now "Cape Merchant," which gave him responsibility for trade matters. Though Smith writes that he knew little of the native language at this point, he managed to communicate well enough. At first the natives at a place downriver he calls Kecoughtan "scorned him, as a famished man," and imagined that he would give up a sword or even a musket for a handful of corn. Smith was not so easily taken in. Hoping a show of force would win the English some respect, he ordered his men to fire their muskets into the air and come ashore.

The people of Kecoughtan village fled into the woods. Smith's men explored the area and found several caches of corn, which they proposed to seize. Smith would not allow that; he foresaw that it would be preferable to establish a relationship of trust with the natives. Besides, he wrote later, he had a feeling that the villagers would come back.

So they did, "with a most hydeous noyse," sixty or seventy of them charging out of the forest, painted black, red, white, and combinations of all three. Those leading the way bore on their shoulders an idol—"their *Okee*," Smith reported—made of animal skins stuffed with moss, painted and decorated with copper chains. The natives did not expect the Okee alone to defeat the English; they were brandishing clubs, bows and arrows, and shields.

Coolly, Smith, and his men held their ground and let fly a volley of shots from their muskets. This brought the Okee and a few warriors to the ground. The rest fled back into the forest. Again, Smith awaited developments, and soon a man cautiously approached to offer peace in return for the Okee. Smith's terms were more generous: if half a dozen villagers loaded his boat with corn, he would give them his friendship, the Okee, and beads, copper, and hatchets besides. The offer was eagerly accepted, and afterward the natives danced "in signe of friendship" (or perhaps simply relief) as the English departed. As Smith had hoped, he had made sure he could return to trade on other occasions.

Smith made several other successful short trips of this kind, but as events would prove, he could never leave the fort for long without some mischief brewing among the colonists. This time, Wingfield and Kendall managed to convince a group of followers that trying to get through the winter at Jamestown would be riskier than taking the pinnace and attempting to return to England. Unfortunately for them, Smith returned in time to discover the plot and foil it. Smith writes that matters had gone so far that the plotters had seized the boat; he ordered gunners on shore to fire falcons (small cannons) at them, forcing the men aboard to surrender.

In Smith's version of the affair, Kendall was killed in the struggle over the pinnace. Wingfield tells a different story. He claims that the trouble began when Ratcliffe, the new president, beat James Read, the colony's blacksmith, with a stick. Read retaliated, striking back at Ratcliffe. Under the laws of the colony and of England, the blacksmith's action was a capital crime, for Ratcliffe, as a royal official, stood in place of the king. It was not long before a gallows had been built and Read was marching up the steps. At that point, he asked to speak privately with Ratcliffe and revealed a plot—a "mutiny," Wingfield calls it, using a word he was fond of—led by Kendall. Once again, the details of this supposed mutiny are obscure, but the outcome, in Wingfield's account, was not. Kendall was executed; his judges retained the proper forms to the end, for because Kendall was a gentleman (unlike the blacksmith), he was entitled to a firing squad instead of the gallows. No one recorded whether Kendall was pleased at this little show of noblesse oblige, but Wingfield adds one further detail that has frustrated historical researchers ever since. Before his execution, Kendall objected that President Ratcliffe had no right to pass judgment on him, because the president's real name was Sicklemore, not Ratcliffe. Apparently this argument had substance, because in the end the other councilor, Martin, was called on to sentence Kendall to death.

Whether he was Sicklemore or Ratcliffe, no one has ever been able to trace the origins or family of this mysterious leader of Jamestown, nor even to find out why he chose to sail to America under an assumed name. Details are sparse in all accounts of the early years of Jamestown, and in this case the colonists had responded to adversity by executing one of their own. It was not a picture that the sponsors of the colony back in England wanted to present publicly, for they hoped to attract new financial backers and new colonists. In 1612, when Smith first wrote of this part of Jamestown's history, he said, "These brawles are so disgustfull, [that] some will say they were better forgotten, yet all men of good judgement will conclude, [that] it were better their basenes should be manifest to the world, [than] the busines beare the scorne and shame of their excused disorders." For good measure, Smith adds that a short time later he had to thwart yet another attempt to seize the pinnace and leave—this time led by President Ratcliffe/Sicklemore and Gabriel Archer, who as secretary had been accepted as an ex officio member of the council.

By now it was early December and there was still no sign of Newport and the relief ship. Yet thanks to Smith's ability to obtain food from the natives—and the colonists' own ability to take advantage of the bounty that nature provided—there was no fear of hunger. Smith wrote, "the rivers became so covered with swans, geese, duckes, and cranes, that we daily feasted with good bread, Virginia pease, pumpions [pumpkins], and putchamins [persimmons], fish, fowle, and diverse sorts of wild beasts as fat as we could eat them." In Smith's colorful language, "none of our Tuftaffaty humorists desired to goe for England." This was a contemptuous reference to the fancy clothes that English gentlemen sported, even when they were sojourning in the wilds of America.

Though well fed for the present, the Jamestown colonists were facing considerable uncertainty. The abundance of available food would not last forever, and no one really knew when Newport might arrive from England. Smith realized that another bout of illness or hunger would discourage the colonists so much that he could not stop them from doing what had been attempted at least twice: abandoning Jamestown and giving up the effort to establish an English foothold in the New World.

Smith decided to go upriver to trade with the natives for food while supplies were still plentiful. He could hardly have suspected that he was about to embark on a journey that would transform him from an adventurer on the make into an American icon who would be remembered forever.

7

The Great
American Myth

∞

THE ALGONQUIAN-SPEAKING NATIVE PEOPLE of Tidewater Virginia consisted of about thirty distinct groups.
Each had its own name for itself, which was also the
name of the village where the group lived. Anthropologists today
refer to all these groups collectively by the name Powhatans. At
the time the Jamestown settlers arrived, Powhatan was the name
of the principal chief of the area. A remarkable man born around
1540, he had succeeded to the leadership of six villages when he
was a young man. He proved to be an aggressive werowance and
by the time Smith met him late in 1607 he had conquered virtually all his neighbors from the fall line of the local rivers down to
Chesapeake Bay.

The political system of the Powhatans is difficult to characterize. Philip Barbour, the editor of the definitive edition of
Smith's works, calls Powhatan a "despot," perhaps too harsh a
word. Helen Rountree, today's principal authority on the native
people of the region, terms Powhatan the "paramount chief."
Though he had increased his power and control primarily through
combat and conquest rather than diplomacy, those he ruled
seemed to accept their status with little or no complaint. As
Smith had discovered on his trip up the James with Captain Newport, each group had its own werowance (male or female), who
commanded honors and respect. Yet they in turn acknowledged

Powhatan as their overlord, and when he asked (or commanded) them to act in concert, they did so.

Powhatan was in no rush to meet the English colonists, though he had been informed of their arrival in Chesapeake Bay even before they chose Jamestown as a location for their settlement. Smith was later to learn that the appearance of the three English ships had provoked an order from Powhatan that resulted in the slaughter of a group of natives living south of Chesapeake Bay who had previously resisted the paramount chief's rule.

For the native people of Tidewater Virginia had seen Europeans before and Powhatan wanted to present a united front to this latest group of newcomers. As noted in chapter 3, Thomas Harriot and other members of Raleigh's 1585 colonizing expedition had spent the winter in the Chesapeake Bay area. But even before then, probably beginning around 1550, Spanish ships from Spain's colony in Cuba had landed along the mid-Atlantic coast of North America. One of these expeditions, around 1560, had taken a Native American boy away from his homeland. Converted to Christianity, the boy became known as Don Luis and received an education in Havana, Mexico City, and finally Madrid. Spanish Jesuit missionaries offered to bring him back to America, hoping that he would help to convert others. Don Luis led them to Chesapeake Bay and the Jesuits established a mission on the York River, which enters the bay just north of the James. It was not long before Don Luis found that despite his education, his true loyalties lay with his own people. When the Jesuits demanded that he refrain from the traditional ways he had adopted, he arranged for them to be killed. In 1572, a Spanish military force arrived, heard the story from a Spanish boy who had been spared in the massacre, and hanged five natives. Don Luis, knowing what the Spaniards would do, had slipped into the forest and escaped punishment.

That incident, thirty-five years before the arrival of the Jamestown colonists, was still in living memory for many of those born in Tidewater Virginia—and certainly one who recalled it vividly was Powhatan, who must have been in his late twenties when it occurred.

Nor was that the only event that should have made the Native Americans wary of European visitors. In 1588 another Spanish expedition to the area took two native boys as captives, who soon died. Around 1605, yet another vessel entered the bay, sailing up the Rappahannock, the next major river north of the York. A landing party of Europeans (no one has ever identified what nation they were from) clashed with a group of natives. Muskets were fired, the local chief fell dead, and several other natives were taken on board the European ship, never to be seen again.

Smith knew nothing of this background except for the extended visit by Harriot's party, which had been amicable on both sides. Since the arrival of the Jamestown settlers, Powhatan had chosen to remain hidden, and probably permitted his son Tanx-Powhatan to pose as the paramount chief when meeting Newport's exploring party in May, to see how the English would treat him. Following the instructions of the Virginia Company, Newport had done his best to show the chief honor and respect. But Powhatan the elder remained in his village; his only communication with the settlers had been to send them a deer. That had been in July, at the beginning of the epidemic that ravaged the colony, and the English had not followed up on the gesture, probably indicating to Powhatan that they had no manners. He had noticed, however, that although two of the large ships had left the bay, many of the strangers remained, possibly indicating their intention to stay permanently. He wanted to investigate further, but on his terms.

In the fall of 1607, Smith took a different route than the one Newport had followed. Smith's trading mission followed the course of the Chickahominy River, which enters the James a few miles upstream from Jamestown. Though he returned to the fort with food, he was criticized for not seeking to find the source of the Chickahominy—something the instructions of the Virginia Company had asked the settlers to do for every river they encountered, in the vain hope that one of the streams might be the passage to the Pacific Ocean. So in early December, in a flat-bottomed sailing boat, called a barge, that would be useful in traversing the Chickahominy, which was smaller and shallower than the James, Smith set out on his fateful voyage, taking several comrades from the fort. The party soon added two native guides.

When the Chickahominy became too shallow for even the barge to proceed, Smith left it moored offshore, instructing his men to stay with it until he returned. Taking two Englishmen and the two guides, he set out to go farther upstream in a canoe. After reaching a marshy area, Smith went ashore, intending to shoot some wild birds to feed his little party. He took one of the guides with him, and left instructions for the others to signal him if they were attacked.

In the woods, Smith heard gunfire from the direction of the canoe, but not the agreed-on signal. What had happened was that hostile natives had surprised the others, who had immediately fired their muskets. Smith's two comrades had been slain.

The natives then came after Smith. He estimated that there were two hundred of them (three hundred in another version of the same story), but he fought back despite the overwhelming odds. The guide begged Smith to flee, but he threatened the man with a pistol, forcing him to stand fast. Quickly he tied his guide's arm to his own, using the man as a shield. Smith fired his pistol (a French one, as he recalled when he wrote the story seventeen years later; he must have been proud of it), hitting some of the attackers. Unfamiliar with firearms, the other natives withdrew to a safer distance, from which they fired arrows at Smith. One of them struck him in the thigh but did not penetrate his heavy clothing. He managed to reload his weapon, and for a time held off the natives.

Unfortunately, he stepped backward into a "quagmire," probably quicksand, where he was caught fast. Facing the inevitability of death or capture, he let his guide negotiate the terms of surrender. The guide explained that Smith was a werowance, letting the others know that he must be spared until another werowance judged what his fate would be. After being informed that he was safe for now, Smith cast his weapon aside and let himself be pulled from the bog.

He was taken to the group's leader, the "King of Pamunkey," also known as Opechancanough, a younger brother of Powhatan, the paramount chief. Smith had encountered Opechancanough once before, on the trip up the James River with Captain Newport in June. On that occasion, Opechancanough had invited Newport to spend the night in his village, an offer Newport had been ready to accept. However, Smith, Percy, and some of the other Englishmen had suspected treachery. After they insisted on accompanying Newport, the chief had waved them all back to their boat.

Time would show that Smith's distrust of the man was well founded. Opechancanough proved to be an implacable foe of the English. He had not attacked when he first met them because the natives had a tradition of showing hospitality and because old Powhatan had advised—probably ordered—a policy of wait-and-see toward the newcomers. Powhatan was aware of the power of their weapons, and though he did not fear the English, he thought they might be useful in defending his people against their enemies above the fall line, perhaps even in expanding Powhatan's empire. Powhatan, as Smith was to discover, was a man who did not act rashly.

Now Opechancanough and his warriors were away from their village on a hunt for deer; encountering Smith's men by chance, Opechancanough had seen no reason not to respond as he would have to any intruders. Smith later learned the terrible fate of George Cassen, one of the men he had left downriver with the barge. Cassen had ventured ashore, despite Smith's specific order not to, and had been taken captive. The natives bound him to a tree and built a fire. They hacked off his fingers and toes, tossing them into the flames, and then, using the sharp edges of mussel shells as knives, flayed him alive, finally releasing Cassen from agony by setting fire to the tree, around which they danced and sang.

Cassen, while trying desperately to bargain for his life, had revealed that Smith had gone upstream, and the natives followed. When they found the two Englishmen Smith had left at the canoe, they killed them—quickly, this time. Smith was later shown the body of one of them, with twenty arrows in it. He escaped a similar fate only because of the quick thinking of his native guide in calling him a werowance.

Sizing up the situation, Smith began to play his assigned role. It wasn't difficult for him. When he was brought before Opechancanough, he displayed the most impressive object he possessed, a pocket compass. After describing its use, he began to expound on the nature of the world. Smith claims to have "demonstrated . . . the roundnesse of the earth . . . and how the Sunne did chase the night round the world continually; the greatnesse of the Land and Sea, the diversitie of Nations, Varietie of complexions, and how we [the English] were to them [the natives] Antipodes, and many other such like matters"—a remarkable discourse for someone who knew only a smattering of the natives' language. Smith says his listeners "stood as amazed with admiration," but they may simply have been baffled.

Having a greater ring of truth is Smith's description of the natives' reaction to his compass: "Much they marvailed at the playing of the Fly and Needle, which they could see so plainely, and yet not touch . . . because of the glasse that covered them." Smith gave the compass, set in an ivory case, to Opechancanough as a present, but neither that nor the geography lesson persuaded the native werowance to set him free. Instead, the natives tied him to a tree and gathered round with arrows strung in their bows. This was certainly a test, and Smith passed it, forcing himself to show no fear. Opechancanough raised the compass as a signal, and his warriors lowered their weapons. They then marched Smith to a nearby town, where women and children gathered to look at him. The men put on a display of marching and dancing that was punctuated by what seemed to Smith like cries of "hellish notes and screeches." Smith, trained in the military, was impressed by the good order the dancers preserved in their movements, noting their use of "officers and serjeants" to give commands. Seventeen years later, when he wrote his history of Virginia, he remembered the dancers' appearance in vivid detail: "being strangely painted, every one [with] his quiver of Arrowes, and at his backe a club; on his arme a Fox or an Otters skinne . . . their heads and shoulders painted red, with Oyle and Pocones

Smith appears twice in this 1624 engraving of his capture by
Opechancanough's men. At bottom, in a test of courage while
bound to a tree, he faces the natives' drawn bows. At top, the
natives stage a dance of triumph around him. Because Smith was
identified by his native guide as a werowance, or chief, his life
was spared and he was taken to the paramount chief, Powhatan.

[vegetable dye] mingled together, which Scarlet-like colour made
an exceeding handsome shew; his [each man's] bow in his hand,
and the skinne of a Bird with her wings abroad [spread] dryed,
tyed on his head, a peece of copper, a white shell, a long feather,
with a small rattle growing at the tayles of their snakes tyed to it,
or some such like toy."

After the dance concluded, Smith was escorted to a longhouse
where "thirtie or fortie tall fellowes did guard" him. They brought
enormous quantities of food—enough for twenty men, by Smith's
estimation. He was too nervous to eat much, so his captors put

the excess into baskets suspended from the ceiling. About midnight another colossal meal arrived. Smith offered some to his guards, but they refused it, causing him to suspect it was poisoned. The next morning, still more bread and venison was set before him. At that time, the guards ate some of the food that had hung in baskets all night. Smith was relieved to learn that the food wasn't poisoned, but he drew another, more frightening, conclusion: that the natives were fattening him up to eat *him*.

Certainly he was well treated, for a prisoner. As the winter nights grew colder, a man gave Smith his own fur cloak. It was a payback for some "beads and toyes" he had received from Smith when Newport explored the upper reaches of the James River in June. Opechancanough came to confide in Smith that he was planning to attack Jamestown. If Smith would agree to give advice and help, he would be given "life, libertie, land, and women." Whether Opechancanough was serious or this was merely another way of testing the captive, Smith found a way to foil the plan.

Two or three days after Smith was placed in the longhouse, a native broke in and tried to kill him. The guards prevented the man from doing any harm and told Smith that his assailant's son had been shot and wounded by Smith during the fracas when Smith was taken captive. Smith said he had "a water" at the fort that would cure the young man. Opechancanough refused to let him fetch the medicine himself, but Smith proposed another idea. Taking a page from a notebook he carried, he wrote a message to his friends at the fort. He told Opechancanough that if he sent men to Jamestown with the note, the English would send certain items to a specified place where the messengers would wait.

Even though, according to Smith, it was "as bitter weather as could be of frost and snow," the native messengers set out through the forest. Three days later they returned, reporting that all had transpired as Smith had said it would, "to the wonder of them all that heard it." For the natives drew the conclusion that Smith could either predict the future or "the paper could speake." The art of writing had not yet reached Virginia. The incident added to Smith's prestige, for he now appeared to be a shaman as well as a werowance.

The natives' amazement also settles a minor historical controversy. Some scholars have asserted that Opechancanough was in fact the same person as the Don Luis who had been captured by Spanish sailors, taken to Cuba and Spain, and finally returned to Chesapeake Bay in the 1560s. If this were true, Opechancanough would have been familiar with the uses of writing and would not have been awed by Smith's "miracle" (nor by the glass that covered his compass).

Smith's captors now brought him on a tour of the area, displaying him like a trophy to other groups within Powhatan's domain. Finally they returned to Pamunkey, Opechancanough's home village, and tested Smith's magic against theirs. Once more he was placed in a longhouse, where a large fire was burning in the center of the room. Then, in Smith's words, "came skipping in a great, grim fellow, all painted over with coale, mixed with oyle." Around the man's head and shoulders and even covering his face were snake and weasel skins stuffed with moss. In a "hellish voyce" with "most strange gestures and passions" and using a rattle to punctuate his song, he began to chant. As he did he drew a circle of cornmeal around the fire. When that was finished, "three more such devils came rushing in." These were painted half black, half red, with streaks of red along their cheeks. The new trio danced around Smith, chanting, for a while, and then three more "as ugly as the rest" entered the longhouse, painted in a slightly different color combination. All seven of the native shamans now began to sing, their music sounding like a cacophony to Smith. Afterward, the first man, the "chiefe Priest," put four grains of corn on the ground and then, "strayning his armes and hands with such violence" that the veins in his body swelled and sweat broke out on his skin, began "a short Oration." After a response from his companions, he continued the process of placing corn grains until there were two full circles of them around the fire. The ceremony was completed with small sticks, which were laid down, accompanied by chants, in between the circles of corn.

The elaborate rites took much of the day, during which neither Smith nor the shamans had tasted food or drink. Now "they feasted merrily." For three days the shamans appeared and performed the same ritual. Smith was eventually able to obtain an explanation of its meaning. It was intended to divine whether Smith's intentions toward the natives were benign or hostile. The cornmeal-and-grain design on the floor was a cosmography. The natives "imagined the world to be flat and round, like a trencher [plate] and they in the middest." Thus the first circle of cornmeal was their country, the circles of corn grains the sea, and the sticks Smith's country.

This test of Smith's motives was necessary because he was about to be taken to meet the paramount chief, Powhatan himself. Werowocomoco, Powhatan's "capital," as Smith called it, was located on the York River, only about twelve miles from Jamestown. (Archaeologists announced in 2003 that they have rediscovered the precise site, helped by a map drawn by Smith.) Unlike the English, who had built in a swampy spot to make it easier to load and unload their ships, the Powhatan villages, though close to the river, were on high ground. Nearby were planted fields of corn, tobacco, beans, and sunflowers. When Smith entered the stockade of poles that surrounded the town, he found people "wondering at him, as [if] he had beene a monster." He was led inside Powhatan's longhouse, which was larger and grander than any dwelling he had seen so far. (The name Werowocomoco, in Algonquian, means "king's house.") Made of a framework of young saplings covered with bark and thatch, the dwelling was perhaps fifty or sixty yards long and had several rooms inside. The entrance led into a winding corridor meant specifically to slow any hostile intruders.

Finally, Smith entered the central room, a scene that he recalled vividly. He had seen werowances before, but the paramount chief's court was in its way as awe-inspiring as any in Europe. Along each side of the long throne room stood two rows of men, and as many women behind them. Smith estimated there were at least two hundred of these "courtiers." All were painted red from the shoulders up, and wore crowns of feathers and chains of white beads, probably made from the shells of oysters. At Smith's entrance, the whole assembly gave a great shout.

One of the women stepped forward; Smith recognized her as the "Queen of Apamatuck" whom he had seen on the first journey of exploration with Captain Newport. She brought him water so he could wash his hands. A second woman offered him a bunch of feathers to use as a towel. Smith did not realize it, but this was an honor usually reserved for the paramount chief himself.

The only sources of light were a fire burning in the center of the room and a hole in the roof overhead to let out smoke. Gradually, as Smith's eyes adjusted, he saw, at the far end of the room, seated high above the floor on ten or twelve mats, the "emperor" Powhatan. Many strings of pearls hung around his neck and he was wrapped in a large robe made of raccoon skins with the tails still attached. On either side of him sat two young women—the most attractive that Powhatan's "empire" had to offer. They would serve as his concubines until they bore him a child. After that duty had been fulfilled, they were free to marry some other man, but the children were left in Powhatan's household.

Powhatan gestured and Smith approached. The two men began "a long conversation," the first of several such discussions Smith and the paramount chief would have during the next year. Smith reports both sides of these talks, and they are particularly interesting from our modern vantage point. Sometimes Smith clearly tells lies to Powhatan, and he believes that his readers who understand that will sympathize with him. However, Powhatan also lies to Smith, and Smith was not in a position to know this— although we are. It is this last element that gives the conversations a strong air of authenticity. Smith could make up his own lies, but he could hardly have put convincing lies in the mouth of Powhatan when he himself could not have known they were falsehoods.

Powhatan began by asking Smith why the English had come to his country. It was an important question for Powhatan. Unbeknownst to Smith, the chief's soothsayers had predicted that a people would come from the direction of the Chesapeake Bay and conquer Powhatan's empire. Smith responded smoothly that the English ships had been in a battle with the Spaniards, their enemies. They had been compelled to retreat, and a storm brought them into the Chesapeake Bay. He told Powhatan, truthfully, that on landing they had been attacked. After that, his story became more creative. The English had gone up the nearest river to get away from the people who had attacked them. When they met other natives, they asked where they could obtain fresh water and were told farther upstream. One of the three ships, the pinnace, had sprung a leak, forcing Smith and the others to find a place to settle while they repaired the damage. In the meantime, "Captain Newport my father" had departed with the other two ships but would eventually return to take the Englishmen home.

Powhatan inquired why the English had gone farther up the river. What were they looking for? Smith replied that they were searching for the saltwater sea on the other side of the mainland. This was true enough, but he embellished his tale by adding that a child of his "father" Newport had been slain by people there. Probably the Monacans, he added. If so, Powhatan would be glad to hear that the English had come to punish *his* enemies to avenge the death of Newport's child.

After thinking this over for a while, Powhatan told Smith that there was indeed a great body of salt water up beyond the fall line. It was not far—five days' travel, or perhaps six, possibly eight. Powhatan was making the story up as he went along. If the English really wanted to find a body of salt water, perhaps he could persuade them to go look for it and not trouble him any longer.

Smith was excited by the story, not knowing that if he traveled west from the fall line he would not reach the other ocean for three thousand miles, considerably more than an eight days' walk. There was a fierce nation that lived near the western shore, Powhatan added. These were the Pocoughtronacks, and they were cannibals, or so the paramount chief told Smith. They had invaded the distant parts of Powhatan's empire the year before and slain a hundred people. Warming to his tale, Powhatan mentioned that there were other people up there who wore clothing like the English did, and sailed in ships just like theirs. It is not impossible that reports of French traders to the north or Spanish conquistadores to the south were the source of Powhatan's story.

Certainly, Powhatan hoped Smith and his friends would be curious enough to go seek them out.

Smith responded by launching into a geography lesson, "describing to him the territories of Europe, which [were] subject to our great King whose subject I was." Though he was not inventing a story, Smith did his best to make his tale as impressive as possible. He glanced around the smoky room, hoping that the people around him understood his meaning. King James's power was awesome; he had an "innumerable multitude" of ships, and his soldiers fought ferociously. One of those "terrible" warriors was Captain Newport, whom Smith impulsively gave the title of "Meworames," which meant "king of all the waters" in Algonquian.

Powhatan seemed impressed by these tales, Smith thought. Perhaps he was, but his next gesture produced a result that Smith had not expected. At Powhatan's signal, men brought two great stones into the hall and laid them on the floor. Two strong young men seized Smith by the arms and forced his head down onto the stones. Brandishing clubs, other warriors approached—ready, as Smith thought, "to beate out his braines." As he understood the situation, this was to be his place of execution, and unlike the other times he had escaped from deadly peril, there seemed to be no way of getting out of this situation. If John Smith ever felt fear (and he does not admit that he ever did), now was surely the time.

Of course, as everybody knows from one version of the story or another, Smith was about to become immortal.

Pocahontas, "the King's dearest daughter," who was probably no older than eleven, stepped forward and spoke. If she did this of her own accord, she must have been a bold child indeed—the name Pocahontas is thought to be a kind of nickname bestowed by her father, and is usually translated as "little wanton one." The hall was hushed as she spoke rapidly to her father, seemingly trying to persuade him of something. Smith understood that she was pleading to spare the prisoner's life—*his* life.

Smith detected no sign of sympathy from the old chief. He felt the stares of all those lined up in the hall waiting to witness his execution. Pocahontas, seeing that her plea was ignored, rushed

This engraving, done by Robert Vaughan for the 1624 *Generall Historie of Virginia*, is the first depiction of Smith's rescue by Pocahontas. Powhatan, her father, is seated at upper right, and Pocahontas is kneeling in the foreground, next to Smith, on his back and awaiting the deathblow. Presumably, Vaughan was guided by Smith in illustrating what was to become one of the best-known scenes in American history.

to Smith's side, knelt, and looked up at the warriors about to dash out his brains. She laid her own head on Smith's to prevent the executioners from using their clubs. Smith felt the warmth of her slight body, perhaps the rapid beating of her heart. He knew it would be no protection and waited for the deathblow.

The tableau is suspended in time, the inspiration for countless paintings, sentimental prints, literary re-creations, advertisements, and in 2003 a Disney cartoon feature. Even though Pocahontas was a preadolescent child and Smith a twenty-seven-year-old military veteran, a romantic tradition has grown up around the scene as well, turning Smith and Pocahontas into colonial America's Romeo and Juliet. (In some retellings of the tale, Pocahontas even marries Smith, though her actual English husband was John Rolfe, who kidnapped, converted, and wed her in 1616.)

Powhatan, as the story goes, felt his heart touched by his daughter's defense of Smith and ordered his men to put down their clubs. According to Smith, the chief gave the assembly practical reasons for showing mercy. The Englishman could, said Powhatan, make hatchets from the strange shiny material that the Jamestown settlers used, and supply bells, beads, and copper trinkets for Pocahontas. Smith's life was spared, apparently so that he could become a servant for the little girl who had saved his life.

Did it really happen? And if it did, was Smith's understanding of the events correct? Or was it *supposed* to happen this way? Some modern ethnologists now explain the event as a ritual, intended to initiate Smith as a member of the tribal community. If so, the entire scene had been scripted—including Pocahontas's intervention—though of course Smith did not know that.

Others have questioned—and still do—whether the incident occurred at all. This skeptical view was first expressed in a cogent form by Henry Adams, the nineteenth-century writer and editor who was the grandson and great-grandson of presidents. He seems to have been acting in part from personal ambition. Adams, then twenty-eight years old, published his first attack on Smith in 1867, two years after the end of the Civil War. Forty years later he admitted that a mentor had "suggested . . . that an article . . . on Captain John Smith's relations with Pocahontas would attract as much attention, and probably break as much glass, as any other stone that could be thrown by a beginner." The Smith-Pocahontas story was indeed a large target; it had been part of American iconography even before there was a country named the United States. Pocahontas, through the son she later bore John Rolfe, had many descendants among upper-class Virginians, who revered her not only as John Smith's savior, but also as a royal Virginia ancestor, the mother of the colony and the state. Smith himself was remembered as the man who, through strength of character and will, had enabled the colony to survive, thus preserving England's presence in the New World. Because of him, Virginians could claim for their state the distinction of being the place where the United States had begun. They had dominated the new nation for most of its early years; four of the first five U.S. presidents—all except John Adams—were Virginians.

Henry Adams, like his illustrious forebears, was a New Englander. He resented what he saw as Virginians' arrogance, all the more so because of Virginia's leading role in what New Englanders called "the Rebellion" of the Southern states. His attack on Smith would be a step toward substituting Massachusetts for Virginia as the true foundation place of the United States, at least in the public mind.

Adams's mentor, the historian John Gorham Palfrey, had earlier published a massive work, *History of New England,* that was a major attempt to raise the Puritan founders of Massachusetts above Smith and other Southerners in the American pantheon. Writing in 1858, the year after the Supreme Court issued the notorious Dred Scott decision, ruling that a fugitive slave had no legal rights, Palfrey slyly expressed his antislavery (and hence anti-Southern) sympathies when he noted, "A fugitive slave was to be the founder of Virginia." He refers to Smith—a gross exaggeration, for Smith was in no sense "the" founder—but Smith's critics have not always been scrupulously honest themselves. Calling Smith a "fugitive slave" alludes to his earlier adventures in the Turkish empire. There, Palfrey accepts Smith's version of events, though Smith provided no more evidence for his story of life as a slave than he did for the tale of his rescue by Pocahontas.

At Palfrey's urging, Adams challenged Smith's credibility chiefly on the grounds that Smith did not publish the full story of his salvation until 1624, after Pocahontas was dead and could not confirm or deny it. The only document in which Smith related the tale earlier than that was a letter he wrote to Queen Anne, wife of King James I, on the occasion of Pocahontas's visit to England in 1616. But even this letter did not appear in print until 1624, seventeen years after the original incident occurred, and one would have thought Smith should have mentioned it earlier. The only previous reference in print was part of a single sentence that appeared in a book about New England that Smith published in 1622. It reads, "It is true . . . they shot me, slue three of my men, and by the folly of them that fled tooke me prisoner; yet God made Pocahontas the Kings daughter the meanes to deliver me." Smith's long delay in telling the story in print is pretty much the heart of the case against his veracity; it was even cited as evidence that the event never happened in a book on Pocahontas published in 2004.

Smith had many opportunities to tell the story in more detail, but did not. Only a few months after his supposed rescue, an English captain who had brought supplies to the colonists set sail for home, carrying a long letter in which Smith relates the events that had occurred in Virginia up till that time. Appearing in book form in 1608—edited and excised by an unknown editor—the document makes no mention of Smith's remarkable escape from death due to the surprising intervention of the native princess. Smith does mention Pocahontas in another context, calling her "a child of tenne yeares old."

Smith wrote a longer history of Virginia in 1612, four years after his return to England, which he was able to guide through the press himself. Several other colonists are listed as coauthors of the work, and they contributed information about events that happened after Smith left Jamestown. Here Pocahontas is mentioned by name, but Smith still does not allude to her role in rescuing him—naturally enough, since this was a history of the colony, not of his personal life. Referring to her as she was in 1609, he says Pocahontas was then "at most not past 13 or 14 years of age." Confirming that she was no older than twelve when they met, he ruled out any possible romantic attachment, specifically denying that he had planned to "have made himselfe a king by marrying Pocahontas, Powhatans daughter." One would like to know more about the accusations that compelled Smith to issue this denial.

In the 1612 account, Smith does cite a *different* occasion on which Pocahontas gave him key, if not lifesaving, help. That incident, when "in the darke night [she] came through the wild woods" to warn him that her father intended to set an ambush for him and his men, is also mentioned in the 1624 *Generall Historie*. But it is *only* in the 1624 book that Smith recounts the famous rescue that has become one of the few scenes in American history that "everybody knows"—even if they only know it from a grossly distorted motion-picture version.

In searching the record to determine if Smith made up the story or not, it is interesting to examine an account written by an otherwise anonymous "Gentleman of Elvas" (a town in Portugal), who was a companion of the Spanish explorer Hernando de Soto. De Soto and his men, on the expedition that would eventually reach the Mississippi River, landed in Florida in 1539. There they found a Spanish noble, Juan Ortiz, who had been taken prisoner by a group of natives when he came ashore with another exploring party twelve years earlier.

Ortiz told his countrymen that after his capture, he had been brought before a local chieftan named Ucita. "By command of Ucita," the account goes on, "Juan Ortiz was bound hand and foot to four stakes, and laid upon scaffolding, beneath which a fire was kindled, that he might be burned; but a daughter of the Chief entreated that he might be spared. Though one Christian, she said, might do no good, certainly he could do no harm, and it would be an honor to have one for a captive; to which the father acceded." So Ortiz's life was spared.

It is easy to see the similarities between this obscure tale and Smith's account. Could Smith have read it? Certainly, for Richard Hakluyt published his English translation of the Gentleman of Elvas's book in 1609. (The original was in Portuguese.)

Even assuming Smith did read this story, that does not prove he used it as inspiration for his own autobiographical account in 1624. Smith's defenders who are aware of the Elvas account (not all acknowledge it) generally contend that it is evidence that the "ritual" Smith describes—chief's daughter appeals for a prisoner to be spared; he is then accepted into the tribal group—was common among the Native Americans of the eastern seaboard. Thus the story of Juan Ortiz only serves to confirm the authenticity of Smith's report.

Two days after the rescue, if that is what it was, Smith relates that he was taken to a "great house in the woods" and left alone before a warm fire. A large mat, hanging from the roof, divided the house. Soon, from behind it, came "the most dolefullest noyse

[he] ever heard." Powhatan, painted black and looking "more like a devill [than] a man," appeared, followed by two hundred other men "as blacke as himselfe." To an Englishman of the time, black was the color that the devil was most commonly depicted as in illustrations, so Smith readily made the connection that he was confronting demons, but as before he earned respect by showing no fear.

This was actually the final stage in Smith's initiation ceremony. Powhatan told him that they were now "friends," in Smith's terminology—probably "kin" from Powhatan's viewpoint. The chief suggested that Smith now return to Jamestown and find suitable presents for his new father. Two of the large English cannon and a grindstone would be appropriate, thought Powhatan. In return, he would "esteeme" Smith as his son, giving him the tribal name Mantaquoud and making him werowance of a territory called Capahowosick.

Smith readily agreed, as he would have to any proposal that would bring him back to the fort. With a dozen of Powhatan's men as escorts, he set out, walking across country, toward Jamestown. For some reason, the escorts moved slowly despite Smith's urging, and they had to camp for the night in the forest, raising Smith's fears again that their true purpose was to kill him. "But almightie God," Smith writes, acknowledging divine assistance as he commonly did, "had mollified the hearts of those sterne Barbarians with compassion." What he did not know was that his companions at Jamestown had sterner hearts than his new brothers, and that malicious tongues had turned the community against him in his absence.

8

Conflicting Agendas

THE COMPANIONS OF THE UNFORTUNATE George Cassen, having heard his death agonies, had fled back down the Chickahominy in the barge. They reported that Smith and the two men he had taken with him were probably dead as well. Gabriel Archer, the former law student and friend of Bartholomew Gosnold, had then taken the opportunity to get himself elected to the ruling council—a procedure not covered by the Virginia Company's orders. Evidently Archer had revived the proposal to lead the remaining colonists back to England in the pinnace.

The effect of Smith's sudden reappearance, not only alive but with an escort of Powhatan's men, temporarily upset Archer's plans and caused a sensation in the fort. As usual, Smith assumed his right to command. He showed his native escorts (his new "brothers") two demi-culverins, iron cannons, that Powhatan had requested as a gift. Weighing some 4,500 pounds each, the guns proved "somewhat too heavie" for them to carry, Smith recalled with a touch of humor. So did the millstone that Smith presented as a second "gift." More to the point, Smith arranged a demonstration of one of the demi-culverins, loading it with rocks and gravel. He fired at a tree loaded with icicles. The resulting roar, followed by the shattering of tree branches, ice and all, was sufficiently impressive for Smith's purposes. The natives "ran away halfe dead with feare" and had to be coaxed back. As consolation,

Smith presented them with some "toyes"—gifts for Powhatan, his women, and the children. Smith knew that the thing the escorts would speak of most when they returned was the massive power of the cannon, and that suited him quite well.

Now that Smith had made friends of his enemies, however, he was confronted with another threat: his countrymen and fellow colonists decided to kill him, for his unexpected arrival had put a crimp in the scheme to abandon the colony. Archer—who had attended Gray's Inn, one of the Inns of Court in London where law students received training—attempted to employ his interpretation of the law to get Smith out of the way once and for all. He turned to the Bible and invoked the Levitical law of "an eye for an eye." Smith had caused the death of his men (the two who had gone with him in the canoe) and thus his own life should be forfeit, Archer claimed.

Wingfield, still a prisoner, was a witness to this—no doubt getting some wry enjoyment of Smith's plight, though he noted in his journal that naming Archer to the governing council was itself an illegal act. Since Wingfield had no ax to grind in this dispute, he is believable when he reports that Smith was put on trial the very day he returned from captivity, and was sentenced to be hanged the next day, "so speedie is our lawe there [in Virginia]."

And so yet another day dawned that looked as if it must certainly be Smith's last. The gallows stood ready for him once more, and his new friends, the natives, had gone back to Powhatan. Then came a shout from a lookout on duty at the riverbank. A ship flying the English colors was approaching from the bay.

Newport had returned, literally in the nick of time to save Smith. The reader of Wingfield's account can sense his clenched teeth when he wrote, "it pleased god to send Captayn Newport unto us . . . whose arryvall saved Master Smyths leif." Imagine Newport's thoughts when he learned that of the six men who had formed the governing council when he left, Gosnold had died; Ratcliffe had been exposed as an imposter; Wingfield was a prisoner; Kendall had been executed; and Smith was under sentence of death. Newport apparently dissolved the legal judgment against Smith and assumed command of the situation, as naturally as the ship's captain who arrives at the end of the novel *Lord of the Flies* to find that a group of good English schoolboys has descended into savagery. No more is said in any of the colonists' accounts of Archer's interpretation of the law of Leviticus. Archer himself was summarily dismissed from the council, and Newport introduced Matthew Scrivener, a new arrival, as the latest council member, appointed on the orders of the Virginia Company. Archer was defeated for now, but would not forget the slight to his vanity.

Captain Newport had brought eighty new colonists; arriving in the midst of a fierce winter, these newcomers were only additional burdens, needing both food and shelter. Moreover, less than a week after Newport arrived, a fire broke out within the fort. Despite the frantic efforts of the colonists to control it, all but a few of the dwellings were consumed in the flames. The small church (along with the hapless Reverend Hunt's small library), the food storehouse, and the ammunition dump all went up in smoke.

Fortunately, Newport's ship had not yet been fully unloaded, and its provisions were saved. Also, Powhatan was demonstrating his generosity toward his new son by sending venison, corn bread, and other foods to Jamestown. Quite often Pocahontas herself would accompany the bearers of these gifts. There is no doubt that she was sincerely attached to Smith, and his writings about her reveal affection that he showed to few others, English or Native American.

Smith had earlier told Powhatan that Newport was his biological father and would soon return. The appearance of the English ship confirmed the natives' opinion of him as a prophet. Powhatan sent word that Smith and Newport were welcome to visit him. Newport was enthusiastic. While he had been in London, the directors of the Virginia Company had stressed that they expected the next voyage to show a profit. They wanted to see some gold ore in the cargo hold of Newport's ship when he returned. Newport felt that if there were sources of gold in Virginia—and he had no doubt that there were—Powhatan must know their location. He sent generous presents to the paramount chief and set out in the pinnace and barge with Smith, Scrivener, and about thirty other men, heading for Werowocomoco. As usual, word spread across land faster than the boats could go down the James and up the York to Powhatan's "capital," and when the English arrived they were greeted by a cheering crowd of several hundred people. The reception was a bit too over-whelming for Newport, so he stayed in the pinnace while Smith went ashore. Significantly, Smith took twenty men wearing "jacks," quilted leather vests that were thought to be protection against arrows. He would never again place himself wholly at the mercy of Powhatan.

The paramount chief put on an impressive display for his vis-itors. Forty or fifty platters of fine bread were set out in front of his house when the English arrived. Inside, Smith found the scene the same as before, writing that the old chief presided "with such a Majestie as I cannot expresse, nor yet have often seene, either in Pagan or Christian [lands]." Powhatan bade Smith to come sit next to him, and Smith presented him with gifts brought by Newport: a shirt of red cloth, a white greyhound, and a hat in the latest London style, resembling (and named after) a loaf of sugar. Orations followed, as they do at any formal banquet. Three of Powhatan's "nobles" extolled the friendship that would forever endure between the English and the Powhatans. The "Queen of Apamatuck" once more appeared, this time to serve Smith a meal of turkey and bread.

Powhatan courteously waited for Smith to finish eating and then got down to business. Smith was a little more confident this time that he would live through the conversation, but both he and the chief spoke as carefully as if they were engaging in the opening moves of a chess game. "Your kinde visitation doth much content mee," Powhatan said. With a look of concern, he added, "Where is your father Captain Newport? I much desire to see him." Smith responded with what Powhatan already knew: that Newport was still on the pinnace anchored in the river. But he assured the chief that Newport would visit on the following day.

Powhatan turned to another matter. "With a merrie counte-nance" that acknowledged Smith had gotten the better of him at their previous meeting, he asked where the cannon were that Smith had promised. With a straight face, Smith responded that he had offered Powhatan's men demi-culverins, "but they refused to take them." Powhatan laughed aloud, for his men had told him of the guns' great weight. He requested that the next time Smith should send him "some of lesse burthen."

The chief moved on to discuss the men Smith had brought, who were waiting outside. Powhatan would agree to honor them by meeting them. The men were ushered into the longhouse two at a time, for Powhatan, like Smith, was wary: he was not about to entertain so many that they might pose a threat. Each man received a present of several pounds of corn bread. When the introductions were over, Smith reminded the chief that he had promised corn and land for his new son. That would come, replied Powhatan, but first Smith and his companions should lay down their arms in front of him, as a sign of their submission to his authority.

That was a request Smith would often have to deal with. On this first occasion he came up with a smooth excuse for sidestepping it: "I tolde him that was a ceremonie oure enemies desired, but never our friends." Even so, he continued, Powhatan should not doubt that the English were his friends. The next day, Newport would give the chief one of his sons, "and not only that, but when he [Powhatan] should think it convenient," the English would conquer the neighboring "country" of the Monacans and its ruler, delivering them to Powhatan's "subjection."

This promise contented the paramount chief, who now gave a "lowd oration" to the assemblage, proclaiming Smith to be a werowance. He ordered that all his subjects should "esteeme" the English, who were henceforth not strangers but Powhatans, and that the "Corne, women, and Country" belonged as much to them as to his own people.

Smith expressed his thanks for such a generous sentiment. In a remarkable gesture of respect, Powhatan stood and escorted him from the longhouse. When they reached the river, however, Smith saw that the tidal waters had receded, leaving his boat, the barge, stranded in the mud. There was no way to move it, and now a cold rain began to fall. Powhatan offered Smith a place to stay for the night. The English were shown to a longhouse where bows and arrows hung on the walls. Smith, finding this an ominous sign, ordered that two sentinels stand guard at each entrance to the house all night. However, when invited, he returned to Powhatan's lodge for another meal, after which the two men talked for hours. Unfortunately, Smith does not tell us the details—only that a man with a torch lit the way for him back to his longhouse.

In the morning, Powhatan appeared and escorted Smith to the river. On the banks were scores of canoes—in effect, the chief's navy. He described to Smith how he sent his men in them down the river, into the bay, and through the surrounding region, where they would collect tribute from his many subjects. He was clearly trying to impress his new son, perhaps to convince him that it would be better to join the native forces and become a true Powhatan.

The discourse was interrupted when they sighted Newport coming ashore with Scrivener. Powhatan would not receive such a guest casually on the riverbank, and so went back to his longhouse to prepare a suitable welcome. Newport had his own plans for making a proper impression. As the natives crowded around to see him, he had a man go before him to clear the way by blowing a brass trumpet, something the natives had never heard.

Inside Powhatan's longhouse, all was the same as the day before. Newport produced a finer token of friendship than any Smith had offered, giving Powhatan one of his "sons," a thirteen-year-old cabin boy named Thomas Savage. Though this seems startling to us today, it evidently was acceptable to young Master Savage. In the first place, the fact that he had chosen to venture onto the Atlantic, bound for a new world, with a good chance he would die on the way, says much about his prospects in England. He could probably see that Powhatan's people were well fed and decently housed—much more so than the half-starved, hapless Jamestown colonists whose rude huts had just burned to the ground. Indeed, from the standpoint of sheer survival, young Thomas's choice turned out to be the right one, for he is the only

English settler from the first two voyages to Jamestown who has descendants living today.

Powhatan, not to be outdone by Newport's generosity, later reciprocated, presenting Newport with a young man named Namontack, who had guided the English from Jamestown to Werowocomoco. Smith, ever wary, described Namontack as Powhatan's "trustie servant, and one of a shrewd, subtill capacitie." Namontack would serve as Powhatan's eyes and ears in the English camp and even travel to England with Newport.

Several days of feasting and dancing followed, with the English spending the nights in the boats, for Smith did not fully trust Powhatan's intentions. The day after Newport arrived, Powhatan entertained his guests at breakfast. He asked why they had brought their arms, since he was their friend and did not himself carry bow or arrows to the meal. Smith replied that the chief should not take it as an unfriendly gesture; it was merely the custom of the English in their own country. Powhatan seemed satisfied with the answer, but Smith thought it wise that some-one—either he or Scrivener—be stationed by the barge at all times, so the English would not lose their lifeline to the pinnace, anchored in the middle of the river.

Newport began to discuss the business of trading; the English needed to replenish their stores, having lost much in the fire. On previous occasions, Smith had conducted trade with the natives on a piece-by-piece basis. He would present, say, a string of beads and negotiate a certain amount of corn or venison for it. When that deal was completed, another trade item would be brought out, and so on.

Powhatan announced that he was too great a man "to trade for trifles" in this "pedling manner." Addressing Newport, he said, "I esteeme you a great werowance," a man equal to himself. There was no need to haggle. Let Newport lay down everything he had brought to trade. "What I like," said Powhatan, "I will take and in recompence give you [whatever] I thinke fitting their value."

Smith saw through this "auncient tricke," and said (in English) that Powhatan intended to cheat the English. But the proposition appealed to Newport. By agreeing, he would demonstrate his own "ostentation of greatnes," as Smith sarcastically termed it. Among other desirable objects, Newport had brought a dozen large copper kettles, all of which the paramount chief took as soon as they were brought out, as well as some metal hatchets that were far better than any tools the natives had. For all this, Powhatan gave four bushels of corn; the English, says Smith, had expected twenty hogsheads (large barrels) of the grain. Smith remarked that the corn would have been cheaper in Spain, where prices were notoriously high.

The disagreement resulted from the fact that Smith and Newport now had conflicting agendas. Newport aimed to win Powhatan's friendship and goodwill so that the chief would tell him where to find the gold that the Virginia Company wanted. Smith, however, was thinking of the welfare of the colony; to survive, it would have to obtain sufficient corn and other food from the natives. By virtually giving away valuable trade goods, Newport was making future trade negotiations more difficult.

Disliking the whole procedure but unwilling to argue with Newport in front of Powhatan, Smith displayed some blue beads of fine quality that had come from one of the glass factories at Venice. Powhatan was going to give two pecks of corn for these, but Smith—who preferred getting fair value to being esteemed as too great a man to haggle—demanded more. He praised the beads "as being composed of a most rare substance of the colour of the skyes, and not to be worne but by the greatest kings in the world. This made [Powhatan] half madde to be the owner of such strange Jewells." In the end, the old chief offered several bushels of corne for the beads, "yet [they] parted good friends."

The chief was gracious; when the English returned to the pinnace, he sent them bread and venison, enough for fifty to sixty people. The next day, however, Powhatan sent a son to ask the English not to bring their muskets and pistols ashore, for they frightened the women and children. Newport would have agreed to the chief's request, but Smith insisted on arming the men. When confronted by Powhatan, Smith made up another story: the people who had slain his brother (Newport's "other son") had similarly persuaded the English to go unarmed, and then betrayed their promise of friendship. That did not stop Powhatan from continuing to try to persuade Newport to order his men to lay down their arms as a sign of friendship and respect.

The English remained at Werowocomoco for several more days. Much of the time was spent in feasting and dancing, but Powhatan presented a plan for the English to go attack some of his neighbors to the west. Newport was tempted to agree, because according to Powhatan that way led to the South Sea, but Smith feared some treachery on Powhatan's part. In the end, the idea was dropped. A messenger from Opechancanough, Powhatan's younger brother, invited the English to come for a visit. Powhatan succeeded in delaying them for a few days; Smith could see that he wanted to keep for himself a monopoly on trading with the English. Smith, thinking this would put the English at a disadvantage, finally persuaded Newport to go. He had saved some of the blue beads, and Opechancanough was willing to pay as handsome a price for them as Powhatan had.

The English returned to Jamestown in early March, bringing with them several hundred bushels of corn, enough to ensure that the colonists—old and new—would be well fed until another supply ship could arrive. In Smith's mind, Newport's work was finished and he should depart for England. Instead, to Smith's great irritation, the one-armed captain set the colonists to work looking for gold. Since it was impossible to carry out a search for the South Sea in the limited time he had, Newport had decided to please his superiors in London by bringing home a cargo of gold ore. Smith was openly contemptuous of these "golden promises" that "made all men their slaves in hope of recompence; there was no talke, no hope, no worke, but dig gold, wash gold, refine gold, load gold."

Besides thinking the search for gold a waste of effort, Smith lamented the fact that, by remaining at Jamestown, Newport and his crew were using up precious supplies. In fact, the crew took advantage of the situation by selling some of the ship's provisions to the colonists. Not surprisingly, the residents of Jamestown preferred the seamen's diet of "pork, beefe, fish, and oile" to their

usual fare of oatmeal and corn bread. The sailors, in return, collected such valuables as rings and furs by turning the ship into a
"taverne," as Smith described it.

When Newport set sail for England at last on April 10, 1608,
his ship now loaded with what Smith called "gilded durt," he also
took two passengers besides the native Namontack. Having no
need for "Parliaments . . . petitions, admirals, recorders, inter-
preters, chronologers, courts of plea, nor Justices of peace" (all elements of the English legal system), Smith had sent Wingfield and
Archer to England "to seeke some place of better imploiment."

Smith, breathing a hearty sigh of relief, could now devote his
attention to putting the colony on a firm basis. He found that the
new councilor, Scrivener, was a kindred spirit. Ratcliffe (or Sicklemore), still nominally the president of the council, was ailing and
played little part in governing. John Martin, the fourth member
of the current council, evidently continued the fruitless search
for "phantasticall" gold. Thus, Scrivener and Smith divided between them the tasks of rebuilding the town and planting the
fields. This year, Smith hoped the colonists would not have to
beg or barter food from the natives; they could grow what English ships did not supply.

Surprisingly, ten days after Newport's departure, a second
ship—the *Phoenix*—arrived, captained by Francis Nelson. The
Phoenix had originally left London with Newport, but a storm had
separated the two ships and Nelson's vessel had been presumed
lost. Instead, he had landed somewhere in the West Indies, where
he was able to find enough food to feed his passengers and crew
without depleting the supplies he had brought for Jamestown.

The arrival of the *Phoenix* changed everyone's mood. Now
there was an abundance of food, surely enough to last the colony
until Newport would return again. Moreover, it was summer and
the colonists could live in tents a while longer; it no longer
seemed so imperative to rebuild the houses. Ratcliffe, and probably Martin, expressed the feeling that something should be done
to fulfill the original instructions of the Virginia Company, so
that Nelson could bring the happy news home when he sailed.
Influenced by Powhatan's tale that the South Sea lay only a few

days' journey above the fall line, Ratcliffe ordered Smith and Scrivener to lead a party of men up there to find it. Smith was torn between what he saw as the necessity of putting the colony on a strong footing and the chance to attain glory as the discoverer of this new, long-sought route to the South Sea.

He chose glory. The colony, for the present, had a surfeit of men, and Smith took command of sixty of them. After six days' training, he felt they needed to fear no one they might encounter— a bold assumption. But events at the fort proved more destructive to his plans than any unknown enemies beyond the falls.

Before departing, Smith got into a dispute with Martin, who had continued Newport's enthusiastic efforts by stockpiling what was thought to be gold-bearing ore. Smith insisted it was only worthless "durt" (which it proved to be) and said that a far more valuable cargo to send back in Nelson's ship was fragrant, and rare, cedarwood. Instead of digging in the banks of the river, the colonists should be cutting down trees.

Smith's temper was on edge because of this unresolved dispute, and that probably contributed to a conflict with the natives that delayed the departure of his exploring party. Earlier Powhatan had sent Newport twenty turkeys; in response Newport gave the chief twenty swords. Evidently liking his side of the bargain, Powhatan had lately dispatched a messenger with another twenty turkeys, this time for Smith. Smith, however, was not inclined to imitate Newport's generosity. For one thing, he was always reluctant to arm the natives, even with swords. Evidently Powhatan sent some men to collect what he felt was due him, and they began to ambush colonists outside the fort, relieving them of their swords.

Smith fumed at these "insolencies," but Ratcliffe rejected his suggestion that the English retaliate with force, for the president wanted to obey the company's instructions to keep relations with the natives peaceful if at all possible. As Smith caustically expressed it, "[O]ur authoritie-bearers (keeping [safely inside] their houses) would rather be any thing [other] then peace-breakers."

Ratcliffe's "charitable humor" continued in force until some of the natives unwisely tried to take Smith's sword. He was having none of that and, "without further deliberation," retaliated, aided by Scrivener and some other like-minded colonists. He chased the offenders "up and downe the Isle," terrifying them with "whipping, beating, and imprisonment." Smith took seven captives back to the fort.

In response, some other natives captured two Englishmen who had carelessly wandered outside the protective confines of the fort, holding them as hostages for the return of their companions. Smith was determined not to negotiate and "sallied out" to rescue his compatriots. Within an hour—Smith gives no other details of his methods—the natives meekly handed over the English prisoners. Smith kept his own captives, questioning them about the motives for their recent hostility. When they refused to talk, Smith took one man out of sight and fired his pistol. Returning to the others, he let them think he had killed the man, a tactic that caused them to confess that Powhatan had sent them to take the Englishmen's weapons and to cut their throats if necessary.

The news of Smith's action traveled fast. In a few days, Pocahontas appeared, bringing presents from her father, along with an apology for the "rash" actions of some of his subjects. The chief's daughter (here Smith calls her "a child of tenne yeares old") appealed to him to release the captives and assured him of her father's love "for ever." This provided a face-saving way out of the situation for both sides, and Smith accepted it. He released the prisoners to Pocahontas, saying that he had spared their lives for her sake.

That Pocahontas was sent on such a mission, and seemed to have previously established a close connection with Smith, is attested to by two other witnesses. This tends to verify Smith's story of her rescuing him earlier. Though Smith does not specifically refer to that in his first account of Jamestown he does say Pocahontas "not only for feature, countenance, and proportion, much exceedeth any of the rest of his [Powhatan's] people, but for wit, and spirit, the only Nonpariel of his Country"—quite an accolade for a ten-year-old girl! Unless, of course, she had done something Smith had cause to feel grateful for.

The other council members disapproved of Smith's treatment of the natives, but as he pointed out, none of Powhatan's people had been killed and the colonists no longer endured the surprise attacks that had previously occurred as often as twice a day. Compared to the way the English treated the Irish, for example, Smith's conduct had indeed been humane. In his later accounts, however, he cannot resist the urge to brag, writing that his actions had brought about "such fear and obedience" among the natives that his "very name would sometimes affright them."

Not all the colonists, of course, put the instructions of the Virginia Company above their own safety. Smith's success in taking strong action certainly increased his prestige and, in effect, his power within the colony. Thus he prevailed in the contest of wills with his fellow council member Martin as to what cargo Captain Nelson should take back to England. The ship was loaded with cedarwood, which proved to be the most profitable item the London Company obtained from Virginia until John Rolfe introduced a new strain of tobacco in 1612.

Nelson also carried a long letter Smith wrote to a friend in England, describing his experiences from the time the three ships had left London in December 1606. Smith little suspected that this manuscript would give him the distinction of being the first American author who wrote in English. The literature of the United States begins with his work. The name of the friend to whom he sent it is unknown, though it may have been one of the Bertie brothers. In any event, the recipient, after cutting parts of the manuscript that he thought unsuitable for the public eye, arranged to have it published as a book with the title *A True Relation of such occurrences and accidents of noate as hath happened in Virginia since the first planting of that Colony.* . . . The first edition did not list Smith's name on the title page, but later printings did, and thus by the time he returned home he found that he had attained a degree of fame as an author.

A True Relation is the first of three works concerning Virginia authored solely or partially by Smith. This one is the most awkward in its language and style, for Smith wrote it in haste as a personal message, and the editorial cuts that were made in England did not improve the work's readability. Smith was no Shakespeare; his sentences run on with only a comma or a colon to separate one from another, and it often takes several close readings for the modern reader to glean even an idea of what he wanted to say.

Pocahontas, as noted above, is mentioned only once in *A True Relation*, leading Smith's detractors to wonder why the story of her saving him was not included. His defenders argue that the tale might have been cut by his friend or another editor, feeling that it was unsuitable for the public. The Virginia Company was making efforts to present the colonizing venture in as favorable a light as possible, and someone may have thought that Smith's narrow escape could discourage others from investing in the enterprise or from volunteering to be colonists. In the published version of *A True Relation*, though Smith describes his capture, he is "kindly welcomed" by Powhatan, who has a feast laid out for him. His report of their first conversation emphasizes Powhatan's description of the country above the fall line, where a large body of salt water can be reached in a few days. This dovetailed nicely with the Virginia Company's hope of finding a profitable passage to the South Sea.

Smith certainly stayed for some time among the Powhatans, for his descriptions of their customs and the order of succession to the paramount chiefdom (it would fall to the younger brothers of Powhatan, and afterward not to their children but to the children of their sisters) are accurate, according to modern ethnologists. He may have been a braggart, but he was also a keen observer.

John Martin, who had never fully recovered from the epidemic that had struck the colony in its first summer, decided to return to England on Nelson's ship. No doubt he also wished to lodge a complaint with the Virginia Company regarding Smith's peremptory refusal to load the ship with gold ore instead of cedarwood. Smith could not have been sorry to see him go. Anas Todkill, who describes himself as Martin's servant, writes that in the year his master spent in Virginia he had left Jamestown only twice. Todkill remained in Virginia, now in the service of a man he clearly respected: Captain John Smith.

Smith despised idleness above all else, and could not let the ailing Martin depart without one final jibe, writing that he left for England because he was "desirous to injoy the credit of his supposed Art of finding the golden Mine." By the time Smith wrote that, in 1624, of course it was clear there was no such mine, but he would in time have cause to regret his contemptuous treatment of Martin. Back in England the members of the King's Council for Virginia would listen closely to what the well-connected Martin had to tell them.

9
Seeking the Future

ON JUNE 2, 1608, SMITH, with thirteen other men in the barge, acompanied Nelson's departing ship as far as Cape Henry. Smith waited until then to place his manuscript aboard, perhaps making changes right up until the last minute. As the *Phoenix* headed into the Atlantic, he turned north in search of the river that would take him to the South Sea. The James had already been explored to the fall line, and Smith had seen the York and Chickahominy as well. But if Powhatan's word could be trusted, there was an even larger river north of these that might lead toward his goal. According to Powhatan, the name of the river was Patawomek. Today we call it the Potomac.

Smith would have liked to have taken the new council member Scrivener along, but President Ratcliffe had shown a "disturbing" tendency toward "prodigalitie" in the use of the colony's resources, distributing food and drink liberally among his cronies ("parasites," Smith called them). Smith left Scrivener at the fort, hoping he could manage to keep a check on Ratcliffe while Smith was away.

Instead of heading up the western side of the bay, Smith crossed to the eastern shore first. He may have felt that here he was more likely to find natives who were not part of Powhatan's empire. After naming an island at the southern tip of the peninsula for himself, he encountered two natives brandishing "long poles" like javelins. Though outnumbered, they brashly demanded to know who the English were. Since they spoke the same language as Powhatan's people, Smith conversed easily with them, convincing them that his intentions were friendly. They in turn directed the English to their werowance, a man Smith described as "the comliest, proper, civill Salvage we incountred." His name was Kiptopeake. A town and a state park named after him are found in the vicinity today.

He told Smith a ghostly story. Two children of his group had recently died. Afterward their parents had dreams and visions that caused them to revisit the children's bodies. As was customary in the region, the dead had been exposed on platforms, awaiting burial after the elements had reduced them to bones. But the children's bodies had not decomposed; in fact they retained "delightfull countenances, as though they had regained their vitall spirits." Many people came to witness this strange phenomenon, the chief told Smith, but afterward, for some reason that no one understood, those who had seen the bodies began to die. Few were spared, and the werowance was mourning for the loss of so many of his people. It is possible that Kiptopeake's people had contracted some disease that the English brought, but the fact that no other Europeans had preceded Smith to this place makes it unlikely. Still, the werowance's tale, from the vantage point of four centuries, is like an eerie prophecy, a foretelling of what was to happen. The voyage Smith was embarking on would shape his thinking about the extent of America and its suitability for settlement by the English. He would in time write promotional books that praised this new land and described the opportunities that could be found there. He was to become a salesman for America, and his success was destined to destroy the cultures and peoples already there.

Smith traveled on, passing up the eastern shore, searching every inlet and bay to see if there were good sites for harbors or settlements. He was thinking ahead, to a time when the English in Virginia would expand far beyond Jamestown, even though most of those then living at the ramshackle fort would have considered it unlikely the settlement could endure another year. Smith certainly wished to find the river that might lead to the South Sea, but he could also see that America had much to offer as a colonial site—fertile land, fresh rivers and streams, plenty of timber. Best of all, it had vast spaces that to him seemed virtually unpopulated, where English settlers could have all the land they wanted.

Close to the bay, all the rivers were salty, so Smith sailed up one in search of fresh water to replenish the barge's supply. Stopping at a village, he was alarmed when a crowd rushed toward the shore, apparently "with great fury." However, their emotion seemed to shift suddenly to enthusiasm, and they welcomed the newcomers with "songs and daunces and much mirth." The English found enough water at the village to fill three casks, but it was muddy, cloudy liquid that they called "puddle" (meaning that it was the same as that found in a mud puddle). Returning to the coast, they happened on a spot where there was "a great Pond of fresh water, but so exceeding hot wee supposed it some bath." Smith named the place Point Ployer in memory of the French count Plouër who had helped him on his trip through Europe seven years earlier. Again Smith had his farmer's eye out for possible settlement sites, noting that the country nearby was "good to cut for hay in Summer and to catch fish and fowle in Winter."

The English explorers' pleasure at replenishing their supply of freshwater was soon tempered as their boat encountered a fierce storm that caught them far offshore. The barge's mast snapped and the sail was swept overboard. Only by bailing frantically were Smith's men able to keep their craft afloat long enough to reach a small island, which they dubbed Limbo. The storm continued to blow for two days, but the men used the time to sew their shirts together to make a replacement for the sail. Smith seldom let those under his command remain idle for long.

At the next place they stopped, again on the eastern shore, the people they encountered left no doubt about their hostility. Some climbed trees and shot arrows at the English, who anchored their boat offshore (out of the bowmen's reach) and made "all the signes of friendship we could." Smith ordered his men to hold their fire, for on this trip he wished to make friends, not demonstrate the power of English muskets. The colonists slept in their boat safely out of arrow range, and in the morning saw that the natives on shore seemed, as the earlier group did, to have undergone a radical change in attitude. Now they danced in a circle, holding closed baskets, signaling that they contained presents for the English.

Too skeptical to believe that, Smith ordered his men to fire a volley, though the muskets were loaded with small shot that would not kill. The crowd of dancers scattered, running for the shelter of high reeds nearby. Smith's experience as a soldier told him not to pursue, for they might have additional forces concealed there. He waited till dusk to lead his men ashore, preparing the way with another volley of shot. They found a few deserted houses, where cooking fires still smoldered. In each dwelling, Smith left presents: pieces of copper, beads, bells, and small mirrors.

The tactic succeeded. In the morning, four natives in a canoe came paddling up to Smith's boat. The English treated them well, and the four returned with twenty more men. Finally, Smith and his men stepped on shore, where "two or three thousand men women and children came clustring about us, every one presenting us with something." The English distributed beads, which was all they had for such a large crowd, but even a single bead was enough to delight the native children, who had never seen glass. Smith soon had volunteers who were willing to guide him anywhere he wished to go. These natives pointed the way to "a great nation called Massawomekes," which reminded Smith of some natives that Ralph Lane had met during his exploration of the region south of the bay during the winter of 1585–1586. Smith's expedition now crossed the bay to look for them. On the western side, the English encountered some high cliffs. In a sentimental gesture, Smith dubbed them Riccards Cliftes—the only reference to his mother's family in all his accounts of his life after childhood. (Today they are known as the Calvert Cliffs.)

At first Smith did not find the western shore of the bay as hospitable as the opposite side. It was mountainous and heavily wooded, and seemed to be populated only by wolves, bears, and deer. The eerie loneliness began to tell on the nerves of his men, who feared that they had gone beyond the point where humans could live. No one knew if this seemingly endless bay would lead to the South Sea or to some desolate area from which they would never find the way back. Their bread had become damp and rotten—though Smith remarks with approval that his men's stomachs were so good they could eat it anyway. The men pleaded with him to turn back. In his two versions of the story, he quotes in full the speech he made to them at this time, so he must have been proud of it.

He reminded them of Ralph Lane's journey, when, in a similar situation, Lane's crew had wanted to retreat. Lane pointed out that they had a dog on their boat, and that if they boiled it with sassafras leaves (for flavor, evidently), it would be sufficient food to last them. Though Smith had no dogs, he reminded his men that he had shared all the suffering with them "in the worst which is past." He promised that should they encounter hardships yet to come, he would take the brunt, eat the worst portion of any food they had. "As for your feares that I will lose my selfe in these unknowne large waters, or be swallowed up in some stormie gust; abandon these childish feares, for worse [than that which] is past is not likely to happen. . . . Regaine therefore your old spirits for returne I will not (if God please) till I have seene the Massawomecks, found Patawomek, or the head of this water you conceit to be endlesse."

Nonetheless, he ventured south and within a few days, on June 16, they did reach the mighty Potomac, which Smith estimated as being nine miles wide at its mouth. The countryside still seemed deserted. Smith and his companions sailed thirty miles upriver before seeing any people. Then they encountered two men in a canoe who led them up a stream "where all the woods were lay'd with ambuscades [ambushes]." Three or four thousand men (by Smith's count) appeared on the bank, "so strangely paynted, grimed and disguised, shouting, yelling and crying as so many spirits from hell could not have shewed more terrible."

The sight was intended to terrify, and would have daunted most people. But Smith ordered his men to aim their muskets low, and when they fired, the musket balls splashed harmlessly, but visibly, across the water. Combined with the sharp crack of the firearms, the demonstration caused the natives to lay down their weapons.

It didn't take Smith long to negotiate a truce. He reports, somewhat matter-of-factly for such a sweeping accusation, that the natives here told him that they had been told to attack the

English on Powhatan's orders. Furthermore, it had been "the discontents" at Jamestown who had actually encouraged Powhatan to kill Smith and his companions. The reason for this betrayal? Because "our Captaine did cause them [the Jamestown malcontents] to stay in their country [Virginia] against their wills." Unfortunately, Smith gives no more details—not to mention any evidence—but the accusation indicates that Jamestown's problems of disunity and disloyalty did not end with the departure of Wingfield, Archer, and Martin.

Going farther up the Potomac, Smith found himself momentarily gripped by the "gold fever" that he had found so ridiculous in Captain Newport. At the fall line he saw a stream running over the top of a cliff as high as a tree. At the bottom, the water had left a "tinctured spangled" deposit that had gilded the ground. Smith and his men climbed to the top and found sand mixed with shining, yellowish flecks. He describes the method the natives used to extract the metal by running water through a hole in a pot, washing away the dross and leaving the supposed gold behind. The natives, he wrote, "sell it all over the country to paint there bodies, faces, or Idols; which makes them look like Blackmores [Africans] dusted over with silver."

Smith took several bags of the golden sand away. Unfortunately, when it was assayed in England it proved as worthless as Newport's "gilded durt." He saw, however, that the surrounding country held more treasures than gold. "Bevers, Otters, Beares, Martins and minkes are found, and in divers places [an] aboundance of fish, lying so thicke with their heads above the water . . . [that] we attempted to catch them with a frying pan: but we found it a bad instrument to catch fish with." Smith and his companions had brought no fishing nets, and were literally famished in the midst of plenty, reduced to eating fish that they found washed up on the shore.

Having gone up the Potomac as far as was possible in a boat, Smith decided to return to the bay. He could not have guessed that at one of the places he sailed past, there would one day stand the capital of a great nation, founded by descendants of the English who settled in Virginia. Not even Smith could see that far ahead.

Smith's map of Virginia, specifically the Chesapeake Bay area, with west at the top. Though the English named the southernmost river of the bay after King James I, Smith here gives it the native name: Powhatan. The map is accurate enough to have been used in a boundary dispute nearly three hundred years later. At top left is another depiction of Powhatan seated in his longhouse.

The expedition next ventured up the Rappahannock, where a fast-flowing tide sent the clumsy boat careening out of control. It became grounded on a shoal in the midst of a clump of heavy reeds. Seeing that the shallow water was teeming with fish, Smith drew his sword and began to stab them. His companions followed suit, and in an hour had enough to feed themselves for a day. As Smith was slipping the last fish off his sword, he noticed that it had a long, jagged stinger. Suddenly a sharp pain ran up his arm. The "fish" was a stingray, and its venom caused Smith's hand, arm, and shoulder to swell up alarmingly. In a few hours his companions feared he was about to die and went so far as to dig a grave—"as himselfe directed," for even a dying Smith was, as ever, in charge.

There was on the voyage an English doctor named Russell, who had only recently arrived in the colony on Nelson's ship. Seventeenth-century English medicine had not progressed far beyond the theories of Galen, but Dr. Russell had a "precious oyle" that he applied to Smith's wound, with such miraculous effect that by suppertime Smith was able to eat the fish that had attacked him. Once more, Smith had cheated death, possibly winning new confidence from the men who followed him.

Smith decided to return to Jamestown. When the barge reached the mouth of the James River, where the friendly Kecoughtans lived, the natives saw Smith's bandaged arm and a wound suffered by another colonist and assumed the English had been in a battle. The gifts, including bows, arrows, and spears, that Smith's company had received on the journey, were mistaken for trophies of war. Smith saw no harm in acknowledging that yes, he and his men were returning victorious from battles with the Massawomeks and that these were their spoils.

"The rumor went faster up the river than our barge," wrote one of the men on board, and by the time they reached the next village on the James, the natives were prepared to give them a heroes' welcome. The English festively trimmed their boat's sail with strips of cloth, making it so colorful that when the barge finally reached Jamestown, a lookout at first mistook the craft for a Spanish frigate.

The barge's decorations turned out to be the only sign of rejoicing at Jamestown. Most of the new colonists—those brought by Nelson or Newport's second voyage—had now fallen ill. Scrivener, the new council member, was one of those stricken, and he had not been able to keep President Ratcliffe from making unwise choices. Smith was livid as he received complaints about "the pride and unreasonable needlesse crueltie of the silly President." Ratcliffe and his cronies had "riotously" consumed far more than their share of the food stores, and "to fulfill his follies" the president had ordered the construction of what Smith called a "pallace" in the woods.

The other colonists furiously demanded that Smith depose Ratcliffe from office. Smith could have assumed the title of president and governed the colony as he pleased, but he had had a tantalizing glimpse of greater glory. He had already found gold, or so he thought; why not win additional glory by becoming the discoverer of the direct passage to the South Sea? (It would only have added to his satisfaction that Newport had tried, and failed, to find that elusive passage.) So he left Ratcliffe in place, but appointed some officers—"more honest" ones—to assist Scrivener in supervising the colony. Smith and his men set off once again, less than a week after returning.

A cold wind, blowing from the north, kept Smith and his companions anchored at the end of the James River for several days. The Kecoughtans, who had given Smith's men a warm welcome the week before, again "feasted us with much mirth," for they assumed the English were embarking on another punitive expedition against their common enemy, the Massawomeks. Smith, remembering the pyrotechnic skills that had served him well in eastern Europe, fired off a few rockets after nightfall, cementing his reputation among the natives as a mighty magician.

Finally getting under way, the English at first made good progress, but as they advanced to the upper part of the bay, the illness that had devastated the colony now reappeared among the voyagers. Counting Smith, only five of the fourteen men on the trip had been "seasoned" by earlier exposure to the disease. The other nine now were lying feverish and weak in the bottom of the boat. Thus, when Smith spotted seven or eight canoes paddled by the reputedly fierce Massawomeks, he seemed to be thoroughly outnumbered. However, seeing some of the natives drawing their bows, he tried another of the tricks he had used during his military career. He spread a tarpaulin over his incapacitated men and propped their empty hats and muskets along the side of the barge. Then he raised his sail and headed straight for the canoes.

Seeing what was apparently a confident and powerful enemy bearing down on them, the natives could not believe that Smith was bluffing. They turned and headed for shore, where they landed. Once again, following his previous practice, Smith stayed around to befriend those who at first feared him. Making signs that he wished to parley, he finally attracted two men in a canoe to approach the barge. The Massawomeks spoke an Iroquois dialect unrelated to the Powhatans' Algonquian tongue, but Smith was able to communicate with them in sign language. When he presented one of the men with a bell, the others signaled to the shore and an exchange of gifts followed.

The Massawomeks had been on a hunting expedition and their gifts were commensurate with their mission. The English boat was loaded with venison, bear meat, bearskins, bows, arrows, clubs, and shields. Smith saw fresh wounds on the natives' bodies; they said they had fought with the Tockwogh people, who lived farther up the bay. Smith headed in that direction, and some days later entered the Tockwogh River (today the Sassafras) on the eastern shore. A "fleet" of boats appeared, carrying armed natives, who surrounded the English. Fortunately, one of the natives spoke Powhatan's language, and Smith invited him to parley. When the man saw the Massawomek weapons and shields in the boat, Smith let him believe that the English had captured them in battle.

The principle that "the enemy of my enemy is my friend" held as true in America as anywhere else, so the Tockwoghs brought the English to their village for a welcoming feast, "stretching their best abilities to expresse their loves." Smith noticed hatchets and knives made of brass and iron; Powhatan's people had none like these. The Tockwoghs told him their metal tools had come from the Sasquesahanocks, "a mightie people and mortall enemies [of] the Massawomeks." They said Smith's boat was too large to reach the place where the Sasquesahanocks lived, for there were hazardous rocks in the waterway. So Smith requested that a messenger be sent with an invitation for them to pay him a visit.

Sure enough, in a few days, some sixty Sasquesahanocks appeared, having traveled down the opposite side of the bay. The water was choppy and their canoes could not safely cross. Smith took the barge to pick them up, and even though they had never before seen a sailing ship, five of the newcomers' werowances stepped aboard. Smith described the Sasquesahanocks as "gyant-like" people, who brought presents that included tobacco pipes three feet long.

Notwithstanding their height, they seemed impressed by the notably short Captain Smith. The English were accustomed to gathering daily for a prayer service at which a psalm was read aloud. The natives recognized this as a religious ceremony and it prompted them to their own devotion—with Smith as the object of worship. According to one of Smith's companions, "they began in a most passionate manner to hold up their hands to the Sunne, with a most fearefull song. Then imbracing our Captaine, they began to adore him in like manner." Embarrassed, Smith scolded them, but the natives "began an Oration of their loves," accompanied by dancing "done with a most strange furious action." At the end, they covered Smith with a large painted bearskin and lowered a long chain of white beads, weighing six or seven pounds, around his neck. Each of the five werowances stepped forward to stroke Smith's neck and ask him to remain with them and be their "Governour and Protector . . . to defend and revenge them of the Massawomeks."

As politely as possible, Smith declined the honor, but promised that he would return to visit the following year. The Sasquesahanocks had in fact given him information that made him want to move on as soon as possible. The Massawomeks, they said, inhabited a land on a great water beyond the mountains. Smith interpreted that to mean the St. Lawrence River, which would mean that French trappers and traders were the source of the metal tools he had seen earlier.

Somehow, Smith felt, the Chesapeake or one of its tributaries must lead to the St. Lawrence or even to the South Sea. He continued to make his way north, sometimes naming the natural features for people from his past. He dubbed the highest mountain in the region Peregrine's Mount, after the current Lord Willoughby, and to a nearby stream he gave the Willoughby family name. (Philip Barbour identifies Peregrine's Mount as the present-day Gray's Hill, in Cecil County, Maryland.) Evidently Smith missed the mouth of the Susquehanna River, which, if he had followed it, would have led him as far north as today's New York State.

Smith could find no way to proceed beyond the northern reaches of the bay, so he went south and ventured up the Pawtuxent, one of the rivers he had not yet explored. He met some friendly natives, among whom was a man named Mosco. Smith had seen him before on the Potomac River. Mosco was easy to recognize because, unlike the other natives, he had a thick black beard. Smith speculated that his father had been a French trapper.

Mosco did not seem to be closely affiliated with any particular native group, and he now attached himself to the English as their guide and interpreter. He accompanied them back to the bay and up the next river Smith explored—the Rappahannock. Smith saw him as a man on the make, so when the English came to a Rappahannock village and Mosco warned that the people would be hostile, he ignored the advice. He thought Mosco wanted the English to trade only with friends of his. Nonetheless, Smith was careful. He called to a group standing on shore and asked them to exchange hostages so that neither side would attack the other. Several Rappahannocks, showing they were unarmed, waded into the waist-deep water and brought Smith one of their compatriots, receiving in return Anas Todkill, the man who had left the service of John Martin to stay with Smith in Virginia.

Todkill, clearly a brave man, was to become one of the few men Smith trusted completely. He did not intend to wait meekly on shore until he was exchanged again. While the natives were distracted, he moved toward a stand of trees beyond the beach and saw several hundred men hiding there, evidently preparing an ambush should the rest of Smith's men come ashore. Todkill tried to slip into the water and swim back to the boat, but some of the natives seized him. At that, he called out to Smith, warning of the trap. As soon as he did, the native hostage on the barge jumped overboard; the man Smith had assigned to guard him shot him as he headed for shore.

An all-out battle began. Smith commented that the shields the English had received from the Massawomeks came in handy, for his crew had used them to erect a superstructure in the front of their boat. The Rappahannocks' arrows ("more than a thousand Arrowes," Smith wrote) bounced harmlessly off the shields. The natives, on the other hand, had no defense for the English musket balls, and when they had exhausted their supply of arrows

SEEKING THE FUTURE   165

they fled. Todkill, caught in the crossfire, had fallen to the ground but was miraculously unhurt, though covered with the blood of some of his captors.

Preparing to go farther into what now seemed like hostile country, Smith ordered his men to enlarge the superstructure of shields, enough so that every man could be sheltered by them. This defensive tactic soon proved its worth, for the Rappahannocks concealed themselves along the river by attaching shrubbery to themselves. "[W]e tooke them for little bushes," Smith wrote, not realizing what they really were until arrows began to strike the shields on the boat. Smith and his men fired a volley of shot, apparently with little effect, for after the boat had proceeded upriver half a mile, the "bushes" rose and began "dauncing and singing very merrily."

Not long after, the English reached the point at which the water became too shallow for the boat to proceed (about the location of today's Fredericksburg, Virginia). They went ashore to mark the territory by carving their names on trees and nailing brass crosses into the trunks. (None of these have ever been discovered by modern explorers.) Their sentinel was first made aware that the Rappahannocks had followed them when an arrow struck the ground at his feet.

A "hundred nimble Indians [were] skipping from tree to tree, letting fly their arrows as fast as they could." Smith and his men returned fire with their muskets. On shore the English were at a disadvantage, for their shields were still on the boat, while the natives could conceal themselves among the trees. The faithful Mosco seemed heedless of the danger, for he ran back to the boat for more arrows, and fired back so rapidly that it seemed as if the English had many native allies. After half an hour, the hostile forces melted into the forest. Mosco ran after them and discovered a wounded man lying on the ground. Smith had to stop his trusty guide from beating the man to death ("never was Dog more furious against a Beare," Smith recalled).

The English surgeon who had cured Smith of the stingray venom bound up the native's wounds and encouraged him to eat something. Fortunately, Mosco—whose mood had improved because the English had helped him gather all the spent arrows lying on the ground, for him a windfall in trade goods—knew the man's language. Smith wanted to ask him some questions. After determining the names of four local "kings," he asked why the man's people had attacked when the English had come in peace. "[H]e answered, they heard we were a people come from under the world, to take their world from them." Smith asked the captive how many worlds he knew of. "[He] replied, he knew no more but that which was under the skie that covered him," where lived also the Powhatans, the Monacans, and the Massawomeks, who dwelled higher up in the mountains. What lay beyond the mountains? asked Smith. Only "the Sunne," came the answer, disappointing Smith, who was always hoping that someone would point out for him the way to the South Sea.

Smith won over the man, whose name was Amoroleck, with his usual tactics of gifts and kind treatment. Amoroleck agreed to mediate between the English and the local kings, one of whom was his brother. As the English started downriver toward the bay, however, arrows began to land in the water around the boat. Both Mosco and Amoroleck shouted that the English were friends, but the war cries of the attacking force made them impossible to hear. The natives followed along the shore, shooting arrows at the boat, for more than twelve miles. Finally Smith found a broad place in the river where the English could lay anchor beyond the reach of the archers. Night fell and those aboard the boat tried to rest.

As the sun rose, they were able to display their captive, Amoroleck. Mosco made a speech explaining how well the Englishmen had treated Amoroleck, mentioning that he himself would have killed the man had not the English intervened. On Smith's authority, he announced that Amoroleck would go free if his compatriots offered friendship. As before, the offer drew a response. Several men swam to the boat. One of them offered Smith his quiver of arrows—no truer sign of peace and friendship.

In due course, the four "kings" Amoroleck had spoken of came to visit, and both sides exchanged presents. The English balked only at giving away their pistols, which the natives took to be handsome tobacco pipes. As the English departed, they left behind "four or five hundred of our merry Mannahocks, singing, dauncing, and making merry."

So it went throughout the rest of the summer of 1608, with Smith using combinations of force and kindness, always with the aim of winning the friendship of the peoples who lived in the Tidewater region. In most cases, he succeeded. If from the comfortable vantage point of four centuries, some may wish to characterize him as an interloper whose real motive was to dispossess the natives from their land, he might argue that there seemed to be more than enough land for all, and that his methods were far more benign than those of the Spaniards who had conquered, enslaved, tortured, and sought deliberately and systematically to destroy the cultures of the people who were unlucky enough to encounter them. We could observe that the English treated the white, Christian Irish with far more cruelty and ferocity than Smith ever displayed toward Native Americans. The blame should not fall entirely on Smith for the fact that those who followed in his wake would in time dispossess and decimate the Native Americans.

As the days grew shorter and the weather cooler, Smith realized it was time to return to the fort. Ratcliffe's term as president would expire in September, and his obvious successor was Captain John Smith. Disappointingly, Smith had failed in his main objective for the summer: to find a navigable waterway to the South Sea. Of course, we know there was none to find; the Pacific was three thousand miles away, and the journey would not be made, from where Smith stood, for another two centuries.

Yet Smith had accomplished a great deal. He had explored most of the nearly two-hundred-mile-long bay and many of its tributaries. He had somehow acquired the surveying skills to make a map of the territory so accurate that it would remain in use until the middle of the nineteenth century.

Smith must have dreaded returning to the fort for other reasons. He did not know what further plots and dissension might have gone on in his absence, but it seemed right to assume there had been some. Still, the twelve men who, along with Smith, had survived the Chesapeake Bay exploration (one had succumbed to disease) now had the utmost confidence in his ability to lead and keep them alive. They would prove to be invaluable allies if there were any at the fort who still wanted to put Captain Smith to death.

10

Smith vs. Newport

O N SEPTEMBER 10, 1608, "by the Election of the
Councell, and request of the Company, Captaine Smith
received the Letters Patents [as President]: which till
then by no meanes he would accept, though he was often impor-
tuned thereunto."

This paragraph, which opens the seventh chapter of Smith's
Generall Historie of Virginia, shows him at his worst. It was not
enough to write that he was elected president, a title that de-
volved on him by default and his skill (and luck) at eliminating all
the other original council members except Ratcliffe, who had to
relinquish the office after his term was up. No, Smith must also
describe his new appointment as coming at the "request of the
Company"—a phrase that has led some biographers to describe
him as the first popularly elected leader in America. Moreover,
Smith adds with false modesty that although he was often impor-
tuned to accept the office earlier, he declined it. Smith was brave,
smart, and hardworking, but modesty was not one of his qualities, which may help explain why he has attracted so many enemies from his time to ours.

As president, though, he set to work with typical energy and
decisiveness. He halted once and for all the construction of Ratcliffe's "Pallace" and began reconstruction of the church and
storehouse, along with additional buildings to shelter the supplies the colonists expected to arrive soon from England. He also

brought a greater degree of military discipline to the colony. He regularized the order in which men stood watch, personally training those who were to serve on guard duty. No man was exempt as each Saturday Smith drilled the company on a field near the fort, which "we called Smithfield." No doubt some had other names for it. Natives would gather to watch "in amazement" these curious goings-on.

Smith even found a post, and the rank of lieutenant, for George Percy, who had for long seemed to stay in the background even though his noble family was the most illustrious of any represented at Jamestown. Lieutenant Percy was entrusted with the barge and sent out to trade with the natives, a task Smith had previously reserved for himself, so he must have developed considerable confidence in Percy.

As chance would have it, Percy was thus the first to encounter Captain Newport returning from England once again; his ship was just entering the bay as Percy reached the mouth of the James. On this visit, unfortunately, Smith and Newport were destined to clash bitterly. Newport's offense, in Smith's eyes, was to deliver and carry out orders from the Virginia Company that contradicted what Smith thought was best for the colony. One would think Smith would have retained a certain amount of affection for a man who had saved him (twice) from the gallows, but by the time Newport left, he carried a carefully sealed letter from Smith to the directors of the Virginia Company suggesting that they could save money by dispensing with Newport's services in the future.

It is not clear how long Smith had served as president when Newport arrived—it may have been as little as nineteen days—but he certainly did not have enough time to put the colony on the kind of footing that he hoped to. Now here was Newport with the news that the directors of the Virginia Company had ordered him not to return without a cargo showing at least two thousand pounds' profit for the voyage. Furthermore, Newport should accomplish one or more of three other tasks: first, find the passage to the South Sea; second, find indisputable evidence of deposits of silver or gold ("a lumpe of gold" was preferable), since Smith's prediction that the previous cargo of ore was indeed "durt" had proved true; and third, find one or more of the survivors of Raleigh's colony, or their descendants. To accomplish these goals, Newport was to have the full support of the colonists at Jamestown.

Worse yet, someone in London had hatched the bright idea that the English should hold an official coronation ceremony for Powhatan, thus winning the chief's undying gratitude—or so it was assumed. To accomplish this assignment, Newport came supplied with a crown and what the Virginia Company directors thought were suitable gifts: a bedstead and mattress, a china basin and pitcher made for a bedroom night table, and other "costly novelties" that Smith accurately judged would have been valued less by Powhatan than an ordinary piece of copper.

To add to Smith's headaches, Newport had of course brought additional colonists, including the first two women—only two, who must have felt themselves overwhelmed in the otherwise all-male community. The women were of less concern to Smith than some skilled workers from Germany and Poland who also arrived with Newport. Their role was to begin making salable products, such as glass, pitch, tar, and soap ashes (an ingredient used in soap that was scarce in England), to help put the colony on a paying basis. Profit was definitely on the minds of the Virginia Company directors at this stage of the venture.

Finally, the company's instructions (addressed to the president by title, not name, and thus delivered to Smith by Captain Newport) reprimanded the council for arguing among themselves and forming "factions." Whoever was president now was firmly directed to follow the orders of Captain Newport. For good measure, Newport had brought two newly appointed members to the council, Captain Richard Waldo and Captain Peter Winne, described by Smith as "two auncient Souldiers, and valiant Gentlemen, but yet ignorant of the business [of colonization]." The additional members were important because they meant Smith could be outvoted. Previously, since the president had two votes, and there were only two other council members, Smith could guarantee at least a tie on any matter up for decision.

Besides the gifts for Powhatan, Newport had brought a seemingly clever invention that was intended to overcome the obstacle that had previously prevented him from exploring beyond the fall line. This was a boat that could be broken into five pieces so that it could be easily transported overland, past the falls, and then reassembled on the other side to allow the explorers to continue their journey upriver.

Smith raised objections to all of Newport's proposals, causing Newport to accuse him of trying to hinder the projects that the company wanted to complete. Even Smith's report of his recent exploration of the Chesapeake drew criticism, for Newport disapproved of the "crueltie" Smith had shown in dealing with the natives.

Newport made the coronation of Powhatan his first order of business. He decided to go to Werowocomoco by ship, which would require traveling down the James and back up the York River. Furthermore, he intended to take 120 men with him, draining the colony of its labor force and effectively putting an end to all the building projects Smith had planned. So Smith volunteered to go overland—a distance of only twelve miles—to ask Powhatan to come to Jamestown for the ceremony. "And where Newport durst not goe with less than 120 [men] he [Smith] onely tooke with him [four]," Smith wrote later. This was not the last of the barbs Newport would suffer from Smith's pen.

When Smith and his companions arrived at Werowocomoco, they found that the old chief was away, visiting some other village. A messenger went to inform Powhatan of Smith's arrival, and the five Englishmen settled down to wait, making a fire in an open field to keep warm. Pocahontas and "her women" decided to surprise Smith and his friends with an entertainment. The visitors suddenly heard "such a hydeous noise and shreeking" coming from a nearby copse that they jumped to their feet, muskets ready for what Smith thought was an attack by "Powhatan with all his power." Instead, Pocahontas emerged from the woods to assure Smith that no harm was intended. She was "willing [for] him to kill her" if she betrayed his trust.

Sure enough, a short time later, thirty young women emerged from the woods, nearly naked, wearing only a few green leaves before and behind. Each had painted her body in a different design and had donned some element of costume. The one Smith assumed to be the leader, for example, wore a pair of deer antlers on her head and an otter's skin around her waist. Another carried a quiver of arrows and a bow, in Diana-like fashion. Others held swords, clubs, or what Smith called a "pot-sticke." This "anticke" reminded Smith of an English masque, even though he described it as having "savage" aspects: "These fiends with the most hellish shouts and cryes . . . cast themselves in a ring around the fire, singing and Dauncing with most excellent ill varietie, oft falling into their infernall passions, and solemnly againe to sing and daunce; having spent neare an houre in the Mascarado . . . they departed."

That turned out to be only a prelude to a more passionate scene. Smith wrote that the women went to their lodgings and invited him to follow. (He wrote "him," not mentioning if his companions were included.) He was no sooner within the house when "all these Nymphes . . . tormented him [more] then ever, crowding, pressing, and hanging about him, most tediously crying, Love you not me? love you not me?" Afterward the women laid out a feast "consisting of all the Salvage dainties they could devise." More dancing and singing accompanied the meal.

Finally with the "mirth being ended," the women took firebrands—for by now night had fallen—and led Smith through the village to a house where he could sleep. He draws the curtain on the evening's activities at that point. But other English visitors to Jamestown recorded that Powhatan women customarily welcomed male visitors by sleeping with them. In view of the nature of the ceremony that led to this moment, it seems likely that such a gift was offered to Smith.

Did he accept? As far as is known, from the several books he wrote about his life and what others wrote about him, Smith never consummated a relationship with a woman. If that does not seem to match the image of the freebooting Elizabethan adventurer, it may be possible to consider the alternative: that Smith preferred men to women as his sexual partners. (Though there is no evidence that he ever had sexual relations with anyone.)

Consider the words he uses in the passage above to describe a scene that might be another man's fantasy: as an unmarried man in his late twenties, he is surrounded by nearly naked women, probably in their teens, who "tormented him," "crowding, pressing, and hanging about him, most tediously crying." Are those the expressions a man would choose if he found women sexually desirable?

In any event, business soon superseded thoughts of pleasure. Powhatan arrived and received the invitation from Smith, who noted that "Father Newport" had more gifts for the chief at the fort, and if Powhatan came to accept them, Newport would then begin his campaign of revenge against their common enemy, the Monacans.

Powhatan, described as a "subtile Savage" by Smith, responded with all the dignity of royalty: "If your King have sent me Presents, I also am a King, and this is my land. . . . Your Father is to come to me, not I to him . . . as for the Monacans I can revenge my owne injuries." The old chief then began to draw on the ground a map showing all the territory within his empire. Smith paid close attention and the two men conversed for some time. Again Smith does not reveal what was said, except to mention that Powhatan now denied that there was any salt water beyond the mountains. Smith should have paid attention to this, but the reports he had from other natives were too hopeful for him to believe what Powhatan said.

Smith took Powhatan's reply back to Newport, who set out by land for the chief's capital, taking fifty good marksmen with him. The presents, being too bulky to carry, had to be transported by boat, a distance of nearly one hundred miles. After the English arrived in Werowocomoco, they had to wait for the gifts to catch up. Eventually, all was in readiness for the "coronation." The water basin, bed, and mattress were neatly arranged before Powhatan. Newport produced a scarlet cloak for the chief to wear, but it required Namontack—who had been to England and back—to reassure the chief that none of these strange things were intended to harm him.

Now, however, there was the matter of actually placing a crown on Powhatan's head. Smith doesn't describe how lavish an object it was, but it soon became clear that Powhatan did not know its "majesty nor meaning." What he did know was that the English wanted him to kneel to receive it ("bend the knee" would have been sufficient, says Smith), and Powhatan adamantly knelt for no one. The English tried "perswasions, examples, and instructions," to no avail.

Powhatan evidently was a tall enough individual that none of the Englishmen could place the crown on his head *unless* he lowered himself. So a group approached him from behind, and while some leaned hard on his shoulders they were able to get him to stoop a little as three men rushed to crown him.

To complete the debacle, as soon as the crown was in place, someone fired a pistol as a signal to an honor guard waiting in the boat, who then, as arranged, fired a volley as a salute to the new "king." Unfortunately, the king thought he was under attack, and started up "in a horrible feare." Eventually someone made it clear that the muskets had been fired as an honor, and calm was restored. Remembering his manners, the king looked around for a gift to bestow on Newport and came up with a pair of "old shooes and his mantell." Presumably Powhatan thought those were the equivalent to the honor he felt had been shown him. (There is in the British Museum today a mantle made of feathers that has traditionally been regarded as the one Newport received on this occasion.)

Newport now turned to another matter. He wished to go upriver to the country of the Monacans and punish them for killing his other son. Actually, this fiction was a cover story for Newport's true purpose: to find the South Sea. He asked Powhatan to contribute some scouts and warriors, making this a joint effort. The old chief flatly refused, saying that he had given Namontack to the English and that was all the help they were going to get.

Newport decided to go anyway, snubbing Smith by leaving him at the fort while taking along 120 men of less experience, including newcomers Captain Waldo, Captain Winne, and Francis West, the younger brother of Lord De La Warr, a member of the king's privy council who was about to become a major player in the story of Jamestown. Scrivener and Percy also went. In the end, the expedition failed to accomplish its purpose, partly because the much-heralded collapsible boat was a failure. As Smith wrote in a scathing letter to the Virginia Company, "If he [Newport] had burnt her [the boat] to ashes, one might have carried her in a bag; but as she is, five hundred [men] cannot, to a navigable place above the Falles." Evidently the boat was much too cumbersome for even Newport's large force to portage across country and reassemble.

Newport was also distracted because he thought he had discovered a lode of silver. Precious metals still retained their glitter for him, because he knew that his superiors in London would be pleased by any proof that Virginia held such treasures. Once more, however, the "ore" samples he stopped to gather proved worthless.

On the journey, Newport found it necessary to employ Smith's methods of dealing with the natives, which he had previously chastised Smith for. According to the anonymous chronicler of Newport's expedition, the English came upon two Monacan towns, where "the people neither used us well or ill, yet for our securitie we took one of their petty Kings, and led him bound to conduct [show] us the way." Thus when the English arrived at another town, they found that word of their arrival had as usual preceded them; when they tried to trade for corn, the natives claimed to have none, having already hidden their supply.

Meanwhile Smith was making the most of his assignment to command the fort, which housed some ninety men and the two women. He wrote that the 120 members of Newport's expedition were "the best men he could chuse." Presumably that left Smith with the weak, the sick, and the lazy. He dealt with the situation the same way he would later, when the colony faced starvation: he divided them into groups. The Polish and German glassmakers needed sand for their work so he sent them across the river to build a workshop and shelter. Other newcomers, skilled in making tar, pitch, or soap ashes, were similarly dispersed.

Smith was left with a group of what he elsewhere called "Tuftaffaty humorists," an irresistible phrase that refers to those who dressed fashionably in the latest clothing fad, a silken fabric with decorative tufts. A full twenty-five of the seventy new colonists

Newport had brought on this supply (known as the "second sup-ply") are listed in the roster as "gentlemen," that is, men who did not expect to work. Smith was determined to turn them into use-ful members of the community, and took them five miles down-river to cut down trees, learn to make clapboard, and—perhaps hardest of all—sleep in the woods. We know the names of two of these men (Gabriel Beadle and John Russell) because Smith called them "the only two gallants of this last Supply." He does not use the term "gallant" as a compliment; the last "gallants" he encountered were the four Frenchmen who bilked him out of his belongings when he set out on his quixotic quest to fight the Turks.

Smith took these foppish young men under his wing and set a personal example: "lodging, eating and drinking, working or playing, they but doing as the President did himselfe." Within a week, Smith says, these men, raised in luxury and idleness, were actually enjoying the work, "making it their delight to heare the trees thunder as they fell." Their newfound enthusiasm had an undesired result. The hard work "blistered their tendere fin-gers," so that every third blow of the ax brought forth a swear word. Smith, good Christian that he was, felt compelled to pun-ish these offenses. He counted the oaths each man uttered, and at the evening meal a can of water was poured down each man's sleeve for each transgression that day. The penalty seems an odd one—and likely to lead to chaotic scenes at dinnertime—but Smith proudly reports that soon there was hardly an oath heard in a week. The tone of his report changes when he writes about this interlude. He doesn't feel the need to relentlessly justify his actions; instead the reader gets the impression that he was never happier than when he was leading a group of men who were accomplishing some task under his direction. The summer voy-age around the Chesapeake was another such instance.

While Smith was away from the fort, however, discipline suf-fered within. As with Captain Nelson's previous visit, the presence of the sailors caused both colonists and seamen to place personal profit above the good of the colony. The ship's company, as before, had excellent food and drink to offer. Smith lists butter, cheese, beef, pork, aqua vitae, and beer, among other delectables in the ship's larder that seemed far preferable to the colonists' humdrum daily fare. This time, however, the colonists brought a third element into the trade: the natives. The colonists readily exchanged English metal tools for the furs, baskets, and small animals the natives brought to the fort. The sailors, in turn, gave their stores of food for the furs and other native trade goods, which brought high prices in London. Smith wrote that one of the ship's officers sold the furs he obtained in Virginia for thirty pounds, far more than he had been paid for serving on the voyage.

All this was unfortunately detrimental to the colony, for as Smith noted, there were so many eager profiteers within the fort that in six or seven weeks the colonists' supply of tools began to dwindle alarmingly. The figures Smith gives are two hundred to three hundred axes, chisels, hoes, and so forth—reduced to twenty. Ominously, more dangerous things such as pikes, shot, and gunpowder also began to disappear.

Newport and his band of explorers returned to the fort, as described by the anonymous recorder of the expedition, "half sicke, all complaining, and tired with toyle, famine, and discontent." Their expedition had been an utter failure. Soon afterward, Newport and his greedy crew were "dispatched," in Smith's word, taking with them samples of the products the craftsmen had made, the clapboard that Smith and his merry group of woodsmen had provided, and a long letter that Smith had somehow found the time to write. He must have sealed it with a thick coating of wax, for in it he called on the Virginia Company to dismiss Captain Newport, questioned the orders of the company's directors, and presumed to give them advice on how the colony should be run.

It is hard to understand how Smith could have written, and sent, such an intemperate communication. He perfunctorily apologizes in his first paragraph, writing, "I humbly intreat your Pardons if I offend you with my rude Answer." But the tone and the message must clearly have been quite offensive to the very people Smith most needed to curry favor with, if he truly wanted to accomplish the objectives he sets forth.

(Of course, this letter—like the Pocahontas rescue story—did not see print until the third version of Smith's account of Virginia history, the one he wrote in 1624. So he may merely have concocted it to settle old scores against a Virginia Company that by then had turned its back on him. Since the records of the company for this period have long been lost, there is no way of telling when the letter was actually sent, or if it ever was. Captain Newport had been dead seven years by the time Smith published it. Most of those who also might have known of it in 1608 were also unable to confirm or contradict it in 1624.)

Smith evidently was stung by the letter Newport delivered to him containing the company's instructions. It seems to have reprimanded the councilors at Jamestown for quarreling among themselves, and also complained that the colony's leader had sent them merely vague promises, or as Smith terms them, "ifs and ands, hopes, and some few proofes; as if we would keepe the mystery of the business to our selves."

Smith refutes these charges, at least as they pertained to him personally, with a dash of sarcasm: "[As] For our factions," he writes, "unless you would have me run away and leave the country, I cannot prevent them." Referring to the unfulfilled promises that the company received, he denies responsibility: "I have not concealed from you any thing I know; but I feare some cause you to beleeve much more then is true."

Having blamed (but not named) others for the problems of the colony, Smith now turned his guns on his chief target: Newport. Smith had been offended by the older man's refusal to take his advice about how to deal with Powhatan, and even more so when Newport went looking for the South Sea without taking him along.

Smith estimated that the latest voyage cost the company two or three thousand pounds. This investment's only return was less than a hundred pounds' worth of goods. Smith knew that the directors would be displeased and he placed the blame squarely on Newport's shoulders. He enumerates Newport's failures: to find the South Sea, to discover a source of gold, to locate any of the lost colonists. Smith claims that he told Newport he would fail, and adds that the grand expedition of "120 of the best men he [Newport] could chuse" accomplished no more than "might have beene done by one man . . . for the value of a pound of Copper."

Smith doesn't fail to mention his own efforts to establish the industries the company desired—making "Pitch and Tarre, Glasse, Sope-ashes and Clapboard," but cautions against pursuing the projects. He says such things were made in Russia and Sweden, where the poor people who toiled at that labor could hardly earn enough to live. It would be cheaper, Smith advises, for England to buy from those sources than to make such products in Virginia.

Returning to his main subject, Smith accuses Newport of bungling the coronation of Powhatan and failing in the subsequent trade negotiations. Newport had promised to load two ships (the barges) with corn from Powhatan; instead, he returned with only fourteen bushels. Newport even mishandled the supplies that the Virginia Company had sent aboard his ship. Smith says the colony was given only about twenty pounds' worth of food and thus the colonists subsisted on "meale and water" while the sailors made "good cheare" on their well-provided ship. He adds that the soldiers who accompanied Newport said that their officers supported their families from the sale of goods that the Virginia Company sent for the colonists. Clearly implying that Newport and his crew were cheating both the company and the colonists, Smith asks that in the future the company should "let us know what we should receive, and not stand to [rely on] the saylers courtesie to leave us what they please."

Finally Smith comes to the subject that seems to have bothered him most. He says he is enclosing the map he had made on his travels around Chesapeake Bay and its tributaries. He isn't shy about comparing it to Newport's efforts: "I have made you as great a discovery as he, for lesse charge than he spendeth [charges] you every meale." Indeed, he says, Newport and his men lingered at Jamestown so long that they actually became a burden on the colonists. Newport, Smith claims, was said to receive a hundred pounds a year merely for "carying newes." Since any competent ship's master "can find the way as well as he," the company could save that money by doing without Newport's services.

What did the colony need most? Smith leaves no doubt. "I intreat you . . . send but thirty Carpenters, husbandmen, gardiners, fisher men, blacksmiths, masons, and diggers up of trees, roots, well provided; then [rather than] a thousand of such as we have." Smith wanted men who could work, not gentlemen or gallants who consumed food and required shelter, draining the community of strength "before they can be made good for any thing."

As an aside, Smith mentions that he has put aboard the ship the onetime council president Ratcliffe, "now called Sicklemore, a poore counterfeited Imposture," for the colony had no further need of his services. "I have sent you him home, least [lest] the company [colonists] should cut his throat . . . if he and Archer returne again, they are sufficient to keepe us always in factions." (If Smith seems to be a bit obsessed about Archer, who had left the colony eight months earlier, it is only fair to consider that Archer tried to have Smith hanged.)

Smith concludes this remarkable document in the tone of a man explaining elementary facts to schoolboys: "These are the causes that have kept us in Virginia, from laying such a foundation, that ere this might have given much better content and satisfaction; but as yet you must not looke for any profitable returnes: so I humbly rest."

The penultimate word is the only humble thing about this letter. It is hard to see what Smith thought he would accomplish by sending it. In a mood of frustration, many people probably think of writing such letters—perhaps even going so far as to put their thoughts on paper—but most have the good sense not to send them. Sealing the letter and putting it aboard Newport's ship was the act of someone who has let his sense of his own superiority overcome his perception of reality. The rich and powerful leaders of the Virginia Company would demonstrate that they did not like being lectured by a yeoman's son. Coat of arms or no, Smith was still not on equal terms with the people who held the power in England.

11

Smith vs. Powhatan

ONE WAY OR ANOTHER, all of the original council members except Smith had now departed from the scene. Three new councilors had appeared, but Smith still held the title of president, and the two votes that that office carried with it. The immediate concern of the colony was to stock enough food to last the winter. Jamestown could expect no more English ships until spring, and Smith knew he had to obtain any additional supplies from the natives. The ill temper that had prompted the writing of his letter to the Virginia Company carried over into his dealings with the local peoples. The Nansemonds, who lived thirty miles downriver near the mouth of the James, had promised to trade some of their corn to the English, but when Smith went to begin negotiations, they balked. The natives had excuses: the harvest had been poor and they had no grain to spare. More ominously, they claimed Powhatan had ordered them not to trade with the English; in fact, the paramount chief had told the Nansemonds not even to let Smith's men enter their territory.

Smith, offshore with the barges, ordered his forces to fire their muskets into the air as a threat. Instead of fighting, the Nansemonds fled into the woods. Enraged, Smith came ashore and set one of their houses on fire; that brought some of them running back, offering him grain—even as much as half they had—if only he would spare the rest of the village.

Smith wrote, "how they collected it, I know not, but before night they loaded our three Boats" with corn. That was still not nearly enough to see the colonists through the winter, so Smith and Captain Waldo ventured out with two barges to find more. This time, everywhere they went, they found abandoned villages. Word had spread that the English wanted food, and Powhatan had ordered that they not receive any. The natives simply disappeared rather than face Smith.

Smith decided he had to approach Powhatan, but although he and the old chief had conducted several intimate conversations, for some reason Smith judged that this time he could not use a direct approach. Instead, he plotted with Waldo to "surprise" the paramount chief. Smith's account of the proceeding contains a hint that he was starting to see enemies where none existed, for he writes that Captain Winne and Scrivener, the other two councilors, "did their best to hinder that project," and that this resulted from a plot hatched in England "to ruine Captaine Smith."

Before any plot could be carried out, however, Powhatan sent a messenger with an offer of his own. This may have been the old chief's intention all along. Powhatan asked Smith to send some men to Werowocomoco to build a new house for him. If Smith also provided a grindstone, fifty swords, some "peeces" (firearms), a cock and a hen, along with copper and beads, then Powhatan would fill all the English barges with corn.

It was an offer impossible to refuse, though Smith was "not ignorant of [Powhatan's] devises and subtiltie." Nor was Smith willing to give the natives firearms, but that was a detail that could be negotiated. Accordingly, he sent overland a party of men, including three of the Germans, to start work on Powhatan's house. Smith himself set out with the pinnace, two barges, and forty-six volunteers. He stresses the fact that all his men had offered their services freely, for there seem to have been skeptics at the fort who doubted that the mission would be successful. Some whom Smith had asked to go with him found "excuses to stay behind," even though (he adds with typical bravado) everyone knew "Smith would not returne emptie[-handed] if it [corn] were to be had."

It was December 29 when Smith's party embarked, and the weather was already bitterly cold. The English stayed the first night at Warraskoyack, where the werowance was a man Smith trusted. The "king," as Smith called him, strongly urged him to abandon the mission. Failing in that, he said, "Captaine Smith, you shall find Powhatan [will seem to] use you kindly, but trust him not, and be sure he have no oportunitie to seize on your Armes; for he hath sent for you onley to cut your throats."

Smith combined another task with his journey to see Powhatan. He asked the werowance to assign two guards to escort one of Smith's men, Michael Sicklemore, to Chowanoac, south of the bay. This was the place that Ralph Lane, governor of Raleigh's first colony, had scouted in the winter of 1585–1586 when searching for a new site to move his people. Smith felt that if any trace of the Roanoke "lost colonists" could still be found, that would be a likely location. (Sometime later, Sicklemore returned to Jamestown, having found "little hope and lesse certaintie" of the Roanoke colonists.)

The next day Smith reached Kecoughtan, the native settlement at the mouth of the James River, where a major blizzard blew up. "The extreme windy rayne, frost and snow caused us to keep Christmas among the Salvages." Nonetheless, he wrote with what for him was unusual festiveness, "we were never more merry, nor fed on more plentie of good Oysters, Fish, Flesh, Wild-foule, and good bread; nor never had better fires in England, then [than] in the dry smoaky houses of Kecoughtan." He and two other Englishmen went hunting birds to provide additional food for the feast; he reported that in three trips they bagged 148 fowl of various types.

Finally, on January 12, 1609, they reached Werowocomoco. Finding that the river was frozen half a mile out from the shore, Smith, again "by his owne example," led his men ashore, wading through muddy, frozen ooze. They were given shelter in vacant houses and soon Powhatan sent them bread, turkey, and venison in the usual generous quantities. When he and Smith met the next day, however, Powhatan wondered aloud why Smith had chosen this time to visit, for the old chief had extended no invitation, nor did he have any spare corn. Smith pointed out the men standing in the longhouse who had in fact delivered Powhatan's invitation to Jamestown. He asked how it was that the chief had become so forgetful. Powhatan responded with a laugh; it appears he must have enjoyed parleying with the quick-witted Englishman.

They got down to business. On this, the fourth and final time when Smith and Powhatan met face-to-face, Smith quotes the old chief at great length. Powhatan waxed eloquent on the intentions of the English and the plight in which he found himself. He could not have known how prescient he was. Smith, already mapping sites for future settlements, would become the leading English exponent of the colonization of America, which would result in the destruction of the people who already lived there.

Powhatan knew one thing: that the key to the Englishmen's power was their weapons, and he wanted some. When Smith balked once again at giving him muskets or even swords, suggesting that the chief accept copper instead, Powhatan replied that he valued his corn more than Smith's copper, for he could eat the corn, but not the copper.

Smith protested that he was neglecting affairs at the fort to come here in response to Powhatan's wishes, and now the chief would not negotiate. He had demonstrated his "love" for Powhatan by sending men to build him a house, while work in Jamestown went unfinished. "As for swords and gunnes, I told you long ago I had none to spare," Smith said, claiming that he needed the weapons to hunt game. "Yet steale or wrong you I will not," he asserted, "nor dissolve that friendship we have mutually promised," unless Powhatan forced him to defend himself.

Powhatan relented somewhat, agreeing to spare whatever corn he could, but said he needed two days to gather it. He added that he had doubts about Smith's reasons for coming to visit, "for many doe informe me, [that] your comming hither is not for trade, but to invade my people, and possesse my country." Smith could relieve Powhatan of this fear, the chief suggested, by leaving his weapons aboard his ship, "for here they are needlesse, we being all friends, and for ever Powhatans [members of the same tribe]."

Once more, with that last phrase, the chief was inviting Smith to become a member of Powhatan's people. After Smith left the conference, he discovered that others from Jamestown had found the offer more appealing than he had. The Germans he had sent to construct a house for Powhatan had compared conditions at Jamestown with those at Werowocomoco and decided that their chances of survival were better with Powhatan. They had, in Smith's view, turned traitor; it was they who had told Powhatan that the English were not temporary visitors, but intended to stay permanently, taking whatever land they needed. Smith was stunned by this discovery, for in fact he had assigned one of the treacherous Germans to serve as *his* spy in Powhatan's capital.

The Germans' actions may seem strange to us, but they most likely regarded Powhatan's people as no more "savage" than Marco Polo considered the Chinese, among whom he lived for sixteen years. The Germans could expect Powhatan to treat them well in return for their services and skills.

When the corn arrived, Smith and Powhatan again sat down to discuss trade terms. Powhatan made a last effort to persuade Smith to lay aside his weapons. Eloquently, the chief described the reasons why he preferred peace to war. He began by recalling battles of the past, saying that he had seen the deaths of all his people three times, that he was the last survivor of those generations. "I know the difference of Peace and Warre better than any in my country," he said. "But now I am old and ere long must die." He wished for his successors—his brothers, sisters, and the children of his sisters—to live in peace with the English, but Smith's weapons made everyone afraid.

"What will it availe you," the chief asked Smith, "to take that by force you may quickly have by love, or destroy them that provide you food?" He pointed out that he and his people could hide their provisions and flee into the woods, where the English would not find them. He hoped they would not have to do that. "Thinke you," he asked, "I am so simple, not to know it is better to eate good meate, lye well, and sleepe quietly with my women and children, laugh and be merry with you . . . [than to] be forced to flie from all, to lie cold in the woods, feed upon Acorns, rootes, and such trash, and be so hunted by you, that I can neither rest, eate, nor sleepe?"

The chief's regard for Smith was high enough (or he pretended it was) that he described how fearful the Englishman's looming presence would be when Powhatan took to the woods with his people: "My tired men must watch, and if a twig but breake, every one cryeth there commeth Captaine Smith: then must I fly I know not whether: and thus with miserable feare, end my miserable life, leaving my pleasures to such youths as you." Powhatan added a cautionary thought: Smith too might come to a miserable end, if he could not find enough food. All of this could be avoided, the old chief said, "if you would come in [a] friendly manner to see us, and not thus with your guns and swords as [if] to invade your foes."

In the face of this seemingly conciliatory offer, Smith remained firm in his determination to keep his weapons. He reminded Powhatan that "the vow I made you of my love, both my selfe and my men have kept," despite the fact that Powhatan's men had broken the chief's pledge of friendship. Even so, Smith added, the English had curbed their desire for revenge; otherwise, Powhatan would have "knowne as well the crueltie we use to our enemies, as our true love to our friends." Powhatan's people frequently came to Jamestown with their bows and arrows, and the English accepted that as their custom.

Dismissing Powhatan's threat to go to war and hide the corn to starve the English, Smith declared that to the English, fighting wars "consist our chiefest pleasure." He added, "for your riches we have no use: as for the hiding [of] your provision . . . we shall not so unadvisedly starve as you conclude." The English, Smith claimed mysteriously, had a way of finding hidden things that was "beyond your knowledge."

"Many other discourses they had," Smith recalled, "till at last they began to trade." Scholars have long wished to know what was discussed during those "other discourses," for there are strong indications that it was on this occasion that Powhatan revealed to Smith what had actually happened to the survivors of Raleigh's lost colony. William Strachey, who arrived at Jamestown in 1610, after Smith had departed, was the secretary for the colony under its governor Sir Thomas Gates. Strachey wrote an account of his experiences, *Historie of Travell into Virginia Britania*, in which he states that "the men women, and Children of the first plantation at Roanoak were by practize and Comaundement of Powhatan . . . miserably slaughtered without any offence given him." Strachey says that Powhatan ordered the massacre on the advice of his "Priests."

Furthermore, the Reverend Samuel Purchas, who carried on Hakluyt's work after the latter's death, and who published much of Smith's writings on the New World, wrote that Powhatan had admitted to Smith that he had personally witnessed the slaughter of the Raleigh colonists, and even showed Smith some of the "utensills" that the dead colonists had possessed. Purchas could only have learned this from Smith. Both Strachey and Purchas mention the deaths of the colonists only briefly, as if the news were common knowledge. Strachey even says that "his Majestie," King James I, had been informed of the news.

If Smith had known of the sad fate of the earlier colonists *before* this encounter with Powhatan, he would not have sent Michael Sicklemore to search for them. Since this was the last time Smith and Powhatan were ever to meet, it must have been now when Smith learned of their fate. However, Smith himself fails to mention this startling news in his account—and it would have been far more interesting to the English readers of his day than any story he could tell about little Pocahontas. Indeed, it is precisely because Smith did *not* mention the slaughter, by Powhatan, of the Roanoke settlers that historians have to this day continued to refer to them as the "lost" colonists. (That also indicates how completely historians have relied on Smith's accounts for parts of Virginia's early history.)

So why didn't Smith mention Powhatan's admission of responsibility for the deaths of the survivors of Raleigh's colony? Smith includes his conversations with the old chief in two of his three accounts of Virginia; one was published in 1612 and the other in 1624. The earlier of these works was published at Oxford, possibly because the Virginia Company blocked its publication in London, where Smith's other books were printed. The second was written by Smith as a kind of "official" history, partially sponsored by the company. In both cases, declaring that Powhatan had ordered the slaughter of the remnants of Raleigh's colonists would have produced negative publicity that neither the company nor, in the latter case, Smith himself wanted. In 1624 Smith was trying to obtain financial backing for another trip to the New World. His task would have been made more difficult if people regarded the Native Americans as bloodthirsty savages.

Smith's reaction after his final meeting with Powhatan certainly indicates that he has just made a disturbing discovery. Even at the end of their discussions, Powhatan was still trying to gain his confidence: "Captaine Smith," he said, "I never use any Werowance so kindely as your selfe, yet from you I receive the least kindnesse of any." The chief compared Smith to Captain Newport, who had treated Powhatan with respect and generosity. Possibly with another smile flickering across his face, the chief said, "Captain Newport you call father, and so you call me; but I see for . . . us both you will do what you list [please], and we must both seeke to content you." This was a perceptive thought, and shows that Powhatan had earlier observed Smith's conflicts with Newport.

Once more Powhatan insisted: if Smith truly loved him, he would prove it by coming to Powhatan without his weapons. This was, as events showed, Smith's last chance to become a member of Powhatan's tribe, but Smith did not see it that way. His analysis was that "the Salvage" was only seeking the chance to cut his throat. Something must have made him feel such distrust.

Smith tried some delaying tactics of his own. After firmly declaring where his allegiance lay ("Powhatan you must know, as I have but one God, I honour but one King; and I live not here as your subject, but as your friend"), he made a promise: "to content you," he told the chief, he would leave his arms behind when he visited the chief the following day. Smith's true intentions are revealed in a marginal note that appeared in the published version of his account: "Captaine Smiths discourse to delay time, till he found oportunity to surprise the King."

Powhatan was no more easily deceived than Smith by such professions of good faith. Leaving some of his women to talk with his visitor, the chief slipped out of the longhouse and, as he had declared he would, disappeared into the woods. He and Smith would never see each other again.

While Smith chatted with the women, some of Powhatan's men surrounded the house, waiting to ambush him when he emerged. Smith, who had brought only one companion, became enraged when he discovered the attempted ambush, and blasted his way through the crowd: "with his pistoll, sword, and target [shield] hee made such a passage among these naked Divels; that at his first shot, they . . . tumbled one over another, and the rest quickly fled some one way some another."

When Smith reached the river, he found the rest of his men waiting at the bank, having brought the barges ashore when the ice broke up. An old man arrived, bringing Smith "a great bracelet and a chaine of pearl"—presents from Powhatan as an apology for his sudden departure and the alarm Smith had suffered from the gathering of men outside the longhouse. The gift-bearer, "an ancient Oratour," made a speech in which he repeated Powhatan's request that Smith put aside his weapons, which had frightened Powhatan's people.

Instead, Smith loaded his boats with the corn he had traded for, enlisting some of the natives—at gunpoint—to help in the effort. By the time they finished, the tide had gone out, stranding the English boats on the freezing mud. Smith could only lead his men to a nearby house, where they prepared to spend the night.

Powhatan was not far off, and that night he planned, Smith says, to catch the English unawares and kill them. The bearer of this surprising news was none other than Pocahontas herself, saving Smith's life a second time. As Smith recalled it, "Powhatan . . . was making ready his forces to surprise the house. . . . [Nevertheless] the eternall all-seeing God did prevent him, and by a strange meanes. For Pocahontas his dearest jewell and daughter, in that darke night came through the irksome woods, and told our Captaine great cheare [food] should be sent us by and by: but Powhatan and all the power he could make, would after come kill us all, if they that brought it could not kill us with our owne weapons when we were at supper. Therefore if we would live shee wished us presently to bee gone."

Smith attempted to reward Pocahontas with some gifts, "but with the teares running downe her cheekes, shee said shee durst not" accept them, for if Powhatan saw her with the gifts, "she were but dead, and so shee ranne away by her selfe as she came."

Sure enough, "eight or ten lusty fellowes" soon appeared, with "great platters of venison" for Smith and his men. They asked only that Smith and his men extinguish their matches—the slow-burning fuses that were used to ignite the charges in their muskets—because the smoke made them ill. Smith not only refused, he made the gift-bearers taste every platter of the meat before allowing his own men to eat it. Throughout the night, more "messengers" kept arriving, "to see what newes." Forewarned by Pocahontas, Smith and his men kept awake and vigilant, muskets primed, until dawn.

Both sides continued the charade of friendliness as the English launched their boats. Smith even left behind the Germans to finish the house he had agreed to build for Powhatan, as well as a marksman named Edward Brynton to shoot birds for the chief's dinner.

Smith was later to regret the trust he placed in the Germans, for Powhatan sent two of them overland to Jamestown, where the unsuspecting Captain Winne was in charge. They told him that Smith had sent them for more arms. At the fort they enlisted six or seven more men in their conspiracy and carried away from Jamestown a haul of eight muskets, shot, powder, fifty swords, and eight pikes, which they subsequently delivered to Powhatan. The Germans' reward for this remarkable act of treachery was that "they should live with Powhatan . . . free from those miseries that would happen [to] the Colony."

Unaware of all this, Smith reached Pamunkey, where Powhatan's younger brother Opechancanough was werowance. At first the village seemed nearly deserted, but the chief appeared after a short time and opened trade negotiations, telling Smith that the following day the natives would have more corn for him.

Accordingly, Smith came to the chief's house the next day, accompanied by fifteen men. Opechancanough seemed to have "a strained cheerfulnesse" and spoke at length about what he had done to keep his promises. It was a delaying tactic, for suddenly one of Smith's companions, a Master Russell, came into the house and told him that some seven hundred armed natives had surrounded the dwelling. Though Opechancanough did not understand Russell's English, Smith saw by the fearful look on the chief's face that he realized his true intentions had been discovered.

Some of Smith's own men began to show fear when they understood the situation. But once more Smith rallied his company with a speech, which he quotes verbatim fifteen years after the fact, so it was no doubt improved by some editing. He begins by complaining about the "malicious Councell with their open mouthed Minions"—in other words, his bosses in England—alleging that they would accuse him of being a peace-breaker if he acted in self-defense by attacking the natives. He wished that those who called him an oppressor (and the natives "saints") were here in his place. This decidedly reads like something he tacked on when preparing the manuscript for publication in 1624.

Smith told his men to prepare to fight. He reminded them that on another occasion, he had by himself faced down two or three hundred natives. Now "wee are sixteene, and they but seaven hundred at the most." The odds in favor of survival had actually improved. He told his men that merely discharging their muskets would be enough to frighten away their enemies. "Yet howsoever," he added, "let us fight like men, and not die like sheepe: for by that meanes you know God hath oft delivered mee, and so I trust will now . . . promise me you will be valiant."

Smith turned to Opechancanough, speaking now in the chief's tongue: "I see . . . your plot to murder me, but I feare it not." He pointed out that as yet no one had been hurt on either side, and laid down a novel challenge: he and Opechancanough would put aside their weapons, shields, and armor: "My body shall be as naked as yours." Then the two would fight in hand-to-hand combat on an island in the nearby river. The victor "shall be Lord and Master over all our men." The stakes in the battle would be

Opechancanough's corn against the copper Smith had brought to trade: "the Conquerour take all."

The challenge was no doubt prompted by Smith's memories of the siege of the city on the Plains of Regall where he had first won glory by defeating the three Turks in single combat. If Opechancanough had accepted Smith's offer, yet another scene might have been added to the Englishman's catalog of valor.

Opechancanough no doubt felt he had no need to fight Smith. It appeared that the werowance had the situation in hand, so why give even odds to the Englishman? Even inside the house, the English were outnumbered, for Opechancanough had forty to fifty personal guards there, in addition to the seven hundred men outside. Soothingly, the werowance assured Smith that there was a "great present" for him at the door; all he had to do was step outside and receive it.

Instead, Smith took the initiative—so boldly that it caught Opechancanough by surprise. The native men wore their hair long on one side, while shaving it close on the other. Though Opechancanough was taller than Smith by at least six inches, Smith reached up and grasped the werowance's long hair. At the same time, he pressed his cocked pistol against Opechancanough's breast. He moved so swiftly that none of the bodyguards were able to respond. Now they were certain that any hostile move would result in their chief's death.

Smith marched "the trembling King, neare dead with feare," out the door. The assembled warriors, stunned at seeing their chief a prisoner, lowered their bows at Smith's command—and then were forced to listen to another of Smith's orations:

"I see," he began, "the great desire you have to kill me, and my long suffering [tolerating] your injuries hath imboldened you to this presumption." He recalled his promise "before the God I serve" to be their friend. "If I keepe this vow, my God will keepe me, you cannot hurt me, [but if] I break it, he will destroy me. But if you shoot but one Arrow to shed one drop of bloud of any of my men . . . you shall see I will not cease revenge (if once I begin) so long as I can . . . finde one of your Nation."

Smith proclaimed, "Here I stand, shoot he that dare." If no one dared (and no one did), then, he reminded them, they should

C. Smith taketh the King of Pamaunkee prisoner 1608

Another of Smith's exploits that was illustrated in *The General Historie of Virginia.* While he and his men were outnumbered at least fourteen to one by Opechancanough's forces, Smith seized the native commander by the hair and took him hostage—turning the tables on the man who had captured him earlier. Note the height disparity between the two men.

carry out their promise to load his ship with corn, "and so you shall, or I meane to load her with your dead carcasses." There was a carrot along with the stick, however. "If as friends you will come and trade," Smith said, then "your King shall be free and be my friend, for I am not come to hurt him or any of you."

At once the natives put away their bows and arrows and rushed to bring out their commodities to trade. Even then, Smith could not rest. He tried to, for the tension of the moment had "overwearied" him, and he lay down to sleep inside Opechancanough's house while the work of loading the boats went on.

Then, he writes, "fortie or fiftie of their choise men each with a club, or an English sword . . . began to enter the house." The noise they made stirred Smith from his slumber. He reached for his sword and shield, and with the help of a few companions charged the natives, driving them out of the house faster than they had entered.

Such exploits, which strain credulity, may seem to appear with almost monotonous regularity in Smith's writings. This latest one, however, first appeared in print in 1612, at a time when many of those who were witnesses to it were still alive. It is significant that those of Smith's companions who disliked him—Wingfield and Percy were two of the most articulate—never questioned the truth of his accounts. They had other epithets for him, but they did not call him a liar.

12

Smith Takes Charge

W HILE SMITH WAS OFF COLLECTING food supplies, council members Matthew Scrivener and Captain Waldo, along with nine other men, took a boat
across the river to the Isle of Hogs. A storm blew up, overturning
their craft, and all were lost. Richard Wiffin, one of the original
colonists, volunteered to take the grim news to Smith. Wiffin
went first to Powhatan's village, expecting to find the English
there. He was received cordially and stayed overnight, but soon
realized that there was something amiss. Pocahontas helped him
get away and gave him directions to Opechancanough's village.
Smith's account says that she deceived the men her father sent to
pursue Wiffin, sending them in another direction—yet another
instance of Pocahontas endangering herself to help the English.

Wiffin finally located Smith, who told him to keep the news
of the deaths from the other Englishmen for the time being.
Smith wanted to complete his trade mission. In the midst of additional accounts of hairbreadth escapes—poison was yet another
of the methods the natives tried—he surprisingly takes a final
swipe at the now dead Scrivener, alleging that he had received
instructions from London (presumably through Newport) "to
make himself . . . Caesar" in Virginia, and "began to decline in his
affections for Captaine Smith, [who] ever regarded him [Scriv-
ener] as [highly as] himself." Making such an allegation reflects
badly on Smith, and is further indication that some of his enemies might have been imaginary.

For good measure, Smith tosses another criticism of Newport into the story. Returning to Jamestown with some 479
bushels of corn that he had browbeaten the natives into giving
him in trade, he remarks that it could have been much more had
the gathering of corn been done in October, November, and
December, when the natives' storehouses were full from the harvest. At that time, Newport could have filled a ship with corn,
Smith claims, but he was too busy searching for the South Sea in
the Monacan country above the falls.

Sometime in early 1609, Captain Winne died. He had not
been in Virginia long, and it was probably the harsh winter and
exposure to the now endemic typhoid fever that did him in.
Touchingly, he had written a friend in England at the end of
November, "I am now willing here to end my dayes for I fine
[find] it a farr more pleasant and plentifull country than any report
made mencion of." His death left Smith as the sole council member, with no provision for appointing others, even if he had wanted
to. At least some of the colonists must have been made appre-
hensive by this development. Smith was no doubt the best person
to keep the colonists alive, but he would also be sure to make
them miserable in the effort.

Smith assembled the company and gave a speech that, while
not particularly stirring, was plainspoken. He began by cautioning
them not to think "that either my pains [efforts], nor the Adventurers purses [referring to the Virginia Company's investors] will
ever maintaine you in idlenesse and sloath." He admitted that
some among the colonists worked hard, deserving of "both honour and reward," but the majority had to become "more industrious, or starve."

In the past, the authority of the council had protected those
who did not work. No longer, Smith promised. Now "power rest-
eth wholly in my selfe: you must obey this now for a Law, that he
that will not worke shall not eate," unless illness excused them.
Smith left no doubt about the ratio of hard workers to idlers:
"the labours of thirtie or fortie honest and industrious men shall
not be consumed to maintaine an hundred and fiftie idle loyterers." This was nothing less than a revolutionary change in the

social structure of the colony. Most of the gentlemen in the fort had expected that they would not have to do much, if any, physical labor in the New World. Their role was to plan, to lead, to command. Smith was now setting forth what was to be part of the American ideal: that here men were equal in status and each one was required to make his own way.

In case there were any who resisted this idea, Smith concluded with a not so veiled threat: "there are now no more Counsellors [besides himself] to protect you, nor curbe my endevours. Therefore he that offendeth, let him assuredly expect his due punishment." For good measure he erected a large chart on which he daily recorded the work done by each man "to incourage the good, and with shame to spurre on the rest."

What the highborn gentlemen of the colony thought of this decree is difficult to ascertain. None of them had been required to do manual labor in England—that was the essence of their class privilege. Only Percy among these first Virginia gentlemen still present in the colony recorded his thoughts. Percy was unequivocal in his contempt for Smith the yeoman's son, calling him "an ambitious unworthy and vainglorious fellow." Later, however, he was to find that in Smith's absence, things began to unravel.

In the midst of Smith's efforts to inculcate a work ethic in the community, he faced a growing security problem: the "Dutchmen" (as he calls the Germans) continued to pilfer gunpowder, ammunition, swords, and tools for Powhatan, going so far as to instruct the natives in the use of firearms. The Germans had become Powhatan's permanent guests and in addition seemingly had collaborators within Jamestown itself. One day Smith heard that one of Powhatan's Germans, "a stout young fellow" disguised as a native, had gone to the small glass factory that had been built in the woods a mile from Jamestown.

The visit was actually part of a plot—hatched both by natives and by colonists hostile to Smith—to ambush the colony's leader. Smith, without giving details, says he eluded some forty men waiting to kill him, but then encountered the "King" of Paspahegh, "a most strong stout Salvage." The werowance, seeing that

Smith was armed only with a sword, attempted to shoot him with his bow. Smith ran forward before the king could notch his arrow and grabbed the bow. The two grappled in desperate combat. The king, being the taller of the two, maneuvered them into the river, where he hoped to drown Smith. The Englishman, however, got a tight grip on the king's throat, strangling him until he was so weak that Smith was able to draw his falchion. But as he prepared to cut off the king's head, the native begged for mercy. Smith fought back his rage, realizing that the werowance was worth more alive than dead. He took him back to the fort and imprisoned him.

Smith sent a message to Powhatan that he would hold the man until the paramount chief ransomed him by sending the traitorous Germans back to Jamestown. But the old chief protested that the Germans did not want to return (probably true), and he refused to have his own men carry them on their backs.

Smith permitted the wives and children of his royal prisoner to visit and bring him presents. Due to the guard's negligence, Smith wrote, the king escaped. Smith sent fifty men to recapture him, but when that effort failed, Smith himself led a force downriver. His anger caused him to act more ruthlessly than ever before. He burned houses, seized the natives' canoes and fishing nets, and killed several men.

Approaching another village, he first encountered resistance, but when the natives recognized him they laid down their bows. A negotiator named Okaning stepped forward and announced that the Paspahegh werowance, the man Smith was pursuing, was among those present. But he appealed to Smith to forgive him, for "the fishes swim, the foules fly, and the very beasts strive to escape the snare and live. Then blame not him [for] being a man." He reminded Smith that the captain himself had once been a prisoner and at that time Powhatan had mercifully spared his life. Finally, and most telling, Okaning pointed out that the English were accustomed to enjoying the fruits of the natives' labor—the corn and other crops that they grew. He repeated the threat that Powhatan had made: "[W]e know you cannot live if you want [lack] our harvest. . . . If you promise us peace, we will beleeve you; if you proceed in revenge we will abandon the Country."

Smith accepted this as wisdom, and left the Paspaheghs and their werowance in peace. When he returned to the fort, however, he found another problem: a native had stolen a pistol. Smith apparently felt he had to take severe action against the theft of weapons, so he took two of the thief's companions, who were brothers, imprisoned one, and sent the other to find the pistol. If he failed to return within half a day, Smith declared, he would hang the man's brother.

The man returned with the pistol before midnight. Unfortunately, his brother had been held in a room where a charcoal fire was burning. The fumes had overcome him, and he appeared to be dead. The surviving brother "most lamentably bewayled his death, and broke into such bitter agonies" that Smith sought to console him. If they promised never to steal again, Smith said, he would bring the dead man back to life. With a combination of brandy and vinegar poured down the unconscious man's throat, Smith performed what seemed like a miracle. Now, however, drunk from the strong liquor, the prisoner appeared to be insane, a condition that caused his brother as much grief as his apparent death had. Smith promised that this too could be cured, and gave the prisoner a comfortable place to sleep it off. In the morning the man had recovered, except for some burns he had received from the charcoal fire. With salve on these, the two brothers were sent on their way, along with some copper presents Smith had given them.

The word soon spread that Smith was such a powerful magician that he "could make a man alive that was dead." As a result, people throughout the region began sending pilfered objects back to Jamestown, including some the English had not realized were missing. Thieves were occasionally sent to Jamestown as well, to receive whatever punishment Smith levied.

By the spring of 1609, Smith was able to make a list of his accomplishments. The small factories had begun to produce glass, tar, pitch, and soap ashes; the fort had its first freshwater well, twenty more houses, a roof on the church, and a guardhouse on the narrow isthmus that connected Jamestown to the mainland. Three sows that the fort had been provided with had increased to more than sixty pigs, so many that Smith had to move them to another island, with people to tend them and make clapboard in their spare time. The other colonists, compelled to work or starve, had managed to bring between thirty and forty acres of land under cultivation, and the English could now look forward to a harvest in the fall.

A crushing blow, however, threatened to negate all these accomplishments: the corn supply accumulated by Smith from the natives through threats, violence, and promises of friendship was now found to be "halfe rotted and the rest . . . consumed [by] . . . thousands of Rats." The vermin had come over on English ships, for rats had previously been unknown in Virginia. "This did drive us all to our wits end," wrote Smith, for it meant the colonists would be forced to survive on what they could hunt or gather from the wilderness.

Smith wrote that, for a time, the natives living nearby supplied the colonists with squirrels, turkeys, deer, and other wild beasts, but that was only a stopgap solution. He decided on a drastic step: he would break up the colony at least until the time came to harvest the crops they had planted.

He assigned about seventy people to make camp on the shores of the bay "to live upon Oysters," which were so plentiful that they could simply be picked up from the bottom. Another twenty men, under Percy's leadership, he assigned a more difficult task: from a base at Point Comfort at the mouth of the James River, they would try to keep themselves alive by catching fish, something that, surprisingly, the colonists had not yet been able to do effectively. Young Francis West was sent upriver to the fall line with twenty more men, in hopes that they could hunt enough game to survive. Smith reports that this last group fared poorly because all they could find was a few acorns, of which "every man had their equall proportion."

Smith, as he customarily did, took the hardest task for himself. He kept the remaining 150 colonists, most of whom he regarded as "gluttonous Loyterers" who "would all have starved or have eaten one another" had he not compelled them to gather their own food. Left to their own devices, they would soon have bartered every object in the fort to Powhatan's people to obtain food. Once, Smith wrote, they heard the old chief was offering to trade a basket of corn. Smith bought half to placate them, "yet to have had the other halfe, they would have sould their soules, though [the corn was] not sufficient to have kept them a weeke."

Smith's plan was successful. He pointed out with pride that the colony lost only seven people during the spring and summer months, not counting those who drowned. He recalled some of the food they ate, though he fails to give recipes: "We had more Sturgeon, then could be devoured by Dog and Man, of which the industrious by drying and pounding, mingled with Caviare, Sorell and other wholesome hearbes would make bread and good meate: others would gather as much Tockwhogh roots, in a day as would make them bread [for] a weeke."

Perhaps it was not surprising that the colonists Smith had kept under his wing were ungrateful, even going so far as to want to take the pinnace back to England. "Thousands were their exclamations, suggestions, and devises," he wrote, "to . . . have made it an occasion to abandon the country." Smith assembled his malcontents and, addressing them as "fellow soldiers," made another speech, this one ranging between boasting and threats. He began by expressing his disappointment that there were any among them so false to say—or so "simple" as to believe—"that I either intend to starve you, or that Powhatan at this present [time] has corne for himselfe, much less for you, or that I would not have it, if I knew where it were to be had." In any case, he continued, "I will doe my best for my worst maligner," though if he were to find anyone else trying to make off with the pinnace, he would send them to the gallows.

"You cannot deny," Smith reminded his restive company, "but that by the hazard of my life many a time I have saved yours." Now, he insisted, "I protest by that God that made me . . . you shall not onely gather for your selves, but [for] those that are sicke." No capitalist, Smith—he sounds here more like a socialist: "The sick shall not starve, but equally share of all our labours." He issued another of his harsh decrees: "[H]e that gathereth not every day as much as I doe, the next day shall be set beyond the river, and be banished from the Fort as a drone, till he amend his conditions or starve."

The groans that must have greeted this rule can be imagined, but Smith describes the reaction more delicately: "This order many murmured was very cruell." Yet it worked, and the company survived—if unhappily.

Another problem, threatening to become a major danger, was the continued disloyalty of the Germans who were living in Powhatan's village. Smith assigned a Swiss to spy on them, presumably because he spoke German, but he too became a turncoat. Evidently the rewards Powhatan offered to "defectors" from Jamestown were tempting. Smith also implies that the Germans hoped to ally themselves with the Spanish if a punitive expedition arrived from Florida. The Germans went so far as to propose to Powhatan an attack on the fort. With his help, they would burn the pinnace and the colonists' houses. Smith got word of this when two of the plotters "whose christian hearts relented at such an unchristian act" revealed it to him. He thought that this could be an opportunity to ambush the attackers, but several of his officers, including George Percy, suggested that they take the offensive and "cut [the Germans'] throats before the face of Powhatan."

Before any of these plots and counterplots came to fruition, an English ship arrived, bearing unwelcome news. Events in the wider world beyond Virginia were about to engulf Smith's efforts.

The Spanish ambassador to England, Don Pedro de Zuñiga (who also served as the king of Spain's chief spy), had continued to warn his monarch about England's Chesapeake Bay colony. Zuñiga had frequently protested to King James and his officials that the English were settling on land claimed by Spain.

The ambassador's intelligence was often quite good. The files of the Spanish archives in which his dispatches survive contain the only known copy of a map Smith drew of Jamestown and the surrounding region, very early in his stay there. It may be a copy of a map Smith included with the manuscript of *A True Relation*, the letter he sent to an anonymous friend in England in 1608.

King James and his courtiers had diplomatically fended off Zuñiga's complaints, but they knew that Jamestown was a potential source of conflict, something James abhorred, and did not seem to be producing anything of great value to England, despite all the optimistic predictions. Moreover, the ex-councilors Smith had sent home in disgrace had given the King's Council for Virginia their own versions of what had gone wrong and what needed to be done at the colony. Smith would have done better to keep them under his eye, for they did more harm in London than they might have in Jamestown. His own irate and intemperate letter—if indeed he had sent it—could not have helped matters.

Led by Sir Thomas Smythe, governor of the East India Company, a group of wealthy merchants and other influential men proposed that the Virginia Company be reorganized. The expeditions to "Northern Virginia" had failed to establish a permanent colony, and now Jamestown in the south appeared to have serious administrative problems. Perhaps, the new investors suggested, the enterprise should be transformed into a joint-stock company like the East India Company. That way, more funds could be raised and the governance of the colony could be made more efficient.

After some consideration, the king proved only too happy to shift the burden of financing—and the complaints regularly delivered by Zuñiga—to a private group. Smythe became treasurer of this new Virginia Company, and within a few months the venture had attracted more than 650 investors. In addition, a major effort was made to attract new colonists, for the current thinking was that one of Jamestown's problems was that it had too few people. Smith, struggling to feed the ones he already had, might have issued a tart rejoinder, but at least the new company was taking his advice on the *kind* of colonists it hoped to attract. A broadside circulated in London's streets in 1609, "Concerning the Plantation of Virginia," appealed to "workmen of whatever craft they may be, blacksmiths, carpenters, coopers, shipwrights, turners and such as know how to plant vineyards, hunters, fishermen, and all who work in any kind of metal, men who make bricks, architects, bakers, weavers, shoemakers, sawyers and those who spin wool and all others, men as well as women, who have any occupation, who wish to go out in this voyage for colonizing the country with people." In short, the colony needed men and women who were willing to work, not the "Tuftaffaty humorists" who strained Smith's patience.

Besides monetary compensation and an undetermined share in the profits of the company, the would-be colonists were promised "houses to live in, vegetable gardens and orchards and also food and clothing at the expense of the Company"—making Virginia sound a good deal more comfortable than Smith and the others had experienced. So did the numerous tracts that were distributed, poems and plays that were written, and sermons preached about the glorious Virginia venture. As Zuñiga wrote to King Philip III in April 1609, "[T]hey have actually made the ministers in their sermons dwell upon the importance of filling the world with their religion and demand that all make an effort to give what they have for such a grand enterprise."

Led by Hakluyt and Harriot, the Virginia Company's publicity machine was going strong by the time Captain Samuel Argall set sail from London on May 5, 1609. He reached Jamestown on July 10, bearing a letter from the new directors of the company, with the usual criticism of Smith's "hard dealing" with the natives and failure to fill the returning ships with profitable goods. Smith was simply too distracted to pay much attention. Argall seems not to have brought more colonists, for the main purpose of his voyage was to catch sturgeon. Nor does he seem to have told Smith an important fact that would have changed the way Smith acted later: the company had named Thomas West, Lord De La Warr, as governor. De La Warr, the twelfth in his family to hold the title, had served as a soldier in both the Low Countries and Ireland. Though implicated in the Earl of Essex's plot against Elizabeth, he had been pardoned and served on the privy council in both Elizabeth's and James's reigns.

Since De La Warr was not able to leave England at once, Sir Thomas Gates was appointed acting governor, with the kind of sweeping powers Smith had thought the colony's leader should have. Gates had actually been involved in the Virginia enterprise from the beginning. In 1586 he had accompanied Sir Francis Drake when Drake "rescued" the first group of Raleigh's Roanoke colonists. Later, in 1606, Gates's name was listed among those who had petitioned King James for a charter to settle Virginia.

Even so, Gates's appointment was not intended as a slap at Smith, for the new directors of the company also named Smith to head the colony's military garrison. It is possible that Argall had not learned of these appointments before he left England. In any case, Smith's ignorance of them was later to cause misunderstanding and resentment.

Only ten days after Argall sailed from London, seven additional ships started out for Virginia, picking up two more when they passed Plymouth. This flotilla was the ambitious "third supply," on which no expense had been spared in the attempt to put Jamestown permanently on the map. More than five hundred colonists had been attracted to the expedition, lured by the promises of orchards, vegetable gardens, and houses. Christopher Newport, now a vice admiral, commanded the fleet, taking the ships on the southern route, which led to disaster. In the words of one of the other leaders of the expedition, as the ships were "about one hundred and fiftie leagues distant from the West Indies . . . there hapned a most terrible and vehement storme, which was a . . . West Indian Horacano; this *tempest* separated all our Fleet from one another." The harrowing storm lasted forty-four hours, tossing the frail wooden craft like matchsticks. After the winds subsided, four of the ships reassembled, but aboard one of them raged an epidemic thought to be plague.

The four vessels reached the James River on August 11. A lookout at the fort thought they were a Spanish flotilla and spread the alarm. When Smith learned their true identity and saw his old enemy Gabriel Archer step off one of the ships, he was dismayed. With one glance, he assumed the Virginia Company had disregarded everything he had written in the letter sent to England with Newport. John Martin, Smith soon learned, was also among those returning, and in a few days another ship arrived, carrying

John Ratcliffe, alias Sicklemore. These were men of whom Smith had written, "if [they] returne again, they are sufficient to keepe us always in factions." Evidently the leaders of the Virginia Company had taken no notice of Smith's advice—or so he thought.

"Happie had we beene had they never arrived," Smith wrote, "and we for ever abandoned." The three former councilors gleefully related to Smith the details of the new charter, conveniently omitting the role he was to play in the new government. Since the ship carrying the new acting governor, Sir Thomas Gates, had not arrived, it was clearly the right—even the duty—of Archer, Martin, and Ratcliffe to act in Gates's name.

Not so fast, replied Smith, who, although he had not attended the Inns of Court, had picked up some ideas of legal maneuvering. Where, he asked, was the charter establishing a new government in Virginia? Where were the orders that officially relieved him of office?

Actually, three copies of the new charter and accompanying orders had been sent to Virginia. One was in Gates's possession, and the other two were held by Vice Admiral Newport and Sir George Somers, who bore the title "Admiral of Virginia." Unfortunately, a dispute over precedence had led to all three of them traveling on the same ship—one that seemed to have been lost in the storm.

Smith then claimed that in the absence of any charter, his government and his presidency were still secure. Naturally, "the three busy instruments," as Percy called the former council members, disagreed. Smith reported, "It would be too tedious, too strange, and almost incredible; should I particularly relate the infinite dangers, plots, and practices," that "this factious crew" subjected him to.

In addition, he had to face the difficulty of dealing with the large number of new and inexperienced settlers who had arrived—some sick, some ready to look for gold, others wondering where their houses, vegetable gardens, and orchards were. Smith was unimpressed with the quality of the latest arrivals, noting that among them "were many unruly Gallants, packed thither by their friends to escape ill destinies."

Smith decided to use a tactic he had employed before: he would disperse some of his now unwieldy company, sending the more able ones out to fend for themselves. He let Francis West, now a figure of greater importance because his elder brother had been named governor-general of Virginia, take 120 men ("the best he could chuse") up the James River to the fall line. Presumably his earlier experiences would teach him to do more than try to survive by eating acorns.

Martin, the least offensive of the three newcomers, seemed to have recovered from his long illness, so Smith placated him by putting him and Percy in charge of sixty men and sending them to the Nansemond country, on the south bank of the James, near its mouth. The Nansemonds had heretofore been friendly to the English, and Smith hoped the two experienced captains could obtain enough corn to feed themselves and their men.

Smith's trust, however, was misplaced. Martin, apparently nervous at being this far from the fort, angered the Nansemonds by taking their werowance hostage and occupying their village. Percy's story differed from the one Smith reports, however. He said that he and Martin had sent two messengers to negotiate with the werowance, but the natives killed them, cutting and scraping their brains from their skulls with sharpened mussel shells. Percy admits that Martin took hostages and one of them was shot "accidentally."

Relations with the natives were rapidly deteriorating upriver as well. Smith set out in a small boat to check on West and his men; he met West himself, on his way back to Jamestown, apparently frustrated with the situation. Smith continued upriver, and found that the colonists had settled in a spot that was sure to be inundated by flooding at the first hard rainfall. He knew there was a suitable place nearby, but it was occupied by a small group of natives. He sent a message to Powhatan, offering to purchase the site for a quantity of copper, and pointing out that having an English fort there, on the edge of the Monacan country, would be a defensive bulwark for Powhatan's empire. The old chief saw the truth of this; he agreed to allow the English to settle there.

Smith happened to have brought on the trip a fourteen-year-old boy, Henry Spelman, who had just arrived from England. Spelman must have gotten himself into trouble at home, for his family was prosperous enough to have sent him to school or given him a better start in life than packing him off to America. His rich uncle was involved with other overseas voyages, and it was probably through his influence that young Henry shipped out as a colonist. Smith, in much the same way that Newport had bestowed Thomas Savage on Powhatan earlier, now transferred custody of young Henry Spelman to the natives who were yielding their village to the English. Spelman, who spoke none of the native language, misunderstood; he was later to write that Smith sold him to the natives as part of the price of the village. His sojourn with the natives, however, proved beneficial to modern ethnologists, for he wrote a detailed account of the customs and culture of the Powhatans.

Smith's efforts on behalf of West's men went for naught because the colonists refused to abide by the terms he had negotiated. They invaded the neighboring Powhatan villages, "stealing their corne, robbing their gardens, beating them, breaking their houses and keeping some prisoners." The natives complained to Smith that the settlers he had promised would be their protectors had turned out to be worse enemies than the Monacans.

Smith had only five men with him, and West's settlers numbered about 120. So Smith started back to Jamestown, feeling unable to restore order. As soon as he departed, the natives attacked the flimsy fort that West's people had built, slew "many" of the English, and rescued the native prisoners held there.

Having not gotten far because his boat had run aground on a mud bank, Smith soon learned of the attack. He returned and took command, arresting six or seven of the colonists whom he judged most unruly. He negotiated a truce and succeeded in moving the settlers to the site he had intended for them, giving it the wry name Nonesuch. (It was the same name Queen Elizabeth used for her favorite castle.)

West himself now returned to the scene, and the men Smith had imprisoned appealed to him, claiming that they had been acting "for his honor." It was generally known that West's brother was to be the new governor-general, and that fact implicitly gave West the authority to overrule Smith. He did so, releasing the prisoners and moving the whole company back to their original location.

All this makes for a confusing story, and it is even more so in Smith's account. He reverts here to his habit of continually justifying his actions whenever they are questionable. For Smith did face some serious accusations about this incident. Henry Spelman, an eyewitness, later wrote that because of the dispute over the proper location for West's satellite colony, "unkindness" arose between the two leaders. Spelman reported, "Captain Smith at that time replied little, but afterward conspired with the Powhatan to kill Captain Weste, which plot took but small efect."

That judgment might be dismissed as another misunderstanding, due to Spelman's immaturity, but George Percy—who was not at the scene but heard about it afterward from witnesses—wrote that "a great division did grow amongst them [Smith and West]. Captaine Smith, perceiving both his authority and person neglected, incensed and animated the savages against Captain West and his company, reporting unto them that our men had no more powder left than would serve for one volley of shot."

Percy's harsh judgment, that Smith was angriest when his "authority and person" were challenged, is a shrewd one. That was indeed Smith's character flaw, but was the challenge posed by West and his men sufficient to provoke Smith into turning traitor to his own people? In view of everything else known about him, the answer has to be no.

For the present, Smith threw up his hands and left West to his own devices. With his five companions, he boarded his boat and began to ride the tide back downriver to Jamestown. Sitting in the bottom of the boat, exhausted by all he had been through, Smith dozed off. A spark, probably from one of the flintlock matches that were kept burning in case of attack, idly landed on the pouch of gunpowder strapped to his waist. He awoke to find himself on fire; only his tumbling over the side of the boat saved his life. But when his men pulled him from the water, they found he was horribly burned from his waist to his thighs, and on this trip there was no doctor with a healing salve. Smith had to endure the hundred-mile trip to the fort in agonizing pain. He arrived, alive, and his men brought him to bed to rest.

Even in Jamestown, he found no peace nor pity, for Ratcliffe and Archer planned to have him murdered as he lay sleeping. According to Smith, the man chosen to do the job lost his nerve. Now Smith's enemies banded together and demanded his resignation. Smith was too weak to resist. He told the captain of a ship scheduled to leave the next day that he wished to be a passenger.

Still Smith's foes refused to allow him to depart with the honor due him; they treated him the same as Wingfield—packing him off to London with a list of grievances and charges filed by anyone who could think of a decision they questioned or a punishment they resented. Ratcliffe wrote to Lord Salisbury (Robert Cecil), the king's chief minister, "Captain Smith . . . who reigned sole governor, without assistance . . . would at first admitt of no Councell but himselfe. This man is sent home to answer some misdeamenors, whereof I perswade me he can scarcely clear himselfe from great imputation of blame."

On October 4, 1609, as the ship carrying Smith threw off its lines and headed toward the sea, his prospects seemed hardly better than they had when he first landed in chains, almost exactly two and a half years earlier. Whether he was standing on deck or lying in a bunk below, he must have promised himself that he was not finished with America. He would see it again.

As for revenge on those who had wronged him, America itself would take care of that. Smith himself would triumph in a way people who had opposed him never suspected: through the power of his pen.

13

"My Hands Have Been My Lands"

NOTHING IS KNOWN OF SMITH'S ACTIVITIES during the five years after he left Virginia. Presumably he effectively defended himself against the charges that had been made against him in Jamestown, for no punishment was ever levied on him. Since most of those charges accused him of poorly administering the affairs of the colony, it is appropriate to look briefly at what happened in Jamestown after he departed and others were permitted to run things as they saw fit.

Smith's immediate successor was Percy, who became de facto governor, even though he had planned to quit the colony and return to England. The others persuaded him to remain because he was the only figure they could agree on as a leader. Ratcliffe, Martin, and West were newly elected to the council, serving along with "some few of the best and worthyest that inhabite at James-town" as Percy's "assistants," according to Ratcliffe. The phrase he chose suggests that the highborn gentlemen had once more assumed what they regarded as their rightful place in the social order of Jamestown.

Ratcliffe's letter, sent to Lord Salisbury on October 4, 1609, on the same ship that carried Smith, has a tone of confidence, even arrogance. Winter was coming on, but that didn't concern Ratcliffe, for at last Smith was no longer there to harass the gentlemen into performing manual labor, planting and harvesting their own crops. Ratcliffe mentions his long-range plan for provisioning the colony: "[I]f I might be held worthye to advise the directors [of the Virginia company] of their busines: I hold it fitt that ther should be a sufficient supply of victualls for one yeare." He evidently meant the company should *send* that much in the next supply. Meanwhile, he intended to follow Smith's lead in obtaining corn and venison from the natives.

Powhatan, however, proved unyielding. He ordered a halt to all trading with the English, and in Smith's absence the colonists had no leader strong enough to overcome the recalcitrant natives. It would prove to be a hard winter in Jamestown.

Percy himself later wrote an account of that winter of 1609–1610—what he called the "starving time." It makes for depressing reading, as the hapless colonists descended from hunger into savagery. John Martin, whom Percy had left in charge at Point Comfort, the island near the mouth of the James where the colonists had earlier established a base, unexpectedly returned to Jamestown alone. He had left Michael Sicklemore in charge of the garrison, where seventeen of the men mutinied, took a boat, and fled to the natives at nearby Kecoughtan. But the natives were no longer accepting English deserters, and the mutineers were "served according to their deserts," says Percy. None were ever heard from again. A similar fate was in store for Sicklemore, who had taken some of his remaining loyal men to trade with the natives. An English search party later found their bodies with the mouths stuffed full of corn bread. It was clearly meant as a signal that the colonists should no longer try to obtain food from the natives.

Meanwhile, up by the fall line, young Francis West was demonstrating that he was capable of getting into trouble even when Smith was not "conspiring" against him. After losing eleven men and a boat, apparently to the natives, he returned to Jamestown with the remnants of his force. Percy wrote that "in charity we could not deny them" refuge, and the colony's dwindling store of food grew smaller.

Ratcliffe now attempted to imitate Smith's earlier successes, going directly to Powhatan to procure new food supplies. At first the "subtell owlde foxe" (as Percy described him) pretended to negotiate. He had a reason: Ratcliffe had taken as hostages two of the old chief's children. Unfortunately, Ratcliffe was careless enough to let them escape, and when Powhatan learned this, he had his men take the English trade delegation into custody. Ratcliffe, says Percy, was bound naked to a tree with a fire burning in front of him. Native women cut off strips of his flesh with mussel shells and threw the pieces into the flames until death relieved him of his agony. Seventeen of Ratcliffe's men, out of the original fifty, escaped to tell the tale.

Percy once again turned to West, sending him north to the Potomacks, who were, he hoped, outside Powhatan's influence and might be persuaded to trade. Taking thirty-six men in a pinnace, West proved ruthless in pursuit of supplies—even Percy remarks on his "harsh and cruel dealing . . . cutting off two of the savages' heads," as well as the hands and feet of others. The natives gave West what he wanted, enough corn to fill the pinnace, and he turned south, heading for the entrance to the bay. Passing the lightly manned lookout post there, he was hailed by the English commander, who urged him to hurry up the James to bring relief to the colonists. Instead, West hoisted his sails and turned east, bound for the Atlantic and England, "and left us in . . . extreme misery and want," wrote Percy.

West made it back to England, and two years later actually returned to the colony he had deserted, given a new assignment as commander of the fort. Smith must have reflected bitterly on this latest proof that the accident of high birth could excuse incompetence, cowardice, and even treachery.

As the wintry gusts descended on the little fort and its inhabitants, Percy became eloquent in his description: "All of us at Jamestown [felt] that sharp prick of hunger which no man [can] truly describe [unless] he . . . hath tasted the bitterness thereof. A world of miseries ensued." So desperate did the colonists become that Percy was obliged to protect the food storehouse by executing those who tried to rob it.

The colonists ate the horses and then the remainder of their livestock. Next into the cooking pot were cats and dogs, then whatever rats and mice could be trapped; finally, the colonists ate their boots, shoes, and any other leather items in the fort. When those were gone, the settlers ventured into the woods, looking for snakes or frogs and digging in the hard, frozen ground in search of roots—anything that might provide sustenance.

Outside the fort, the colonists themselves became prey for the natives, who ambushed and killed all the Englishmen they could. Powhatan sensed their weakness and now moved to wipe them out. Percy relates that some of the colonists ran away, hoping to find refuge among the natives, but were never heard from again.

Huddled inside the fort, the colonists dug corpses from their graves for food; some, Percy says, "licked up the blood which hathe fallen from their weake fellowes." The most desperate of all was a man who murdered his pregnant wife, "ripped the child out of her womb and threw it into the river and after[ward] chopped the mother in pieces and salted her for his food." After torturing the man to force him to confess, Percy had him executed.

During this time, the long-lost passengers aboard the *Sea Enterprise*, the lost flagship of the fleet that had set out for Jamestown in May 1609, were faring somewhat better than the colonists. A record of their adventures was kept by William Strachey, later to become secretary of the Virginia colony. Strachey relates that the hurricane ("the tempest," he called it, providing the title for the play William Shakespeare wrote after reading his account) that had dispersed the fleet blew him and his companions onto the island of Bermuda. There they constructed two smaller boats and, a full year after leaving England, completed their journey to Virginia, arriving on May 21, 1610.

Expecting to find a thriving, busy settlement, Strachey and the others were shocked when they discovered only about sixty emaciated wretches assembled on the beach crying, "We are starved. We are starved." These were all that remained of the five hundred colonists who had arrived the year before and the one hundred or so that had been there when Smith was governor.

The fort was virtually a ruin. The palisades had been torn down; the gates were off their hinges. Houses whose occupants had died had been torn apart for firewood, though there were, as Strachey noted, stands of trees right outside the fort, should anyone have had the energy to cut them down. Only the natives' fear of firearms had kept Powhatan's people from overwhelming and destroying the English settlement.

Sir Thomas Gates, officially lieutenant governor, now took charge. Archer had starved to death, so only Percy and Martin were left of the leadership group that had sent Smith packing. Since Gates had brought another 150 mouths to feed but had just a few days' food supplies, he made the only choice that seemed sensible: to abandon the colony, pack the survivors aboard the ships, and try to reach England. The decision, says Strachey, met with "a general acclamation and shouts of joy on both sides, for even our owne men began to be disheartened and faint, when they saw the misery of the others."

On June 7, the colonists boarded the two small flimsy vessels that Gates had brought from Bermuda. Gates himself was the last man on shore, for he had to forcibly prevent the bitter colonists from putting the settlement to the torch.

Thus, in the eight months since Smith had left Jamestown, the colony had declined to the point of abandonment. The discipline that he instilled in the colonists, the respect he commanded from the natives, the resourcefulness he showed in making sure there was enough food to ensure survival—without these, Jamestown was unable to persevere. This is not boasting or exaggeration on Smith's part; it is the testimony of others, and should long ago have quelled any doubts about Smith's importance to the establishment of the first permanent English settlement in America.

Permanent it remained, in another of those amazing twists of fate that regularly appear in Smith's story. For as the gangplanks were hauled up and the ships' sails set, another vessel came into view downriver. Lord De La Warr, the appointed governor of Jamestown, had made an unusually speedy crossing of the Atlantic and was now coming up the James with two ships from London carrying three hundred healthy new colonists and a year's supply of food. Percy and his starving companions returned to the fort, no doubt stunned by yet another reversal of fortune and the news that they could not go back to England. Jamestown was saved—just barely.

Smith had reached London sometime in November of 1609 and could conceivably have sailed with De La Warr, who did not embark for Jamestown until April 1 of the following year. That he failed to do so probably indicates he needed time to recuperate from his injuries, though it would have been satisfying for him to return to the colony knowing that he had been named to the governing council, despite all the attempts of his enemies to discredit him and charge him with offenses Ratcliffe had believed he could "scarcely clear himselfe from." Indeed, it was against the interests of the Virginia Company to point the finger of blame at anyone, for at this time the company was assiduously trying to hide its dirty laundry, not air it. Strachey's letter that related the horrifying conditions at Jamestown was suppressed (it's not known how Shakespeare got a look at it), as were all other accounts that hinted at discord, deprivation, or disasters.

Once in England, Smith received another surprise: he was a published author. His earlier letter to a friend had been turned over to someone who edited it (to our loss), cutting sections that he thought "fit to be private." The work was published in book form, at first under the supposed authorship of another man, until later editions acknowledged that Smith was the author. Not a man to willingly allow others to present their versions of his work, Smith linked up with Samuel Purchas and William Symonds, two clergymen-scholars who were following in the large footsteps of Richard Hakluyt. In those days, men who wished to spend their lives in scholarly pursuits after graduating from Oxford or Cambridge obtained sinecures as parish priests in the Church of England. Symonds had received his post through the sponsorship of Robert Bertie, now Lord Willoughby, so it is likely that Smith became acquainted with Symonds through his old friend from Lincolnshire.

Purchas was attempting to carry on Hakluyt's work of collecting and publishing accounts of English voyages of discovery.

He was to cooperate closely with Smith and provide annotations of his work. Purchas's chief fault as a compiler was that he edited and excised too strongly, but in Smith's case he usually did not wield his editorial ax with abandon.

Symonds, Purchas, and Smith set out to publish a book on Virginia, specifically Jamestown, that would be as objective and useful as the work Harriot and White had produced for the Roanoke colony. Unfortunately, Jamestown had no artist to record its scenes. Smith was, however, lucky enough to work with a skilled engraver, William Hale, who executed a precise copy of the map Smith had made of the Chesapeake Bay area. Its accuracy was highly regarded for many years—so much so that in the late nineteenth century it was cited as evidence in a boundary dispute between the states of Virginia and Maryland. Hale included on the map a rendering of Powhatan holding court in his longhouse and a depiction of a Sasquesahanock warrior (one of those whose height impressed Smith).

Smith wrote a section of the work in which he gave a full and detailed description of the land of the Chesapeake region, its resources, and the customs and culture of the people who inhabited it. He also lists some words and phrases in the language of Powhatan's people, including this intriguing one: *Kekaten pokahontas patiaquagh ningh tanks manotyens neer mowchick rawrenock audowgh*, which he translates, "Bid Pokahontas bring hither two little Baskets, and I wil [*sic*] give her white beads to make her a chaine."

Even though Smith did not have the educational background of Harriot, his work is highly regarded as a valuable record of the culture of these Native Americans at the time of first European contacts. He misunderstood some of what he saw; for example, when boys were taken to a secluded place for initiation rites, Smith concluded that they were being "sacrificed." Nevertheless, from all that later investigation and interpretation have turned up, it is clear that he was not inventing his material.

Symonds and Purchas also collected the notes and accounts of others who had been at Jamestown to produce a work known as *A Map of Virginia*. Smith is listed as its principal author, but at least eight other men, including Smith's faithful ally Anas Todkill, had a hand in the writing.

There was apparently some difficulty in getting the book into print. The Virginia Company was trying to make sure that Jamestown was only presented to the public in the most positive way, to ensure that more people would volunteer to be colonists. Printing books was a business that had to be licensed by the crown, and all the printers in London appearently were warned not to print *A Map of Virginia*. There were only two other licensed presses in England, at Oxford and at Cambridge. William Symonds, an Oxford graduate, no doubt put his connections to good use, for the book was published at his alma mater in 1612.

Smith's general responsibility for the text is made clear by a dedication he wrote to Sir Edward Seymour, the Earl of Hertford, whom Smith calls "my honorable good Lord and Maister." Dedications like this were common, to obtain protection and acknowledge the patronage of a wealthy or titled person. Smith, however, puts an unusual spin on it, praising the earl for his "virtue" and then adding, "Though riches now be the chiefest greatnes of the great: when great and little are born, and dye, there is no difference: Vertue only makes men more than men."

This somewhat egalitarian sentiment is followed by a passage that implies Smith's offer to continue in the service of the Virginia Company had been turned down: "I . . . present your Honour with this rude discourse. . . . It is the best gift I can give to the best friend I have. It is the best service I ever did to serve so goode a worke: Wherein having been discouraged from doing any more, I have write this little."

Smith makes a reference to a Renaissance proverb: "Yet my hands have been my lands this fifteene yeares in Europ, Asia, Afric, or America." A man "without lands"—that is, not a member of the gentry—had to use his hands, as Smith had, to make his way in the world. More significantly, he makes here for the first time the claim that he had already been on four continents, though he would not set down the full story of his pre-Jamestown adventures for another eighteen years.

He had much more to do before it was time to reminisce. Probably with the assistance of his titled friends, Lord Willoughby and the Earl of Hertford, he persuaded four London business-men to outfit a voyage to the New World, putting him in com-plete command from the beginning. This was not to be a colo-nial venture; Smith wanted to establish himself first as a man who could earn money for his backers. In theory the purpose of the expedition was to go whaling in the waters where Bartholomew Gosnold had sailed in 1602. For good measure, Smith had prom-ised the sponsors of the voyage to "make trials of a mine of gold and copper," for he well understood that the allure of precious metals could make wealthy men's eyes glitter.

The two ships in Smith's flotilla set sail on March 3, 1614, and less than two months later came in sight of Monhegan Island near West Penobscot Bay in today's Maine. Smith and Thomas Hunt, captain of the second ship, soon discarded the whaling idea after they found that the predominant species of whales in the area were "Jubartes," as Smith called them. They were large, fierce, and apparently not the kind that yielded valuable whale oil.

Still determined to bring home a profitable cargo, Smith set the crews to fishing, drying and salting the catch before storing it in the ships' holds. Meanwhile, he himself took a small group of men and started along the coast, seeking to trade with the natives for food. His sharp eye began to note landmarks, comparing them with maps of the region he had bought in England. He would later write that the maps "did mee no more good, than so much waste paper, though they cost me more."

Smith would make his own map, and it would prove as accu-rate as the Chesapeake Bay one, even though he had less time to scout the coastline here. Originally, he wrote down the native names for places, whenever he could ascertain them. Later, no less a personage than Prince Charles, who had become heir appar-ent to the throne of England on the death of his elder brother Henry, would see the map and suggest names—English ones—for its features. There was no denying a royal request, of course, so Smith complied when he printed the map in his next book, dedicated to Prince Charles. He did provide a list of the original names with the new ones, so we know that the river called Mass-achusetts by those who lived near its banks became the Charles

River; that what was once Aumoughcawgen is today Cambridge; Sowocatuck is Ipswich, and so on.

Interestingly, one of the names Smith originally gave to a place along the coast was neither Native American nor English— it was Smith's attempt to spell a Turkish name: Trabigzanda, the young woman to whom he had once been given as a slave. His Turkish mistress was on his mind. (Not knowing of the meaning the name held for Smith, Prince Charles changed Cape Trabigzanda to Cape Ann, honoring his mother.)

Though Smith's coastal journey was but a brief one, it inspired him with great plans. The region was fertile, teeming with game, and its inhabitants were friendly. Some of them had been trading with French trappers for several years. This would be the place to which John Smith could lead a new group of settlers to found a colony and do it the right way (his way). All he needed was money.

Thus, when he left America in July, he headed for Plymouth, the western port city of England, for there he knew he would find Sir Ferdinando Gorges, governor of Plymouth Fort. Gorges had been a member of the Virginia Company of Plymouth, now defunct, swallowed up by the London Company when the colonial venture was reorganized in 1609. In the same year Jamestown was founded, the Plymouth Company had tried and failed to establish a colony in "northern Virginia"—the area Smith had just visited. Smith had no doubt heard about Gorges years earlier from Bartholomew Gosnold, and realized that he was the most likely person to help put into practice his new plan.

Smith's judgment was correct. Gorges had in fact sponsored a second voyage to "northern Virginia" in 1611, in an attempt to follow up Gosnold's earlier discoveries, but it had accomplished little except to bring some natives back to England. One of these, named Epenow, was shrewd enough to tell Gorges that he knew the location of a gold mine near Cape Cod. Like Smith, he had learned what appealed most to English gentlemen. So in 1614 Gorges had sent Epenow with a fishing expedition to the cape. As soon as the ship approached the coast, however, Epenow spotted some of his friends in canoes, jumped overboard, and was never seen again.

Thus Smith could not have met Gorges at a more favorable moment, for the governor was looking for someone to renew the search for that gold mine, and Smith—confident, ebullient, and with considerable American experience to his credit—was ready to take the role. Of course, Smith had grander plans: he proposed that Gorges sponsor a colony in northern Virginia. It seems to have been at this meeting that Smith coined a new name for the region. The term "northern Virginia" carried unpleasant connotations of the brutally cold winters that previous visitors had described. The weather was in fact among the reasons why the 1607 colony had been abandoned. Smith demonstrated the spirit of a true promoter when he came up with the name "New England," which has stuck ever since. Perhaps he took his inspiration from Sir Francis Drake, his boyhood idol, who when sailing up the Pacific coast of North America in 1579 had dubbed the land New Albion—a more poetic name for Smith's and Drake's homeland.

Though others would be attracted by the name New England, Gorges was not to be convinced merely by a name change that it was worth additional investment to establish a colony there. Smith went on to London, where the sale of his ship's cargo did not quite pay for the voyage. Nonetheless, he was able to raise enough funds for another expedition. He had to dilute his intentions (or mask them) somewhat: this would again be primarily a fishing trip, but it was agreed that Smith and sixteen other men would stay behind as the foundation of a colony.

The plan shows that Smith was either desperate or recklessly overconfident. Given that six hundred people could be reduced to sixty starving wretches during a single winter at Jamestown, where the climate was milder, what chance would seventeen men have in New England?

Perhaps thinking that when push came to shove, Smith would give up the rash idea and concentrate on fishing—as indeed Gosnold had in 1602—Gorges agreed to buy into the venture. When his sponsorship became known, others followed suit, and Smith set out once again with two ships in the spring of 1615. His optimism soon ran afoul of reality. The smaller of the two ships was much swifter than the flagship in which Smith was sailing. It disappeared over the horizon, and Smith's ship proved so shoddily constructed that its masts broke, compelling him to make his way back to Plymouth, using only the spritsail and a makeshift mainmast.

Gorges still had enough faith in the plan to outfit another ship in time for Smith to depart Plymouth on June 24. Unfortunately, a few days out at sea, he encountered a pirate vessel, considerably larger and better armed than his own. His officers advised him to allow the pirates to come aboard. That was foreign to Smith's nature, and for two days he tried to outrun the other ship. At last his officers took control and hove to while Smith retreated to his cabin.

When the pirates boarded, they found that Smith's ship contained nothing of value to them—since they had no interest in colonizing—but more remarkably, some of them discovered who was captain of the vessel and recalled that John Smith had been their companion on some military expedition. Smith does not relate in detail what exploits they had shared, but he does mention that they now invited him to join them, crew and vessel as well, and go off seeking prey together.

Smith declined this friendly proposal, and was allowed to sail on unmolested. By the time he approached the Azores, however, he encountered two more pirate ships, French ones this time. Once more his officers advised him to yield, and as before he refused. The ships exchanged cannon fire, and Smith then declared he would set fire to the powder magazine and sink his ship before he would surrender it. The French sailed away.

A day later, Smith's ship encountered an even more formidable force—four French ships, men-of-war on a privateering expedition. They claimed to have letters of marque from the French government authorizing them to board Spanish and Portuguese ships. The fact that the captains were Protestants, Huguenots from La Rochelle, persuaded Smith to deal with them rather than fight, and he went aboard one of the pirate ships to show his papers. When a storm blew up, he signaled for his own vessel's master to send a boat to pick him up. Instead, the crew set their sails and made their escape. As Smith watched them go, he must have reflected bitterly that the people he had selected to take him to America and undergo the hardships of a colony had proved unworthy of his trust.

In time, Smith would get his revenge, but for now he made the most of the circumstances. The French treated him courteously, in the fashion of an honored prisoner, giving him the "great cabin" to live in. He soon found that they were more pirates than privateers; he remained with them nearly three months, keeping a record of the ships they attacked and plundered. Never one to remain idle, he also wrote the manuscript that would be published as *A Description of New England*, certainly the most influential book ever written aboard a pirate ship.

The French commander had promised to put Smith ashore at some point, but when they reached a small French port, he locked him in the cabin so he could not leave. Putting to sea again, the ships encountered a storm so severe that the crew sought refuge below decks. Smith saw his opportunity and "in the darke night" he launched a boat, taking his manuscript with him. Throughout a "fearefull night of gusts and raine," he drifted, continually bailing water from his frail craft. He made it to an island, where some hunters found him "neere drowned, and halfe dead, with water, colde, and hunger."

The hunters brought Smith to La Rochelle, where he learned that the ship from which he had escaped had been sunk in the storm, drowning its captain and half the crew. He went to local officials to tell his story; there he confronted some of the survivors, who were astonished to see him. They didn't know what others had learned: Smith was a hard man to kill.

A kind Frenchwoman named Madame Chanoyes took the penniless Smith under her wing—another woman who found his charms irresistible. Part of the pirate ship's cargo was salvaged and Smith made a claim for damages. But he grew tired of the pace of the French courts and returned to England, where he had more pressing business: tracking down his officers and crew who had left him to the mercies of the French pirates. He found some of them at Plymouth, where they had divided among themselves his "clothese, bookes, instruments, Armes, and what I had." They had sought to bury him figuratively, "and not only buried mee,

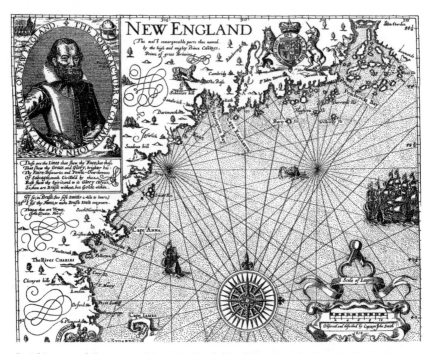

Smith's map of that part of America he dubbed New England. Aided by Prince Charles, the heir to the British throne, he dotted the map with English names that remain today. At upper left is the only known portrait of Smith, who had now assumed the title "Admirall of New England."

but with so much infamy as such trecherous cowards could suggest their villainies."

He "laied by the heeles" the organizers of the mutiny and brought the case to court, where some who were aboard the ship confessed what had happened. What kind of restitution Smith obtained is not known. He salvaged the one thing most important to him: his good name.

Smith next went down to London and began to make arrangements to publish the book he had written on board the French ship. He could not have expected to make much money on it, but it would serve as a promotional piece that would advance his true aim: to found a colony in America. Possibly through one of his noble friends, he even gained a royal patron. The new heir to the throne, Prince Charles, accepted his offer to sprinkle the map of

New England with names of Charles's choosing. The map was engraved by Simon Van de Passe, a Dutch artist who had settled in England. Van de Passe also contributed the only likeness of Smith that exists. At thirty-six, he shows his years of struggle: under a receding hairline and wrinkled brow, somber, wary eyes peer out above a bushy mustache and beard. He wears a wide collar, but not the frilled ruff that adorns the necks of so many noblemen in portraits of the day. Sporting a leather jerkin, instead of a velvet coat, he allows his hand to rest upon the hilt of his sword. This is clearly a soldier, not a courtier.

A Description of New England was published in June 1616. Only sixty pages long, it describes in some detail the region Smith had observed on or near the coast. He goes on to declare the "true" dimensions of North America, arriving at a more accurate estimate than anyone before him. His purpose was to point out that the Spaniards controlled only a small part of it: "more than halfe is yet unknowne." Thus the way was still open for the English to lay claim to large parts of the continent.

This small work was to have repercussions that would resound through the centuries; writing it may have been the most important thing Smith ever did. For he hit on a theme that was to become the foundation of the attraction that drew millions of immigrants to the English colonies and, later, the United States. Smith was doing nothing less than declaring the American dream of opportunity for all: "[H]ere every man may be master and owner of his owne labour and land. . . . If hee have nothing but his hands, he may . . . by industrie quickly grow rich."

It was a powerful message—one directed to Englishmen of the time, who were gradually being denied use of the common land they had farmed for generations—and it would prove to have universal appeal. Smith sounds very much as if he is describing himself when he writes, "Who can desire more content, that has small meanes; or but only his merit to advance his fortune, than to tread, and plant that ground he hath purchased by the hazard of his life . . . what to such a minde can bee more pleasant, then planting and building a foundation for his Posteritie, gotte from the rude earth, by Gods blessing and his owne industrie?"

The marginal note next to this passage marks it as "A note for men that have great spirits, and smal meanes."

Few people had ever before expressed the belief that anyone could be master and owner of his own labor and land. Carried to its logical conclusion, the idea was revolutionary: that society should be a meritocracy in which people could rise through talent, hard work, and ambition. Who more likely to enjoy that opportunity than the talented and obstreperous Captain John Smith?

14

The Dream Survives the Man

IN THE SAME MONTH THAT *A Description of New England* was published, June 1616, a ship carrying an old friend of Smith's came up the Thames to London. Pocahontas was a young woman now, no longer the little girl who had saved John Smith from death. Moreover, she was married to one of the colonists, John Rolfe, and had given birth to his son. All this must certainly have been a surprise to Smith when he first heard of it.

Lord De La Warr, after arriving just in time to save the colony in May 1610, had not stayed long, owing to ill health. Stewardship of Jamestown had first fallen to Sir Thomas Dale and then to Sir Thomas Gates, men whose harsh and strict rule must have caused any colonist to look back with nostalgia to John Smith's time as governor.

Dale had recognized that Jamestown's location was part of the reason why so many of its settlers fell ill and died. He established a second settlement farther up the James River, near the place Smith had earlier chosen and Francis West had abandoned. Dale set three hundred men to the task of clearing a seven-acre site, which they accomplished in ten days. Then they built high watchtowers, providing security against Powhatan's people. This new settlement, called Henrico after James I's eldest son, would in time become larger and more prosperous than the original location of the colony.

Dale got results—but at a price. He levied corporal punishments, including death, for a wide variety of infractions, great and small. Smith's punishment for cursing (pouring water down a man's sleeve) seems like a joke compared to Dale's penalty for the same offense: piercing the offender's tongue with a bodkin, an instrument usually used to make holes in leather. For other offenses, there were worse punishments, according to a complaint filed later: "the slaughter of his Majesty's free subjects by starveing, hangeinge, burninge, breakinge upon the wheele and shootinge to death." Those who tried to escape Dale by fleeing to the natives were later hunted down and burned to death by the English governor. "Some for stealinge to satisfie their hunger were hanged, and one chained to a tree till he starved to death . . . extraordinary publishments, workinge as slaves in irons for terme of yeares (and that for petty offenses) weare dayly executed."

Dale thought he had also found a solution to his problems with the natives. In 1613, Captain Samuel Argall, on another of his visits to the colony, had lured Pocahontas on board his ship and held her hostage. Though Pocahontas had lately been out of favor with her father, Powhatan, the old chief still loved her, and agreed to Dale's demand to return some English captives and provide corn to the colonists once the harvest was in.

An uneasy peace ensued, for the English could not afford to release Pocahontas, although they treated her as befitted a royal captive. Governor Dale sent her to the best part of the colony, Henrico, where she came under the care of the Reverend Alexander Whitaker, a Puritan clergyman and graduate of Cambridge, who had come to America in 1611 with the ambition of becoming "apostle to the Indians." Whitaker was delighted with this chance to further his work, and Pocahontas, already fascinated by the ways of the English, proved an apt and willing pupil. Her knowledge of spoken English increased and she learned to read. She also began to dress as an Englishwoman. Just as whalebone stays in an Englishwoman's gown now shaped her figure, so Whitaker formed her mind. Pocahontas expressed her wish to become a Christian, and took the name Rebecca at her baptism.

The name seems not to have been capriciously chosen. Whitaker no doubt knew of the verse in Genesis 25:23, which reads, "And the Lord said to her [Rebecca] two nations are in thy wombe, and two manner of people shall be divided out of thy bowels, and the one people shall be mightier than the other, and the elder shall serve the younger." In time, that passage would prove eerily prophetic.

One of those who had come to know Pocahontas at Henrico was John Rolfe, one of the men who had sailed for Jamestown on Gates's ship in 1609, been shipwrecked on Bermuda, and arrived in Virginia with the survivors in 1610. Rolfe's origins are something of a mystery. No one has been able to trace his background definitively. What is known is that he had brought a wife with him from England, she gave birth to a daughter on Bermuda, and both mother and child were dead by the time Rolfe reached Jamestown.

Even more mysterious is the origin of the great gift Rolfe brought, or stole: seeds of the fine strain of tobacco that would quickly become the mainstay of Virginia's economy. Powhatan's people grew and smoked tobacco, but it had a harsh, bitter taste. The Spaniards, on their West Indian plantations, grew a much smoother-tasting leaf that was much in demand in the European market. Though the seeds were jealously guarded, somehow Rolfe obtained a supply, and the economic future of the colony was assured.

Because of Rolfe's important contribution, he felt entitled to write Governor Dale with what he evidently regarded as an unusual, if not sinful, request. He wanted to marry Pocahontas. Rolfe's very long letter reveals the mind of a man who has tortured himself on the subject. He rebukes himself with the biblical condemnation of the sons of Levi and Israel for marrying "strange wives." He confesses his fear that his feelings for Pocahontas "are wicked instigations hatched by him who seeketh and delighteth in man's destruction."

Yet Rolfe tries to convince Dale—as he is so obviously struggling to convince himself—that the marriage would be a service to God, to England, to the colony, and to the cause of "converting an unregenerate [Pocahontas] to regeneration." His desire for the brown-skinned teenager is thereby sanctified. Dale evidently agreed, as did Pocahontas, and the couple celebrated their vows in April 1614. Powhatan signaled his consent by sending one of his brothers and two of his sons to the ceremony, though the paramount chief still refused to visit any of the English settlements. Within a year's time Pocahontas gave birth to a son, christened Thomas after Governor Dale. In the spring of 1616, the little family boarded a ship for England.

Hearing of Pocahontas's arrival in London, Smith sent a letter to Queen Anne, making known to her the many ways Pocahontas had helped the colonists—not least by rescuing him from execution, and again by warning him of her father's plans to ambush him in the forest. He urged the queen to treat Pocahontas with the hospitality due to a princess from another nation, one that the English should wish to have as an ally. As Smith puts it, "this Kingdome may rightly have a kingdome by her means."

The existence of such a letter, dated 1616, would put to rest many of the doubts about whether the story of Pocahontas's saving Smith is true. However, the British royal archives do not contain a copy, and the summary of it that Smith published has the same nagging flaw that persistently attaches itself to his tale of rescue: it did not appear in print until 1624, after anyone in a position to contradict or confirm it was dead.

There is evidence that *someone* interceded with the royal household on Pocahontas's behalf, though it would seem to have been to the advantage of the Virginia Company to publicize her visit, for here at last was the "nonpareil of Virginia" herself, of royal blood and proof positive that the Native Americans were peaceful and even susceptible to conversion to Christianity (to the English, a sign of civilization). However, the contemporary letter-writer John Chamberlain, an inveterate gossip who provides many juicy details of seventeenth-century England, wrote of Pocahontas, "[W]ith her tricking up and high stile and titles you might thincke her and her worshipfull husband to be sombody yf you do not know that the poore companie of Virginia . . . [only] allow her foure pound a weeke for her maintenance."

Yet in spite of the paltry sum provided by the Virginia Company, Pocahontas and her retinue (besides her husband and son, she was accompanied by a brother, one of her father's counselors, and several female attendants) were in fact treated as honored visitors. The lord bishop of London entertained her "with festivall state and pompe," wrote Samuel Purchas. The high point of her visit came on January 6, 1617, when she attended a Twelfth Night masque performance written by Ben Jonson specifically for King James. John Chamberlain, ever alert to signals of social hierarchy, noted that Pocahontas was "graciously used" and had been assigned a prominent seat at the performance.

Smith was busy with preparations for another voyage to the New World, but while he was in London one of Pocahontas's companions, Uttamatomakkin, the counselor of Powhatan, came to see him. Powhatan had been told after Smith's departure from Virginia that Smith was dead (no doubt wishful thinking on the part of someone at Jamestown), but Powhatan knew Smith too well to believe he would die so easily. He instructed Uttamatomakkin to look for him in England. Smith heard with a smile the story that, shortly after arriving in London, Uttamatomakkin had found a long stick and, according to his chief's instructions, began to make a notch in it for every Englishman he saw. "He was quickly wearie of that taske," Smith noted.

Still following orders, Uttamatomakkin asked Smith to show him the English god, the king, queen, and prince. Smith pointed out that Pocahontas had already been presented at court and Uttamatomakkin had seen the royal family on that occasion. At first Uttamatomakkin refused to believe it, but Smith assured him that the slobbering, wobbly-legged James was indeed king of England and Scotland. Uttamatomakkin commented on the king's lack of proper hospitality, reminding Smith, "You gave Powhatan a white Dog, which Powhatan fed as [well as] himselfe, but your King gave me nothing, and I am better than your white Dog."

Smith found time to pay Pocahontas a visit at the country house in Middlesex where she was staying. At first she seemed to snub him, turning away, hiding her face, and refusing to speak. Smith had brought friends along, and was embarrassed that he had told them Pocahontas could speak English—but probably even more humiliating was that she seemed to shun him, despite the glowing report he must have given about their relationship. He left her alone for a while, chatting in another room with John Rolfe about events in Jamestown.

Pocahontas's dark mood—whether due to anger or embarrassment or simply surprise at seeing Smith again—soon passed, and she began to speak of the events they had experienced together. There was much that linked them together. She reminded him that he had promised her father "what was yours should be his, and he the like to you." Smith, a stranger in Powhatan's country, had called the old chief his father, "and by the same reason," Pocahontas said, "so must I doe you."

Smith protested that he could not allow her to use that "title" for him, for "she was a Kings daughter." Perhaps he had heard that King James, feeling that the privileges of rank extended to all royal families, had questioned whether John Rolfe, a commoner, should have been permitted to marry Pocahontas, a royal princess.

Pocahontas was insistent, now that she had overcome her initial reticence. A note of teasing is evident in her reply; a hint of the little girl whose name meant "little wanton one" shows through. "Were you not afraid to come into my fathers Countrie," she asked Smith, "and caused feare in him and all his people (but mee)?" After all that Smith had done and dared, she reminded him, how could he fear her calling him father? "I tell you then I will, and you shall call me childe, and so I will bee for ever and ever your Countrie man."

She could not have known how prophetic those words would be—that she and Smith were to be linked together through the centuries, as the nexus between two civilizations, the English and the American. She had saved Smith, and saved the colony in the bargain. In return, his people would destroy hers. The very last words he recorded her saying to him, "your Countriemen will lie much," proved all too true.

They parted for the last time. What farewells were said, Smith does not tell us. Pocahontas's thoughts remained known to her alone, for as far as anyone knows she never wrote them down. In March 1617, she and her husband set out on the return voyage, but she was never to see her homeland again. Besides the plague, London was rife with countless diseases that Pocahontas had never

The only portrait of Pocahontas known to have been drawn from life shows her in English dress. The inscription surrounding her portrait gives her true native name—Matoaka—and the Christian name—Rebecca—that she adopted at her baptism.

been exposed to. Already ill when she boarded the ship, she was taken ashore at Gravesend, where she died. By tradition, she was buried in the little churchyard there, but no stone marks her final resting place among strangers, far from her home.

Smith recorded his contentment that those who were with her at her death witnessed "so religious and godly an end." Rolfe sailed on, leaving his infant son Thomas in the care of a highborn English family. After he grew to manhood, Thomas returned to

Virginia, where he had many descendants. Even today, some proudly claim Pocahontas as an ancestor.

Some fateful Providence seemed to link the fortunes of John Smith and Pocahontas. In the same month she died, Smith was readying another voyage to the New World. Given the imposing title "Admirall of New England" by Sir Ferdinando Gorges, he had hoped to command a flotilla of twenty ships—the largest English colonizing venture yet undertaken. However, willing investors proved harder to come by than Smith expected, and Gorges was more lavish with titles than with money. Smith had, after all, yet to turn a profit for his backers, and the idea that an American colony would in time bring fabulous rewards was still unproved. Men like Smith, who see far over the horizon, often have trouble convincing others what lies there.

So the reality was that Admiral Smith had three ships, not twenty, gathered at Plymouth harbor, and a mere fifteen colonists ready to establish a settlement, instead of the hundreds he might have needed to have any chance of success.

It did not matter, for it was at this point that Smith's phenomenal luck, which had always saved him from whatever perilous situations he found himself in, ran dry. The wind turned against him. Day after day it blew from the southwest, keeping the little fleet from heading out to sea. A week, two weeks, a month . . . surely, Smith must have thought, it had to stop sometime. More supplies had to be carried on board to replace those already consumed. A second month went by and now passengers and crew stole furtive glances at Smith whenever he came on deck to stand in the face of the remorseless wind. He was not a man who cursed, according to one who knew him well, but he must have felt cursed at that point.

A third month passed, and now even he had to admit defeat, for the year was too far gone for him to have time to cross the ocean, clear a plot of ground, and build a fort before winter came. The ships were sent to Newfoundland to catch fish so that the expedition would not be a total loss. Smith bade farewell to those who had volunteered to brave the wilderness of New England with him. There would be another attempt, he promised. He could find new backers, someone who understood what was to be gained, someone who believed in the dream.

He tried. Smith wrote a long letter to Sir Francis Bacon, who had replaced Salisbury as lord chancellor of England. Bacon was one of the most brilliant thinkers of his time, adept in philosophy, a trailblazer in science. If Smith had any hope of finding someone who could fully appreciate the benefits of colonies, it was Bacon. In his letter, Smith gives a full report on all his activities in America, putting the best face possible on them. He apologizes for his presumption in bringing the proposal directly to so eminent a man as Bacon, but cautions, Smith-like, "lett not the povertie of the author, cause the action to be lesse respected." He adds that he does not want riches, but merely the chance to perform this service for England. Five thousand pounds would be sufficient for the task, he promises, and quick profits from fishing and fur trading would make back most of that in a short time. England had already spent more than a hundred thousand pounds in Virginia and Bermuda; why allow that investment to be wasted when such a little more would be sufficient to guarantee success?

Bacon ignored the letter. He was later prosecuted for using his high post to obtain bribes. Smith, even if he could have afforded a bribe large enough to attract Bacon, was not a man to give one. Undaunted, he edited his letter, adding some material from other sources—as authors of the time customarily did—and arranged to have copies printed. These he distributed to many of the "companies," or guilds, in London, hoping that one or more of them would invest in the project. He sent others to "adventurers," wealthy individuals who were known to have invested in other American ventures. Titled *New Englands Trialls* ("trial" meant attempt), the pamphlet summarized the results of a number of earlier voyages to New England, including Smith's own, and described the benefits to be gained from additional "trialls."

The first edition of the pamphlet was published in 1620, the year of the most famous colonial voyage to New England. The settlers, dubbed the Pilgrims by their leader William Bradford, were English religious dissenters who had earlier fled to Holland.

They crossed the Atlantic in the *Mayflower* and landed at a place Smith had already seen, and which Prince Charles had dubbed Plymouth. Learning of their success in establishing a settlement, Smith felt disappointed that they had not asked him to guide them. They had, he wrote, thought "my books and maps were [cheaper] to teach them, than my selfe." They might also have feared that Smith's strong personality would overwhelm their religious purpose.

Two years earlier, the Jamestown colony had also profited from Smith's advice. The Virginia Company, still trying desperately to attract new colonists, had offered fifty acres of land with an annual rent of only one shilling to each person paying his or her own passage to America. It was an offer recommended by Smith in *A Description of New England*, and it proved so successful that it was imitated in some form by almost every later English colonial venture, as well as by the U.S. government in the nineteenth century, to attract immigrants to territories Smith did not even know existed.

The Virginia colony started to grow rapidly. From March 1620 to March 1621, more than a thousand new settlers arrived; the following year saw fifteen hundred more. The profitability of tobacco as a cash crop, and the availability of land, meant that many settlers had moved away from the protection of the forts at Jamestown and Henrico. Plantations had sprung up along the James River.

The natives viewed these developments with concern and distrust, seeing the English encroachment on their lands as a threat. Powhatan had died the year after his daughter Pocahontas. By 1622, his place as paramount chief had been taken by Opechancanough, who had always regarded the English with more hostility than his elder brother. Opechancanough saw only one outcome if the English were allowed to keep sending new colonists: the Powhatans would be driven off their land. The time to strike could not be long delayed, he felt, and on the morning of March 22, 1622, in a series of coordinated moves, the natives attacked the outlying settlements, killing the residents and burning their houses. As many as a third of all the colonists in Virginia were slaughtered.

It was not until July 3 that word of the massacre reached England. The Virginia Company issued a pamphlet purporting to set forth the "facts" in the affair, trying to minimize the damage. Smith saw the event as an opportunity, for who better than he could claim to have controlled the natives while maintaining peace, and even trading with them? He proposed that the company put him in charge of a comparatively small force of a hundred soldiers and thirty sailors. "[B]y God's assistance," he promised, "we would endeavour to enforce the saveages to leave thier Country, or bring them in that fear and subjection that every [English] man should [be able to] follow their business securely."

However, the company had no money to outfit even so modest an expedition as Smith proposed. Moreover, the colonists were already wreaking vengeance for the attack, burning the natives' villages and cornfields, practices they continued for years. Since the battle still pitted firearms against bows and arrows, the natives ultimately were doomed. They had no choice but to move inland, away from the English, not knowing that the English—and others, millions of them—would continue to arrive until they had occupied the continent.

Smith issued a third edition of *New Englands Trialls* later in 1622, adding a commentary on the most recent events in Virginia. Primarily this was an excuse for him to advertise his ability to subdue the natives with far fewer armed men than were in Virginia now: "When I had [only] ten men able to go abroad ... I ranged that unknown country 14 weeks; I had but 18 [men] to subdue them all, with which great army I stayed six weeks before their greatest kings habitations, till they had gathered together all the power they could."

Of particular importance in this edition of the pamphlet, however, is the first mention in print of Smith's rescue by Pocahontas. He writes, "It is true in our greatest extremitie they shot me, slue three of my men, and by the folly of them that fled took me prisoner; yet God made Pocahontas the Kings daughter the means to deliver me." He did not expand on this, waiting until 1624 to tell the full story, but this earlier passage certainly indicates that it was on his mind and was not simply a tale he concocted to add to his reputation. For his purpose in the 1622

account is to stress his military prowess, which is hardly en-
hanced by the fact that he was rescued by a child.

The 1622 version of Smith's pamphlet also shows that he was
feeling aggrieved that others were following in the path he had
marked out. He lists several voyages that had come back recently
from New England, the ships' holds loaded with fish and furs that
brought profits for their backers. "Thus you may see plainely the
yearely successe from New England," he writes; "pardon me
though it passionate me beyond the bounds of modestie, to have
been sufficiently able to foresee it. . . . By that acquaintance I
have with them [the American colonies] I may call them my children, for they have been my wife, my hawks, my hounds, my
cards, my dice, and in totall my best content." The passage is a
rare self-revelation for the ambitious man who indeed had no
wife, no children, and no vices except pride. Pride, as the Greeks
knew, was enough to destroy him.

Others had gone to America and claimed to make discoveries
that were, Smith wrote, "but pigs of my owne sowe." Nonetheless,
despite all the "disasters" that Smith had experienced, "I would
begin again with as small meanes as I did at the first." The reader
may be reminded of his earlier book on New England, in which
he wrote, "Who can desire more content, that has small meanes;
or but only his merit to advance his fortune, than to tread, and
plant that ground he hath purchased by the hazard of his life."

The trouble was, no one would now give him the chance to
begin again. Smith had acquired the reputation of being either an
unlucky man or a reckless one. He spoke of colonies when people
wanted profits; when he promised profits, he could not deliver
them.

Sir Ferdinando Gorges had a variety of ongoing enterprises
in the New World—he issued a patent to the Pilgrims and sought
to commercialize fishing rights to "his" section of the North
American coast—but he had no work for John Smith. The Virginia Company, which might have done well to hire Smith, was
facing a number of problems. In 1621 King James banned the
lotteries that the company had resorted to in order to raise funds.
The massacre of 1622 was followed by a cold, deadly winter that
further took its toll on the colonists at and around Jamestown. In

May 1623 a royal commission began to investigate the financial dealings of the company.

Smith, apparently prompted by someone at the company, was asked to write a history of its affairs in Virginia—not only the events he had witnessed, but those that had transpired since his departure. Typically, he seized on the opportunity to justify and promote himself. He expanded the history's scope to include New England and Bermuda, and obtained the support of a patron—who was, not surprisingly in view of Smith's career, a wealthy woman. She was Frances Howard, known as the "double duchess" because her third husband had held in succession the titles of Duke of Lennox (Scotland) and Duke of Richmond (England). The duchess appears in a full-page engraved frontispiece to the book, and looks well preserved—as a woman in her mid-forties who has had three husbands, each one richer than the one before, should. Smith had dedicated his earlier work, *A Map of Virginia*, to her second husband, the Earl of Hertford, and must have known the duchess from that time.

In any case, having a wealthy patroness freed Smith from any need to conform to the desires of the Virginia Company for favorable treatment. Besides his own memories, he obtained much of his material for this book from the Reverend Samuel Purchas, who was still trying to carry on Hakluyt's work. Smith's history, divided into six parts, ranges widely, from Harriot's account of Raleigh's colony, to Gosnold's 1602 voyage to New England, to an update on the Pilgrims' settlement at Plymouth.

Throughout *The Generall Historie of Virginia*, even in passages virtually lifted from others, Smith's voice predominates, justifying his own actions and urging others to imitate the policies he initiated. In a prospectus for the book, he writes, "[T]hese observations are all that I have for the experiences of a thousand pound, and the losse of eighteen years of time, besides the trials, dangers, miseries, and incumbrances I have endured for my countries good gratis."

During the time Smith was preparing the book for publication, the Virginia Company was sliding into bankruptcy, and it would be dissolved in May 1624. Smith therefore had no need to protect its interests. That was probably why, for the first time, he

Title page of Smith's 1624 *Generall Historie of Virginia, New England, and the Summer Isles* (Bermuda). At top are portraits of Queen Elizabeth, King James, and Prince Charles. The map shows "Ould Virginia" (North Carolina) at left, "Virginia Now planted" (the Chesapeake Bay area) at center, and New England at right. At bottom right of the title panel is Smith's coat of arms, with three Turks' heads, that was awarded to him by Zsigmond Bathory.

includes a detailed account of his rescue by Pocahontas. When he had published earlier accounts of his experiences, the fact that he had been in grave danger would have spoiled the Virginia Company's attempts to portray America as a land of milk, honey, and friendly natives who were ripe for conversion to Christianity.

The massacre of 1622 made that deception impossible to maintain, so Smith acknowledged what everyone knew: that Powhatan's people could be dangerous in defending their territory. Consequently, since Smith had fallen into their hands and yet escaped, had cowed them and demanded their corn, had shown that he could "control" them and befriend them when necessary, it was he who should be assigned to deal with them.

Smith's detractors have asserted that he invented the story of Pocahontas's rescue for this volume. It hardly seems to have been necessary, for many other tales, whose veracity is unquestioned, appear throughout the narrative. Smith's bravery is well attested to without the reader learning that he was saved from death by a mere girl. Indeed, in the dedication he addresses to the double duchess, he gallantly refers to all the other women who had aided him in his lifetime—some of whose stories he would not set down on paper till 1630: his Turkish mistress Tragabigzanda, his Russian benefactor Lady Callamata, the Frenchwoman Madame Chanoyes who had sheltered him at La Rochelle. All had places in his fond memories.

Smith answers his critics, past and present, most effectively when he describes his motivation for writing this book: "I am no Compiler by hearsay, but have beene a reall Actor; I take my selfe to have a propertie in [these events]: and therefore have beene bold to challenge them to come under the reach of my owne rough Pen. That, which hath been indured and passed through with hardship and danger, is thereby sweetned to the Actor, when he becometh the Relator. I have deeply hazarded my selfe in doing and suffering, and why should I sticke [hesitate] to hazard my reputation in Recording?" The words indicate how much pride Smith felt in his achievements, the true scope of his ambition, and how unlikely it would be for him to have made up the story of Pocahontas to embellish his reputation. It was simply not necessary.

In the text of Book IV of the *General History*, Smith reports his testimony given before a commission appointed to investigate the Virginia Company. His recommendation—that the colony revert to direct royal control—was followed, and in 1624 the Virginia Company was dissolved. Little change occurred in Virginia itself. The colonists, who had in 1619 organized the first elected political assembly in the New World, the House of Burgesses, were allowed to keep that institution, though attempts would be made to limit its power. Francis Wyatt, who had been governor since 1621, remained in office. Presumably, since he had been in charge during the massacre of 1622, the "want of martial discipline" that Smith had declared to be the chief cause of the disaster should have been blamed on Wyatt. No doubt Smith was disappointed at not being named to replace him.

King James died in 1625 and his son Charles took the throne. Smith's hopes must have risen, for the new king might well remember the tribute Smith had paid him in inviting him to sprinkle place names through New England. King Charles, however, had his eye on Europe, not America. His sister Elizabeth had earlier married a German prince, Frederick V of the Palatinate, who accepted the throne of the newly created Protestant state of Bohemia. A year later, in 1620, the Austrians and Spanish, both ruled by Catholic monarchs, deposed Frederick, driving him and Elizabeth into exile in Holland.

The English parliament took this as a national and religious insult and wanted to retaliate. James, then still king, as ever had preferred peace to war and had pursued diplomatic solutions. His son Charles, however, was determined to test England's military might, and after taking the throne prepared to send an army onto the Continent.

John Smith, sensing the way the wind was blowing, quickly produced what was intended to be a manual for seamen—or, as he wrote, for those who lacked experience, "and are desirous to learn what belongs to a seaman." Titled *An Accidence* [grammar] *or the Path-way to Experience*, the little book appeared in 1626. It must have done well, for Smith followed it up the next year with an expanded work on the same subject, titled *A Sea Grammar*.

Smith demonstrates in these two works a knowledge of seamanship, and of warfare at sea, which shows that his accounts of having sailed with pirates and predators were not idle boasts. Besides giving an exhaustive vocabulary of early-seventeenth-century ships and naval procedure (some of which was lifted from other books, the custom of writers at that time), Smith describes how to chase a ship, the techniques for boarding a hostile vessel, and (when necessary) how to avoid and escape from a superior force at sea.

In 1630, Smith turned fifty—old age in his era, and certainly he must have felt his years, for it was then that he published his autobiography. This was so uncommon a thing to do in those times that the word *autobiography* did not appear in English until 1809—nearly two centuries later. Except for essentially private documents such as journals and diaries, there is hardly anything like Smith's book before his time. (An illiterate woman named Margery Kempe dictated to scribes what may have been the first English autobiography in 1438, but it did not appear in print till 1936.) Published accounts of travelers who had gone abroad were more common, and the title of Smith's book, *The True Travels, Adventures, and Observations of Captain John Smith, in Europe, Asia, Africa, and America from Anno Domini 1593 to 1629*, makes it seem as if it would be part of that genre.

But Smith is actually somewhat less generous with travel descriptions than the reader might expect. In some parts of his text he merely lists the names of places he passed through—and since he was relying on his ear to determine the spellings, it is sometimes hard to know where he was. It is perhaps a measure of Smith's egotism that he felt the reader would prefer accounts of his exploits to descriptions of the exotic places he had visited.

Here, then, is the only source (other than a few legal records) for the events of Smith's life before he embarked for Virginia in 1606. Here he writes for the first time—sometimes in conflict with the records—about his childhood, schooling, and short-lived apprenticeship. He relates the near drowning on the way to Rome, the Caribbean pirate voyage, his visit to Father Parsons in Rome, his military career, his experience as a slave, and his escape.

What is frustrating to the modern reader is that Smith is not an introspective autobiographer. He does not try to explain the roots of his wanderlust and ambition. From everything that he wrote, we sense his pride, his belief that he was the equal (if not the superior) of any highborn Englishman, but he never declares it. Whenever he has a hair-raising escape from death, he attributes it to God, not to his own tenacious will.

So what remains is a series of events—remarkable events, ones that would not be out of place in an adventure novel—but the man at the center of those events remains a mystery, a figure who fails to convince others of his greatness because he is not real enough to be believable.

That was true even in his own time. Two years after *True Travels* was published, a small volume of humorous verse appeared in London's bookshops. Titled *The Legend of Captain Jones*, it was written by a Welsh clergyman named David Lloyd, and it merrily satirized Smith's claims of derring-do. In the section of the poem in which "Jones" battles some American natives, it reads:

> . . . Now for a verse
> To speak great Jones his deeds, who headlong goes
> Amongst the thickest rancks, cuts, kils and throwes,
> Some by the legs, some by the wast he makes
> Shorter; another by the lock he takes,
> Reapes off his head, wherwith he braines another,
> Then at one stroke kils father, sonne, and brother;
> Few scap'd with life, but strangely happy those
> Which scap'd with losse of halfe a face or nose.

Lloyd refers to Jones's own account of his deeds: "To paint his praise, himselfe hath done enough."

The Legend of Captain Jones sold enough copies to warrant several editions, and either Lloyd or another author expanded it considerably in later versions. Even the engraving on the title page, which shows a mounted horseman in full armor charging an infidel warrior riding an elephant, resembles the engravings that accompanied Smith's book, three of which illustrate the gallant jousts in which he conquered three Turks.

For a satire to be so popular, the original must have been well-known too. We can assume that Smith had achieved a degree of fame through his works. He did in fact display in *True Travels* the final triumph that those three duels had brought him: a coat of arms that the royal herald's office had bestowed on him, recognizing as authentic the letter of patent signed by Zsigmond Bathory, Prince of Transylvania. So Smith had at last attained the social status that a coat of arms carried with it—not in any of the conventional ways his father might have imagined for him, but in his own, uncompromising fashion. The motto he chose for his coat of arms indicates the nature of the man, and the goals he set for himself: *Vincere est Vivere*—"to conquer is to live."

Yet as the years passed, he must have reluctantly faced the knowledge that his final goal—to found a colony and show that it could succeed under his leadership—was never to be realized. Not that he stopped trying to attain it. In his final year, 1631, he published yet another book, titled *Advertisements* [advice] *for the Unexperienced Planters of New England, or Any Where.* There is something plaintive about that final phrase. Anywhere . . . Smith was either looking far ahead or hoping that someone going anywhere would still need his help. He had heard that in 1629 yet another New England colony had been founded, this one at Massachusetts Bay (another place he had mapped), and as ever he felt a proprietary interest in it. The colonies still were, as he had written some ten years earlier, "my children." Now they were growing up without him, and he felt wistful and neglected.

After bringing his readers up to date on the progress of the American colonies, Smith begins to set forth his advice, with the wry comment, "I know how hatefull it is to envy, pride, flattery, and greatnesse to be advised, but I hope . . . wise men will excuse [me] for making my opinion plaine."

Percy had attacked Smith for "being an ambitious unworthy and vainglorious fellow." Smith's offense was that he tried to rise above his station, threatening those like Percy who relied on the accident of birth for their place in society. It is this very quality that marks Smith as the first example of what Jean de Crèvecoeur, a French immigrant to the young United States, would call "the American, this new man." Smith was a self-made man, a term that did not exist in his day. He did what millions who came after him dreamed of doing: he seized the opportunity to invent himself. Smith never shows this more clearly than when he writes in his final book, "[I]t is true, it is a happy thing to be borne to strength, wealth, and honor, but that which is got by prowesse and magnanimity is the truest lustre."

Building a colony, Smith writes, "is not a worke for every one . . . it requires all the best parts of art, judgement, honesty, constancy, diligence, and industry, to doe but neere well." He mentions those in whose footsteps new colonists should aim to follow: Columbus, Cortés, Pizarro, de Soto, Magellan, and of course, "the incomparable Sir Francis Drake." He tells his readers to imitate these "brave spirits, that advanced themselves from poore souldiers to great Captaines," and we know that is the path he planned for himself.

Perhaps he admitted to himself now, past fifty years old, that he would never quite reach that goal, but he never stopped dreaming large: he was planning to write nothing less than a history of the sea when he died. He underestimated his influence, judging that his own career as colonist would in the end serve only as a cautionary tale to others. He prefaced his final work with a poem (apparently his own, showing yet another talent) titled "The Sea Marke." It is told from the point of view of an old wrecked ship that is left on a sandbar, where it rests as a warning to other ships to stay clear.

> I only lie upon this shelfe
> to be a marke to all
> which on the same might fall,
> That none may perish but my selfe.

Smith signed his will on June 21, 1631—using an X instead of writing his name. He must have been gravely ill, for the will was entered for probate just ten days later. His largest bequest— all the lands and houses he had inherited from his father, as well as his hard-won coat of arms—went to Thomas Packer, identified only as one of the clerks of the King's Privy Seal. Packer and Sir Samuel Saltonstall (whose cousin was a founder of the Massachusetts Bay Company) were to serve as executors of the will. Two other men were to share with Packer Smith's library—books were precious things—which was stored in a trunk at Saltonstall's house. Smith left small sums to the widow of his younger brother, to more distant relatives, and to "Mistris Tredway," the last mysterious woman in his life, about whom nothing else is known. He also provided twenty pounds for his funeral, a large enough sum so that his mourners must have had a good time.

Someone identifying himself only as a friend wrote an epitaph in verse on Smith's grave at St. Sepulchre's Church in London. It begins with an acknowledgment that Smith's deeds are almost too great for one man to have accomplished:

Here lyes one conquered that hath conquered Kings.
Subdu'd large Territories, and done things
Which to the World impossible would seem,
But that the Truth is held in more esteem.

It would no doubt have amused Smith if he could have looked ahead four centuries and seen Jamestown today, where, standing on the edge of a continent—now a great nation more powerful than England or Spain ever were—are two statues, one of himself and one of the little girl who saved him from death. He would probably laugh wryly at the thought that this single incident was all most people knew about him, when the countless events of his stirring life—all the heroic deeds, the hairbreadth escapes, the suffering and the glory—are virtually forgotten.

John Smith's dream, that on that vast continent a new kind of society would arise where men with "great spirits and small meanes" could prosper and, yes, grow rich, inspired millions who never knew his name. America was the place he had yearned for his whole life. There his character, determination, and ambition had propelled him to the top of society. He spent the rest of his life trying to return. Though he failed, he pointed the way for others, who were drawn by the promise that opportunity was here for anyone who dared seize it. It was a powerful thought, one that had as much to do with creating the country we have today as anything Smith did to keep Jamestown alive. Smith founded more than a colony. He gave birth to the American dream.

Notes

Prologue

The comments about the scent of America are from David B. Quinn's monumental five-volume collection *New American World: A Documentary History of North America to 1612* (New York: Arno Press, 1979); Verrazano, vol. 1; Barlowe and Archer, vol. 3.

1. Dreams of Glory

All quotations from Captain John Smith come from *The Complete Works of Captain John Smith*, 3 vols., ed. Philip Barbour (Chapel Hill, N.C.: Institute of Early American History and Culture and University of North Carolina Press, 1986).

The quotations from participants in the episode of the Spanish Armada come from A. M. Hadfield, *Time to Finish the Game* (London: Phoenix House, 1964). We have also made use of Garrett Mattingly's *The Armada* (Boston: Houghton Mifflin, 1959).

The Thomas More quotation comes from Penry Williams, *Life in Tudor England* (London: B. T. Batsford, 1964). The act of 1572 dealing with the plight of the poor and the punishment for beggars is quoted in M. St. Clare Byrne, *Elizabethan Life in Town and Country* (London: Methuen & Co., 1954). In describing the world of Smith's boyhood, we have also made use of Barry Coward, *Social Change and Continuity: England 1550–1750* (London: Longman, 1997); Joan Thirsk, *English Peasant Farming: the Agrarian History of Lincolnshire* (London: Routledge and Kegan Paul, 1957); Joan Thirsk, *Tudor Enclosures* (London: Routledge and Kegan Paul, 1959); Clive Holmes, *Seventeenth-Century Lincolnshire* (Lincoln: History of Lincolnshire Committee, 1980); Alan Rogers, *A History of Lincolnshire* (Beaconsfield: Darwen Finlayson, 1970); Roger B. Manning, *Village Revolts: Social Protest and Popular Disturbances in England, 1509–1640* (Oxford: Clarendon Press, 1988); and Albert J. Schmidt, *The Yeoman in Tudor and Stuart England* (Washington, D.C.: Folger Shakespeare Library, 1961). Schmidt's book is also the source of the quotation by Sir Thomas Overbury. An illuminating article is Ian Beckwith's "Captain John Smith: The Yeoman Background," in *History Today*, vol. 26, no. 7 (July 1976).

The wry description of the seal of the King Edward VI Grammar School was provided by William Page in *The Victoria History of the County of Lincoln*, vol. 2 (London: James Street Haymarket, 1906). The story of William Bedell's cruel schoolmaster comes from Bedell's son's account in *Two Biographies of William Bedell*, ed. E. S. Shuckburgh (Cambridge, UK: Cambridge University Press, 1902). In describing Smith's schooling, we have also made use of A. Monroe Stowe, *English Grammar Schools in the Reign of Queen Elizabeth* (New York: Teacher's College, Columbia University, 1908), and John Howard Brown, *Elizabethan Schooldays* (Oxford: Basil Blackwell, 1933). George Smith's will and the inventory of his property are quoted in volume 3 of Philip Barbour's edition of Smith's works.

The quotation from Thomas Raymond is from *Autobiography of Thomas Raymond and Memoirs of the Family of Guise of Elmore, Gloucestershire*, ed. G. Davies (London: Royal Historical Society, 1917). "The Ballad of Lord Willoughby" appeared in Jane West, *The Brave Lord Willoughby* (Edinburgh: Pentland Press, 1998).

Smith's reading matter during his hermitage includes *Don Anthony of Guevara: The Diall of Princes*, in the 1557 translation by Sir Thomas North, ed. K. N. Colville (London: Philip Allan & Co., 1919). The sixteenth-century Peter Whitehorne edition of Machiavelli's *The Art of War*, with the appended treatise on gunpowder that Smith must have read, is available online at www.lib.umi.com/eebo/image/12127. The quotation from the purported autobiography of an English merchant's son is from Louis B. Wright, *Middle-Class Culture in Elizabethan England* (Ithaca, N.Y.: Cornell University Press, 1958).

2. *"To Conquer Is to Live"*

Smith's account of his military career in Europe was long viewed skeptically by historians, primarily because his attempts to spell the names of foreign places that he had not heard for a quarter century at the time of his writing seldom matched any place names that could be found on a map. Bradford Smith's groundbreaking book *Captain John Smith: His Life and Legend* (Philadelphia: J. B. Lippincott, 1953), with its appendix by Laura Polanyi Striker, did much to clarify and confirm Smith's adventures. Philip Barbour in his magisterial biography *The Three Worlds of Captain John Smith* (Boston: Houghton Mifflin, 1964) contributed much additional valuable scholarship to the study of Smith's life, as did Barbour's comprehensive and authoritative notes to his edition of Smith's works. Barbour concludes his biography, "Let it only be said that nothing John Smith wrote has yet been found to be a lie." One could quibble with this judgment, for in certain details Smith sometimes contradicts himself from version to version of his works, but at least his military career can now be correlated with events known by historians to have occurred. We have also consulted Dorothy M. Vaughan, *Europe and the Turk: A Pattern of Alliances, 1350–1700* (New York: AMS Press, 1976).

An interesting book by an Englishman who traveled Europe at about the same time Smith did appears in a modern edition as *Shakespeare's Europe*, by Fynes Moryson (New York: B. Blom, 1967 edition of 1617 original). The information about slave markets in Christian Europe comes from Ernest Stuart Bates, *Touring in 1600* (Boston: Houghton Mifflin, 1971). The quotation from William Lithgow is from his *The Totall Discourse of the Rare Adventures & Painefull Peregrinations of Long Nineteene Yeares Travayles from Scotland to the Most Famous Kingdomes in Europe, Asia and Affrica* (Glasgow: James MacLehose and Sons, 1906). The life and career of Robert Parsons, S.J., are discussed in Michael L. Carrafield, *Robert Parsons and English Catholicism, 1580–1610* (Selinsgrove, Pa.: Susquehanna University Press, 1998), and Francis Edwards, *Robert Persons [sic]: the Biography of an Elizabethan Jesuit, 1546–1610* (St. Louis: Institute of Jesuit Sources, n.d. [1995?]).

The information on tournaments and jousting comes from Alan Young, *Tudor and Jacobean Tournaments* (Dobbs Ferry, N.Y.: Sheridan House, 1987), and from Richard W. Barber and Juliet Barker, *Tournaments: Jousts, Chivalry, and Pageants in the Middle Ages* (New York: Weidenfeld and Nicolson, 1989). The latter book is the source of the quotation from King Duarte's work on jousting.

3. Voyagers West

The quotations from explorers and colonists such as Gilbert, Hayes, Barlowe, Harriot, and White generally come from Quinn, *New American World*, cited above. The source of the term "think tank" to refer to Raleigh's Durham House circle is Karen Ordahl Kupperman in vol. 1, ch. 7 of *North American Exploration*, ed. John Logan Allen (Lincoln: University of Nebraska Press, 1997). We have benefited in other ways from the work of Dr. Allen and his colleagues.

We have also made use of David Beers Quinn, *England and the Discovery of America, 1481–1620* (New York: Knopf, 1974); Michael Foss, *Undreamed Shores: England's Wasted Empire in America* (London: Phoenix Press, 1974); J. H. Elliott, *The Old World and the New, 1492–1650* (Cambridge, UK: Cambridge University Press, 1970); Raleigh Trevelyan, *Sir Walter Raleigh* (New York: Henry Holt, 2002); A. L. Rowse, *Sir Richard Grenville* (London: Jonathan Cape, 1937); David Barr Chidsey, *Sir Humphrey Gilbert: Elizabeth's Racketeer* (New York: Harper & Brothers, 1932); Theodore Rabb,

Enterprise and Empire: Merchant and Gentry Investment in the Expansion of England, 1575–1630 (Cambridge, Mass.: Harvard University Press, 1967); and David Duncan Wallace, *South Carolina: A Short History 1520–1948* (Columbia: University of South Carolina Press, 1961). Background on Richard Hakluyt is in George Bruner Parks, *Richard Hakluyt and the English Voyages* (New York: American Geographical Society, 1928). Hakluyt's report to Queen Elizabeth is in Quinn, *New American World*, cited above.

4. The "First Mover" of Jamestown

The information about Sir John Popham appears in John Aubrey, *Aubrey's Brief Lives* (London: Cresset Press, 1949). Information about London and the London theater came from A. L. Rowse, *Shakespeare the Elizabethan* (New York: Putnam's, 1977), and Lawrence Manley, *London in the Age of Shakespeare: An Anthology* (London: Croom Helm, 1986). In addition to the sources cited above for chapter 3, we have benefited from reading A. L. Rowse, *Shakespeare's Southampton: Patron of Virginia* (New York: Harper & Row, 1965). The source of the quotations from Philip II's spy Pedro de Zuñiga, George Percy, and Edward Maria Wingfield, unless otherwise noted, is *The Jamestown Voyages Under the First Charter 1606–1609*, 2 vols., ed. Philip L. Barbour (Cambridge, UK: Hakluyt Society, 1969). An invaluable source of information about Bartholomew Gosnold is Warner F. Gookin and Philip Barbour, *Bartholomew Gosnold, Discoverer and Planter* (Hamden, Conn.: Archon Books, 1963).

5. A Charge of Mutiny

The quotations from Smith are from the edition of his works ed. Philip Barbour. The quotation from William Harrison is from William Harrison, *Elizabethan England* (London: Walter Scott Publishing, n.d. [1902?]). All other quotations in this chapter are from Barbour's *The Jamestown Voyages*.

6. Disease, Dissension, and Death

The "earlier English visitor" was Ralph Lane, in 1585. Quoted from Michael Foss, *Undreamed Shores: England's Wasted Empire in America* (London: Phoenix Press, 1974). The accounts of Wingfield and Percy are from Barbour, *The Jamestown Voyages*, cited above, and Alexander Brown, *The First Republic in America* (Boston: Houghton Mifflin, 1898).

The epidemic at Jamestown, discussed from a physician's viewpoint, is from Gordon W. Jones, "The First Epidemic in English America," *Vir-*

ginia Magazine of History and Biography, vol. 71, no. 1 (January 1963), and in Wyndham B. Blanton, MD, *Medicine in Virginia in the Seventeenth Century* (Richmond, Va.: William Byrd Press, 1930).

Reverend Hunt's will is printed in the *Virginia Magazine of History and Biography*, vol. 25, no. 2 (April 1917). The source of the statement that the natives had no iron tools is Helen C. Rountree, *Pocahontas's People: The Powhatan Indians of Virginia Through Four Centuries* (Norman: University of Oklahoma Press, 1990).

7. The Great American Myth

The information on the Spanish expeditions to the Chesapeake Bay region is found in Paul E. Hoffman, *Spain and the Roanoke Voyages* (Raleigh: North Carolina Department of Cultural Resources, 1987). The culture of the people who lived in Virginia when Europeans first arrived is described and discussed in Helen C. Rountree and E. Randolph Turner III, *Before and After Jamestown: Virginia's Powhatans and Their Predecessors* (Gainesville: University Press of Florida, 2002); Frederic W. Gleach, *Powhatan's World and Colonial Virginia: A Conflict of Cultures* (Lincoln: University of Nebraska Press, 1997); and Helen C. Rountree, *Pocahontas's People: The Powhatan Indians of Virginia Through Four Centuries*, cited above. The rediscovery of the site of Werowocomoco, Powhatan's village, was reported in the *New York Times*, May 7, 2003, p. A22.

The origins of the Pocahontas controversy can be found in Henry Adams, *The Education of Henry Adams: An Autobiography* (Boston: Houghton Mifflin, 1961); Henry Adams, *The Letters of Henry Adams*, ed. J. C. Levenson et al., vol. 1 (Cambridge, Mass.: Belknap Press, 1982); and John Gorham Palfrey, *History of New England* (Boston: Little, Brown, 1890 reprint of 1858 edition). Discussion of the controversy appears in Robert S. Tilton, *Pocahontas: The Evolution of an American Narrative* (Cambridge, Mass.: Cambridge University Press, 1994).

The sources for the story of the Gentleman of Elvas are Edward T. Bourne, ed., and Buckingham Smith, trans., *Narratives of the Career of Hernando de Soto* (New York: A. S. Barnes, 1904), and Richard Hakluyt, *Virginia Richly Valued* (Ann Arbor, Mich.: University Microfilms, 1966 facsimile reprint of 1609 edition).

8. Conflicting Agendas

The information on Thomas Savage and his descendants is in Martha Bennett Stiles, "Hostage to the Indians," *Virginia Cavalcade*, vol. XII, no. 1 (Summer 1962).

9. Seeking the Future

The quotations are from the Philip Barbour edition of John Smith's *Generall Historie of Virginia*.

10. Smith vs. Newport

Smith's letter is quoted in Barbour's edition of Smith's works. The records of the Virginia Company for this period have not survived.

11. Smith vs. Powhatan

Strachey's account comes from Louis B. Wright and Virginia Freund, eds., William Strachey, *The Historie of Travell into Virginia Britania* (London: Hakluyt Society, 1953 reprint of 1612 edition). The connection between Strachey and Shakespeare is discussed in Charles Richard Sanders, "William Strachey, the Virginia Colony and Shakespeare," *Virginia Magazine of History and Biography*, vol. 57, no. 2 (April 1949). Purchas's quote is from Samuel Purchas, *Hakluytus Posthumus or Purchas His Pilgrimes*, vol. 19 (Glasgow: James MacLehose & Sons, 1906).

A comparison of the different versions of Smith's account of events in Virginia, from 1608 to 1624, is found in Kevin J. Hayes, "Defining the Ideal Colonist: Captain John Smith's Revisions from *A True Relation* to the *Proceedings* to the Third Book of the *Generall Historie*," *Virginia Magazine of History and Biography*, vol. 99, no. 2 (April 1991).

12. Smith Takes Charge

Captain Winne's letter is from Quinn, *New American World*, vol. 5, p. 285. The Percy quote re Smith, the Zuñiga notes, and the directors' new instructions are from Barbour, *The Jamestown Voyages*. The text of the 1609 London broadside is from Alexander Brown, *The Genesis of the United States* (New York: Russell & Russell, 1964 reprint of 1890 edition), p. 248. "One of the other leaders of the expedition" was Smith's old enemy, Gabriel Archer. The quotation is from Brown, *Genesis*, p. 329. Spelman's account is from Edward Arber's edition of Smith's works.

13. "My Hands Have Been My Lands"

The quotations from Smith and the story of the publication of his first book are from the Barbour edition of Smith's works. The quotations from others are from Barbour, *The Jamestown Voyages*; Quinn, *New American*

World, vol. 5; and George Percy, "A Trewe Relacyon," in *Tyler's Quarterly Historical and Genealogical Magazine*, vol. 3 (1922): 259–282.

14. The Dream Survives the Man

The colonists' complaints about Governor Dale are in the *William and Mary Quarterly*, series 2, vol. 18, p. 466. Alexander Whitaker's ambition is described in Frances Mossiker, *Pocahontas: The Life and the Legend* (New York: Knopf, 1976), p. 165. Rolfe's letter is in *Narratives of Early Virginia*, ed. Lyon Gardiner Tyler (New York: Scribner's, 1907). John Chamberlain's comments on Pocahontas's visit to England are from *The Letters of John Chamberlain*, ed. Norman Egbert McClure, vol. 2 (Philadelphia: American Philosophical Society, 1939).

The information on English autobiography is from Paul Delany, *British Autobiography in the Seventeenth Century* (London: Routledge and Kegan Paul, 1969). The poem satirizing Smith's *True Travels* is discussed by Alden T. Vaughan in "John Smith Satirized: *The Legend of Captain Iones*," *William and Mary Quarterly*, series 3, vol. 45, no. 4 (October 1988). Smith's epitaph is in Barbour's edition of Smith's works, vol. 3.

For Further Reading

Abrams, Ann Uhry. *The Pilgrims and Pocahontas: Rival Myths of American Origin*. Boulder, Colo.: Westview Press, 1999. How and why Smith's reputation was besmirched.

Brown, Alexander. *The First Republic in America*. Boston: Houghton Mifflin, 1898. The strongest articulation of the argument that Smith was a liar.

Coward, Barry. *Social Change and Continuity: England 1550–1750*. London: Longman, 1997. A good overview of the social conditions of Smith's youth.

Gleach, Frederic W. *Powhatan's World and Colonial Virginia: A Conflict of Cultures*. Lincoln: University of Nebraska Press, 1997. An informed study of the cultural clash between the English and the Native Americans.

Haile, Edward Wright. *Jamestown Narratives: Eyewitness Accounts of the Virginia Colony, the First Decade, 1607–1617*. Champlain, Va.: RoundHouse, 1998. A useful source for the accounts of those involved with Jamestown in its first ten years, modernized for the general reader.

Hume, Ivor Noel. *The Virginia Adventure: Roanoke to James Towne*. Charlottesville: University Press of Virginia, 1994. A clear and lively account of Raleigh's failed attempts.

Lemay, J. A. Leo. *The American Dream of Captain John Smith*. Charlottesville: University Press of Virginia, 1991. Smith's most ardent modern defender and interpreter.

———. *Did Pocahontas Save Captain John Smith?* Athens: University of Georgia Press, 1992. He says yes.

Price, David A. *Love and Hate in Jamestown: John Smith, Pocahontas, and the Heart of a New Nation*. New York: Knopf, 2003. A lively narrative history of the first two decades of colonization at Jamestown.

Townsend, Camilla. *Pocahontas and the Powhatan Dilemma*. New York: Hill and Wang, 2004. A scholar's successful attempt to present the clash between English and Native American cultures in an imaginative and lively fashion, based on her sound scholarship.

Vaughan, Alden T. *American Genesis: Captain John Smith and the Founding of Virginia*. Boston: Little, Brown, 1975. A useful short account.

Wingfield, Jocelyn R. *Virginia's True Founder: Edward-Maria Wingfield and His Times, 1550–c.1614* Athens, Ga.: The Wingfield Family Society, 1993. Still resentful, after all these years.

Index

NOTE: Page numbers in *italics* refer to illustrations.